Physicality and Acting

Physicality and Acting

Movement Training as a Catalyst for Change

Shona Morris

methuen | drama
LONDON • NEW YORK • OXFORD • NEW DELHI • SYDNEY

METHUEN DRAMA
Bloomsbury Publishing Plc, 50 Bedford Square, London, WC1B 3DP, UK
Bloomsbury Publishing Inc, 1359 Broadway, New York, NY 10018, USA
Bloomsbury Publishing Ireland, 29 Earlsfort Terrace, Dublin 2, D02 AY28, Ireland

BLOOMSBURY, METHUEN DRAMA and the Methuen Drama logo are
trademarks of Bloomsbury Publishing Plc

First published in Great Britain 2026

Copyright © Shona Morris, 2026

Shona Morris has asserted her right under the Copyright, Designs and
Patents Act, 1988, to be identified as Author of this work.

Photograph © Marc Brenner
Image subject: Saskia Reeves

All rights reserved. No part of this publication may be: i) reproduced or transmitted in any form, electronic or mechanical, including photocopying, recording or by means of any information storage or retrieval system without prior permission in writing from the publishers; or ii) used or reproduced in any way for the training, development or operation of artificial intelligence (AI) technologies, including generative AI technologies. The rights holders expressly reserve this publication from the text and data mining exception as per Article 4(3) of the Digital Single Market Directive (EU) 2019/790.

Bloomsbury Publishing Plc does not have any control over, or responsibility for, any third-party websites referred to or in this book. All internet addresses given in this book were correct at the time of going to press. The author and publisher regret any inconvenience caused if addresses have changed or sites have ceased to exist, but can accept no responsibility for any such changes.

A catalogue record for this book is available from the British Library.

A catalog record for this book is available from the Library of Congress.

ISBN: HB: 978-1-3503-6915-3
        PB: 978-1-3503-6914-6
        ePDF: 978-1-3503-6917-7
        eBook: 978-1-3503-6916-0

Typeset by Integra Software Services Pvt. Ltd.
Printed and bound in Great Britain

For product safety related questions contact productsafety@bloomsbury.com.

To find out more about our authors and books visit www.bloomsbury.com
and sign up for our newsletters.

Shore Woman – by Seamus Heaney
(*Opened Ground: Poems 1966–1996*, Faber and Faber, 2002)

Man to the hills, woman to the shore (Gaelic proverb)

'Between parched dunes and salivating wave,
I have rights on this fallow avenue,
A membrane between moonlight and my shadow.'

This book is dedicated to my mother Eva, my son Laurence,
and my grandsons Luke and Raphael.

And for those who come after – and who came before.

Contents

List of illustrations — viii

Part I Origins

1. Introduction — 3
2. First steps — 16
3. Transformation — 32
4. The need for a system and how to place that system in a contemporary context: The traces that matter — 52

Part II The body as a play text

5. Trish Arnold and her legacy — 83
6. First classes — 106
7. Working in three dimensions — 130
8. In Praise of Play: Pure and Expressive Movement in Praise of Play — 157

Part III Movement in the world

9. Chameleon — 173
10. Animal Studies — 192
11. Mask work — 217
12. Neutral Mask and Chorus — 236
13. Actors and play and end notes — 260

References — 269

Illustrations

1	Wolfe Morris in *Ill Met By Moonlight*, directed by Michael Powell and Emeric Pressburger in 1957	19
2	*Discus Thrower in Classical Pose*, Olympia Part 1 Festival of the Peoples 1936, directed by Leni Riefenstahl. Getty	62
3	Oda Schottmüller performing in her solo *Tragoedie* with the mask she had designed, Getty	78
4	Commedia dell'Arte autocours mask work. Lecoq 1977 shows how the work was updated to cover contemporary themes	89
5	'The landlord throws her into the snow' – autocours. Lecoq 1978 shows the use of space and emotion in gesture and physical attitude	90
6	*The Green Table*, choreographed by Kurt Jooss. Getty	97
7	*I'm Sorry For Your Loss* written and directed by Shona Morris at NT Studio 2025. Different energies in the same space. Actors Wendy Allnutt, Leah Muller, Jack Chiswick. Photo taken by Sheila Mars	120
8	Rounding and hollowing – Composite image. Drawn by Peter Shenai	132
9	Image from *Waiting for Godot*, directed by Roger Blin, France 1953. Getty	161
10	*Stuff Happens* by David Edgar at RADA, student production, directed by Ed Kemp, movement Shona Morris. Photo credit RADA/Linda Carter	253

Part I Origins

1 Introduction

Ever since I started to teach movement, I wanted to write about it. To capture in words the magical work I saw in studios and rehearsal rooms, and inspire those who have never seen a movement class or movement session, with how special it is to witness a story evolve through a body in a space. To show how physicality is central to an actor's craft.

This book places movement at the heart of a discussion about how actors are trained, and theatre is made, and introduces Actors' Movement as a 'subject' to students, actors, teachers, directors – anyone interested in theatre. I refer to the innovative teachers and methods that developed it and my own journey with movement, as an actor and movement teacher.

Writing about movement is like trying to catch the wind – a movement class is only ever a set of fluid responses between students and teacher. There are, however, some common principles and there is also a history and a context to movement teaching.

Here are some questions I have been asked about Movement for Actors.

Is it deportment, alignment or learning to bow or curtsey in a play? Does it help us move across a stage, make an entrance or an exit? Is it good 'timing', comedy routines or miming a door (that isn't there)? Or learning how to sit on a chair as a woman in the 1930s or whether to cross your legs in Victorian dress, or button a waistcoat? Learning a dance routine, or a step-ball-change? Or even how to be an animal, or waltz as an old man or act an epileptic fit safely on stage? The ability to multi-role, one actor playing many parts, or feel confident doing a non-naturalistic scene change? Or even, being able to take part in the warm-up without having a heart attack?

I have staged many of these activities and taught many actors how to do them. But these are physical skills. Physical studies for acting go much deeper. Movement teachers are different to the movement specialists employed in theatre, though often the skills and roles overlap. Intimacy co-ordinators, and access advocates have now joined Fight Directors and Movement Directors to co-ordinate physical life on our stages and sets. They keep the work safe and professional through advocating for consent, attending to the individual needs of the actors, whilst recording and choreographing their movement. Nothing physical that you see on stage or in a film is left to chance: all is crafted by movement specialists. All movement practitioners, including movement teachers, work with the body as a site of memory, or of action, of co-ordination, or of communication.

So how does all this relate to a movement class in a drama school? An actor's ability to embrace all these varied and complex challenges will have been explored in a movement class: and the movement class will have 'deepened' their ability to meet them with confidence and full expression. Quintessentially, Actors' Movement classes teach us how to act with the body.

Movement is a vital part of human survival and expression

Let us start from the basic idea that everybody moves.

All movement starts from sensation. A desire triggers an action – we communicate, we play, we work, we fight, we love, we live in society. The first gesture a baby makes is to reach towards an object or point to a loved one, an action that comes from the self and towards another. Movement as gesture is also fundamental to all of us. An actor's metier is to capture human experience in movement, words, body and breath.

The actor is also working with time – in a play or a performance. Their gestures and their actions need to be pertinent, chosen, crafted. To act is to make meaning through movement. Acting is practical, body-based and interpretive. Acting is a physical activity, and physical awareness will be one of the first classes for an actor in training.

Learning about movement is to learn how your own body moves

The actor first encounters movement by learning how their own body moves. Learning the principles of physicality is to learn how the body moves in a space–time continuum. Its connection to the breath, weight, momentum, and to the space around us, is a personal connection to your own body and a personal connection to 'self'. But it places the 'self' in the 'world'.

These classes that teach actors to expand their physical capacity, and be able to move confidently in the space, are technical and craft based. 'Presence' and 'body awareness' are skills that can be learnt. The learning is kinaesthetic and experiential, and for students who have never trained physically before, these are new learning modalities.

Learning to move like other people

How we move, our physicality, expresses who we are and the society we are part of. Actors shape-shift physically, to convey the culture, constraints, social background or status of a character. They stand in the shoes of someone else and see the world through their eyes, feel their feelings and think their thoughts. Acting is transformation, and movement is its pathway.

What is Movement for Actors?

Movement for Actors could best be described as an amalgam of dance and acting. It trains not only the technical principles of how a body moves through space but also explores the reasons behind it. Action and impulse.

The actor might learn a movement vocabulary taught through specific exercises, that seem common to other practices – modern dance or yoga perhaps. But the focus is on physical expression, not on physical excellence. The actor brings the movements to life through their imagination and empathy – pouring themselves into a script, a text, a scene, a production. Movement gives actors skills to physically live inside their character and carve meaning with their bodies. Its techniques keep the actor safe, as they move into more extreme forms of physicality, and spatially aware as they move on complicated sets, or master difficult routines.

An actor needs physical craft to be physically alive on stage, and an imagination to bring it to life.

The body is an instrument: Tuning the instrument

Movement training opens the actor's powers of expression. The body is an instrument and is stretched and expanded with their powers of observation, to be able to work in detail. Tuning the instrument helps the actor find subtleness and ease, as well as punctuation.

Experiment and exploration and pedagogy

Over the years, my fascination with how and why bodies move, and how to teach this, has grown to include many experimental ways of moving, tapping into improvisation and creativity, which lead to story and communication with an audience.

The audience is not always sitting in a theatre – and communication isn't always naturalistic.

Movement training for actors helps them to adapt to different modes of performance. I see this as moving a dial up and down on a sound-desk, a practical, creative and expressive approach to exploring the possibilities of how we make theatre. Some of my exercises are practical and directly applicable to plays and text. Some are exploratory and experiential, to develop expression and teach physical awareness. Some aim to deepen an actor's ability to get inside the intention or action of the role they are playing.

I have crystallized my experience with movement into a pedagogy – a series of exercises that I teach in drama schools. I have asked myself many questions about how to teach these exercises effectively, over many years.

How to develop a pedagogy for movement teaching is also the subject of this book, and the teacher–artists who taught and inspired me. Movement teaching and movement teachers go together.

Movement and the world around us

I have always been curious about how physicality relates to the world around me – as a politic and a point of view. My curiosity intensified when I became a mother and watched my child move and play and considered what helped his development. When I began to write this book, I realized how much my own journey with movement was forged by my political, social and cultural circumstances. This wasn't a comfortable realization, and the more I wrote about movement, the harder it was to ignore my own origins, and what is revealed about us when we move. Movement training for actors is in a political and social context, because we live in the world. The characters an actor plays, and the lives we all lead, are shaped by events and who we are.

The students

The original aim of this book was to consider a common set of principles for movement, offering the exercises and approaches from my body of work, as examples. It still is. But as I started my research, a particular set of global circumstances challenged the practice I teach. It is impossible to keep pace with the speed of the change: what presented as a compelling set of circumstances in 2020, when I started my research, has changed again to encompass a new set of fluid circumstances. This posed many vital questions for me, but the most compelling was how to continue to connect to the students.

How can a student take charge of their training, if their values or background are not shared by their educators? This tension is now at the heart of this book and has recently formed the basis of many discussions in drama schools and the arts. But this tension is not new. I have experienced this myself. I have trained alongside others, thoroughly embracing the journey they provided, while developing my own methodologies and practices as an educator, and sometimes a critique of those practices. However, the context is new. So, this book has shifted. It looks at how to teach movement in a world that is changing and considers how movement training for actors itself developed as a response to a changing world. It asks if movement training needs to change, and if so, what new principles are needed.

'Physicality and Acting: Movement Training as a Catalyst for Change' is what this book is about.

But first I want to take you on a journey, to show how vital movement is to rehearsal and performance, and to outline the beginnings of the practice, and one key event that changed the thinking about movement I describe above – 'The Tsunami in Drama Schools'.

Movement is vital to rehearsal and performance

It is a rehearsal room in Canada on a cold winter's day, and a group of actors kneel in prayer, heads bowed. They are Elders. They hold tightly between them a long red patchwork 'carpet' of cut-up dresses belonging to a young girl. A man steps carefully onto it; he is their King returning from the wars. As a body, the elders breathe and mutter anxiously together, pulling at the fabric as he walks slowly along it. His wife opens her arms to greet him, her face adamantine. His army are rattled by this strange display, and the elders' prayers get louder, but the King continues to walk, masking his unease.

A young woman tethered to a cart watches, a hawk circling in the sky, her movements birdlike, mirroring the hawk. Veiled from head to foot, a large wooden stick yoked across her back, she twists and turns. The man keeps walking, as she thrashes her stick against the cart, a guard unties her, but she flies off the cart in a torrent of words, a prophesy. The man continues to walk, the elders are frozen, the girl screams.

'Crack', says the young girl and falls, throwing the stick across the room.

Silence. Stillness. Breath.

'Shit', she says.

'What?', the stage manager whispers.

'Crack! I said crack! It was meant to be the stick breaking, we haven't got the real one, I said "crack" instead', she says.

Gasps of relief and laughter ripple through the room. The actors relax, Cassandra fist bumps the guard, then signals to the director she is fine.

*

This was a group improvisation for a play. The director had set the scenario that morning. I had run movement sessions on chorus work with the company, and the voice coach and I had worked with Cassandra in preparation for this session. I recall the power of the actors' individual responses as a chorus – the tension, the silence, the musicality of the movement.

We were exploring Agamemnon's arrival back from Troy, from the play by Aeschylus in a translation by Ted Hughes. Every action in the scene needed a physical life, a reason to move, the ability to transmit that, and the skill to be able to repeat it. Apart from Cassandra's prophesy, the improvisation didn't use words, but the movement was acting. The work I had explored with the actors was selected, of course, from my own movement practice. What is this practice?

What are the techniques and systems that help actors move, and make theatre full of life?

I teach a synthesis of the work of Jacques Lecoq, Trish Arnold and Litz Pisk,[1] that I developed along with a set of my own exercises. I developed this practice over thirty years, through teaching in British drama schools. This was balanced with a long period first as artist in residence at The Stratford Festival Theatre in Canada, then as a visiting coach and Head of Movement there, and a movement director. How to develop Actors' Movement was guided by the experience I had working as an actor. As an actor I naturally brought my awareness of movement to my understanding of character, situation and text, and saw the radical possibilities for transformation it offers.

The major discovery I made when researching this book was how movement training has also radically transformed theatre.

Like many people, I fall into several identities in terms of ethnicity, class and demographic. I have always subscribed to putting the work first and subsuming my identity into a role. This has changed, and the outcomes are exciting – as actors connect more viscerally to themselves to create vital forms of original expression. But it still raises the question of how to embrace the complexities of identity when teaching? I still believe transformation is fundamental to acting. Transformation is also radical. There are many paradoxes in these statements, because the times we live in are complex.

The movement syllabus: 'Let the Movement Change You' – A catalyst for change in the body and in theatre

Movement training has had a radical influence on actor training. It was part of the development of new approaches to body-based training in British drama schools, just before and after the Second World War. It intersected with post-war ideas on acting, politics and culture. Though the movement I teach could be considered part of a post-war tradition, I champion

---

[1] All of whom I discuss below.

how I initially encountered it – as an approach that revitalized theatre and expanded its possibilities and radicalized my understanding of theatre.

The actor's experience of a movement class as a guide to how to structure a syllabus

A movement class affects the body, breath and physical awareness of the actor. Training starts slowly, first working with the spine, then out into the rest of the body, to end with creative explorations. The practical training will help actors consider some of these questions. How does the actor move with text, to create a believable physicality on stage? How do they access their imaginations and their emotional life while doing this?

Repetition in the training helps movement become part of an actor's daily practice: like voice exercises or playing scales for singers and instrumentalists.

A community of practice

My first full-time post teaching movement was in 1989, when there wasn't an agreed pedagogy on how to teach movement in the theatre, or even a course on Movement for Actors, but there were brilliant and influential teachers.[2] Over the years I developed my craft and expanded my understanding of the subject, through a 'community of practice' – movement teachers from other drama schools, with similar trainings to mine.

The term 'community of practice' comes from the educational theorist Etienne Wengner who recognized the breadth of learning possible when undertaken as a social activity. This is also how the pedagogy of Actors' Movement – also called 'Pure Movement' – developed and advanced its principles. A 'river of work' we all contributed to, that flows on to the next generation of movement teachers.

This 'community of practice' is not academically recorded or codified, and its essential contribution to movement training has yet to be recognized. A group of practitioners working together, sharing and developing the work, without trying to monetize it, is rare.

Radical European influences

The change that movement brought to theatre training was to see acting not just as words but as a physical, imaginative and collective endeavour. I encountered this while training at the Jacques Lecoq School in Paris from 1976 to 1978, and while there, saw many productions which expanded theatre, beyond text and psychological realism.[3] It was exciting to know that the work we were doing in the beautiful space of Lecoq's school in Paris was a highway to this experimental theatre.

The research for this book revealed that my teaching practice had two sources that complemented each other, both radical in their different ways and both developed in the twentieth century.

---

[2] A post-graduate diploma was offered at Guildhall School of Music and Drama; and the MFA in Movement at Central School of Speech and Drama was offered in 2004.
[3] I discuss these in the next chapters.

One was the development of mime in post-war France, which had so fascinated me and had sent me to Lecoq in Paris.

The other source was the Free Dance practitioners of Central and Eastern Europe in the early twentieth century, who developed a language of physical expression for the body moving in space, to tell powerful stories in dance. Working with a dropped centre of gravity, and a dynamic use of space, freed the body from its social constraints – redefining the dramatic possibilities of dance. Though this seems positive, there are also more troubling aspects to this 'revolution'.

Further research revealed how Free Dance and Expressionism were linked to the work of Rudolph Laban, with his troubling associations with The Third Reich in Nazi Germany, which I had not fully appreciated before (Karina and Kant, 2004).[4] Lecoq's innovations in mime also had their own historical context, more positive, as part of the de-Nazification of Europe. I discovered there is a relationship between politics and movement. This relationship prevails today.

The impact of the pandemic: The tsunami

Since starting to research this book in 2020, the context and culture in which I teach has changed beyond recognition, and I now consider a different catalyst for change: the social justice and Black Lives Matter movements, and their impact on drama schools and the practice I teach.

I acknowledge my positionality in this. I am a white, middle-class woman from a certain generation, who has dedicated most of my life to working in the theatre. My background and my culture determined my view of the world – but at the same time I believed they were sufficiently inclusive to hold a dynamic and creative teaching space.

The impact of what happened in drama schools was felt and seen differently by all of us caught up in it, and the students and younger teachers no doubt will recall this differently, welcoming the changes as do I. And drama schools had long ignored how much change was necessary – focusing solely on the 'work' to determine their relationships with students.

As much as we 'see' the students, they also 'see' us. To teach embodied practices inclusively can only ever be a process in response to what is happening in society, and who we are teaching. It is not enough to refine and discover new exercises or methodologies to open the body and the imagination. Keeping a practice up to date, I learnt, was also to take on board social activism, political theory, identity politics and the impact of online discussions. The boundaries of where classes begin and end became blurred.

So, when I recount the impact of what I describe as the 'tsunami' in drama schools, it is to help our understanding and advance the debate of how we train, who makes the choices and funds what is taught. This can only ever be my version of events – and at the same time – positionality again – my view of my practice, and my demographic, no doubt makes me partial when recounting what happened.

*

---

[4]See Lilian Karina and Marion Kant (2004) *Hitler's Dancers*.

In 2020, COVID-19 and the social justice movements of Black Lives Matter and #MeToo seismically shook the stability of drama schools and conservatoires. The effects of Brexit and the cost-of-living crisis had already meant theatre graduates were facing insecure professional futures. In 2020, the combination of all these factors revolutionized Conservatoire thinking, with an urgency to decolonize its repertoire, alongside more socially aware approaches to teaching.[5] This was in response to accusations of systemic racism within the institutions, which the students themselves had brought to light.

All drama schools and conservatoires faced these crises. In 2021, Guildhall hosted a conference – 'Strengthening Music in Society' – examining how to introduce a more diverse repertoire. Helen Gaunt's keynote speech[6] recognized the importance of artistry and craft, but also the need to broaden the repertoire and change the teaching ethos, to give students more options to work outside of concert halls (Gaunt, 2021).

Discussions about keeping the artistry and craft in place, while broadening the repertoire – 'not throwing the baby out with the bathwater' – were a common concern for many conservatoires, as they scrambled to update their curricula. But the report was clear that the responsibility couldn't just lie with the teachers unless change happened elsewhere within the institutions. The report stated how conservatoires needed to 'transcend embedded power hierarchies' and develop empathy and listening to 'work through inevitable resistances' by *'relating to the ethics of care, tolerance, generosity and nimbleness'*.

*

But by 2021, the impact of COVID-19 had already made us rethink our classes and our pedagogies – and we were already responding to social forces, albeit not consistently nor effectively. No longer could we rely on exercises using touch or 'ensemble' teaching. Students' experience of learning had become atomized, either in small groups (when allowed back into the building) or as individuals in their bedrooms online – postage stamps on a screen. For two years during COVID-19, we pivoted from class to screen, often in the space of a day. This was much harder for students, forced to take movement classes online in bedrooms, cupboards, kitchens, parks or anywhere they could find to continue their training. The cost of this atomized training to the emotional well-being of the students cannot be underestimated.

Today, though most classes are back in the room, how we teach and what we teach has never returned to its previous methodology. Drama school teaching practice, and their teachers' relationships with their institutions changed irrevocably after 2020, with mutual trust and respect replaced by protocols and extensive investigations. Many 'new' practices in drama schools – intimacy co-ordination, check-ins, personal pronouns, the use of trigger warnings, flexibility with attendance, mandatory lesson plans – were in fact being tested during lockdown and its aftermath, in a highly emotionally charged environment, which made tutors nervous, and left students often feeling uncertain about who

---

[5]We had begun an informal process of de-colonization – through training and discussion and some changes to the curriculum – but not formal anti-racist training nor critical race theory.
[6]Principal of the Royal Welsh College: Conference 'Strengthening Music in Society', 16 December 2021, given by The Institute for Social Impact Research in the Performing Arts at Guildhall.

ran the classes. One of the first principles of teaching, in any learning environment, is that the teacher runs the class. If there are no guard-rails, teaching disintegrates. As I show later, letting students teach themselves became a defining part of Lecoq's pedagogy in response to the student riots in Paris in 1968. But as I also show below, the students in 2020 never asked us to stop teaching – just to teach with more awareness about who they were, and what they needed.

Dealing with COVID-19 started as a response to a pandemic, but the wider implications are nothing short of a revolution. These can be characterized in several ways. Drama schools were forced to embrace a curriculum that was more culturally diverse, at pace, with little time to re-calibrate or research. It was no longer enough to teach students a body of work that equipped them for a professional career[7] unless it was contextualized and updated – but there was little time or funding for practical research. It challenged the 'canon' of dramatic literature and psychologically based acting systems but had no methodology to offer any radical alternatives at the pace required.

We were in an unprecedented state of flux.

The full impact at the Royal Academy of Dramatic Art (RADA) came in 2020, after the murder of George Floyd, when we were formally asked to critically assess in public, over the course of many months, our own practices in relation to anti-racism. This was requested by the management as a response to the gravity of a student report – the Student Action Plan, or SAP, COVID-19 and the Black Lives Matter movement were intrinsically linked.

The Student Action Plan, called the Anti-Racism Action Plan

The Student Action Plan, written in 2020, was commissioned by the RADA senior management as a response to a cataclysmic meeting the students had convened. It was written by the students, as a rapid response to the events I describe below.

The students had requested this online meeting between the entire BA student body[8] and every member of the Acting and Production Faculties, to demand change and express their anger and frustrations about systemic racism within the institution. These, we understood, had been expressed for a long time, with little change. As in many institutions, the anger the students felt was catalysed by the murder of George Floyd, and the anti-racist demonstrations taking place all over the world had empowered them. At the meeting, student after student detailed their serious concerns about their experience of racism, in their training, the curriculum, the repertoire and their teachers. The impact was shocking and revelatory.

This is what led to the management's request to draw up a 'Student Action Plan',[9] asking them to detail their concerns in a formal document. They effectively handed the baton straight back to the students, and it became the basis from which to start a root and branch reform to the curriculum – and as it turned out – the teachers.[10]

---

[7]As I mention below, you can of course do both.
[8]These were BA Acting and BA Production. MA Courses were also involved but didn't attend the meeting.
[9]An action plan, in education, is a document that will indicate how to achieve certain educational goals and improve teaching practices – in this case in response to anti-racism.
[10]Staff were given weekly anti-racist training sessions, overseen by Professor Vini Landor from Leeds Beckett University, which formed part of a serious root-and-branch review of curriculum and pedagogy.

Perhaps the management thought this was what the students wanted, their voice being heard, with them being asked to suggest how to update their training. But the introduction to the Student Action Plan tells a slightly different story – one of disappointment with the management and dismay that it was the students who needed to itemize what the institution should, arguably, have already been aware of.

The frontispiece makes for striking reading, and I quote its entirety to give weight to its importance and discuss its impact, since its publication on 29 June 2020.[11]

> RADA Students Anti-Racism Action Plan:
>
> This document has been created by the student body who have been empowered to unite in light of the Black Lives Matter movement. It is a response to a continuous lack of care and concern for Black Students within the institution. It has fallen to students to create this document due to a lack of faith in RADA's management and their lack of desire for change. (RADA, 2020)

Phrases like 'It has fallen to the students' reveal their disappointment at the failure of their institutions. 'Lack of faith' in the management is not revolutionary as a statement and 'lack of desire for change' asks for management, teachers and, by implication all teaching institutions to set the appropriate educational goals to improve anti-racist teaching practices.

It should not have been up to the students to do the heavy lifting here.

The content that followed, in the Student Action Plan[12] was extremely detailed and well written. It levelled criticisms of our practices and our pedagogies and covered every aspect of training as laid out in the students' BA Course Document for RADA which formed the basis of the curriculum. It proposed radical alterations to the curriculum, methodology and pedagogy.[13] There was a call to replace 'male geniuses' like Stanislavski, Chekhov, Brecht, Shakespeare – and to jettison the study of Restoration plays and Greek tragedy, radically altering its repertoire of the last thirty years.[14]

The strategic review that followed the SAP would subsequently also draw attention to the Movement Curriculum because it wasn't codified, and was based on approaches that relied on the teacher to transmit them. The strategic review was made up of tutors, not uniquely students, and some members of Senior Management.

There was a twofold criticism in both reports: (1), that the repertoire needed to decolonize, and (2), that when a subject was dynamic and not codified and experimental (as with movement) it lacked transparency. The other common link in both reports was a concern that Stanislavski-based techniques relied too much on students using their own experiences, which could be traumatizing.[15]

All this was timely and necessary – but the question remains – why had it taken drama schools so long to incorporate these changes in society, many of which were being

---

[11] Many drama schools were grappling with the same issues.
[12] Introduction quoted above.
[13] The Principal issued a public apology to say that RADA was systemically racist, and had committed to a root-and-branch review of its practices, and regular anti-racist training for all its staff.
[14] It was implemented the first two years after the Student Action Plan, when the syllabus was then changed in a later course review.
[15] Many of the 'systems' and the material criticized in this report are still in place in most drama schools.

researched in universities, and all of which affected how young actors placed themselves in terms of identity and experience? Particularly regarding racism?

Was it the conditions of employment and the lack of opportunity for tutors to interrogate their practice? A focus on the demands of a cyclical syllabus repeated every year, often with material recycled yearly. Most contracts in drama schools were not research contracts, and most institutions not part of the Research Excellence Framework in Universities (REF). Was it the rigidity of the management structures themselves, which one of the board members at RADA once referred to as 'command and control'?

I felt the urgency of the weight of a pedagogy and a culture that was characterized as systemically oppressive. This left me to reflect on my part in this and my own practice. Most of these reflections and research were done in my own time and unfunded. Any questions I asked outside of my institution were informal (I couldn't pay anyone for their time), and my institution would not be requesting a report.

This didn't prevent me from researching the provenance of my practice, trying to understand the traces of racism it might contain, and how to change what I taught and how I teach. I spoke to as many practitioners who could spare the time – many of whom were from the Black and Global Majority teaching dance. I reviewed my own practice from the Central European tradition and uncovered uncomfortable facts about the provenance, particularly the views of Rudolph Laban, whose work makes up much of UK drama school practice. I had the opportunity to meet with Marion Kant, co-author of 'Hitler's Dancers', to discuss Laban's association with The Ministry of Propaganda during the Third Reich (Karina and Kant, 2004). Laban's connection to the Ministry of Propaganda is highly contested but, in the light of understanding racism, I was drawn to the evidence and testimony I found. This research made me look deeper at how bodies are socialized and appraised culturally. The book *Stages of Reckoning* (Ginther, 2023) helped me understand my practice in relation to the 'Anti-racist and Decolonial Actor Training' it proposes, which chimed with testimony from the SAP and elucidated how damaging the effects of language and cultural bias can be.

These enlightening and disturbing discoveries and events have led me to consider the entrenched views in my own practice and sent me on a path to change them and re-visit my first love of movement – to free and change theatre.

This book is still about the body and the actor and how to make theatre with physicality. But it is also about the context we teach in, socially, politically and culturally. It doesn't claim to be comprehensive, but it looks at movement teaching as a subject that actors can still rely on to train them for the theatre, in the hope that the questions I ask will keep it relevant.

Some notes when reading this book

Each chapter in the book examines a different aspect of movement training for actors, and can be read separately or as part of the arc of the training I am describing. The description of the exercises follows the journey of my pedagogy, from 'Pure Movement' to 'Expressive Movement'.

- Part I: Origins. This looks at the history of movement teaching and its context. It is also semi-autobiographical, describing my own journey with movement as a template for how different this is, for all of us.

- Part II: The body as a play text. This looks at 'Pure Movement' and how to teach it. 'Pure Movement' was a term that Trish Arnold coined to describe her practice. The name was also used by the community of practice I refer to. I situate Pure Movement in its provenance and look at ways to build a syllabus. It describes some of the key exercises in Pure Movement. It also considers how the relationship between movement and playfulness is germane to acting.
- Part III: Movement in the world. The third part considers the genesis and exercises of 'Expressive Movement' with links to theatre, ancient and modern. 'Expressive Movement' is a term that Trish Arnold suggested to me, to find ways to help actors interpret character and how to work in different registers. 'Expressive Movement' is not the same as 'expressionism'. Expressive Movement is a response to the world around us and a way to work with heightened text.

Many of the exercises for both 'Pure' and 'Expressive' movement are mine – but I also refer to their provenance or what inspired me.

I refer to the terms Actors' Movement or movement for actors interchangeably, to describe physicality in the theatre in general. Threading throughout the book are my reflections on movement teaching in a social and cultural context, often in response to current events.

*

The book follows both a linear and a cyclical structure. It records the pedagogy I taught, as a three-year course, but recognizes that classes and exercises can be taught independently or in different ways. I also add comments and documents, to provide insight and reflections on how to structure movement classes, sometimes describing the pitfalls and mistakes.

I include references to notes and conversations with key practitioners, students and movement teachers. I interviewed many practitioners, taking notes of our conversations and sending them transcripts to check through afterwards. I use examples from productions I have seen, and helped make, and fragments of memory, which I have recycled and created my own pedagogy from.

As each chapter looks at physicality and acting from a different perspective, there might be some crossovers or repetitions of subjects from other chapters, viewed in different lights. This is to help familiarize the reader with the practitioners or ideas as they appear in different contexts.

*

Referencing

Where I refer to plays it is suggested that you use your own copies to find the reference.

When quoting from plays I will provide the edition in the footnotes.

When quoting from artists' notebooks (Trish Arnold's for example), or interviews, they will be appropriately cited. Trish Arnold gave me her notes when she taught me, and they have not been published. She was keen for her exercises and practice to be shared for future generations, and handed her notes to many of the teachers she was mentoring. As I mention frequently in this book, there is no funded research in drama schools to hold and archive much of this practice, which amplifies my frequent explanations and discussions about how this is a 'community of practice'. Informal and unrecorded, and not codified. There is a small archive of Litz Pisk's emphemera held in the library at Central School of Speech and Drama which I also refer to.

When quoting from books or publications, the title of the book will be given, but not the page number.

I have supported my reflections with appropriate references, but this is not an academic book. When I have simplified ideas, this represents only how I have understood my discipline as a practitioner, not as an academic. However, I provide references for my sources.

Occasionally I have combined several experiences as a semi-fictionalized account of events to protect individuals but also to draw together as many strands as possible.

Writing about movement, as I say, is almost impossible. To prepare for this I studied with John Burgess on his playwriting course. Sadly, he died in June 2024, but with every sentence I write I hear his succinct critiques in my head. I haven't always managed to measure up to his call for clarity.

Others I wish to thank for their help and input are: Ayse Tashkiran (for access to the Litz Pisk archive), Lisa Peck, Ingrid Mackinnon, Vanessa Ewan, Angela Gasparetto, Kath Rogers, Amanda Parfitt, Anna Furse, Niamh Dowling, Irina Brown, Gabriel Gawin, Vladimir Mirodan, Annie Tyson, Matthew Wernham, Micaela Miranda, Sarah Miller, Dr Margaret Coldiron, Jane Gibson, Brigid Larmour, Thomas Kampe, David Latham and Marion Kant and many others who gave their time to talk to me, work with me, or inspire me.

Writing this book I have also had illuminating discussions with Mark Evans and Sue Lefton: I have tried to represent their input accurately, but inevitably my understanding will have shifted some of their emphasis to my own and I take full responsibility for any of the views expressed in this book. I thank both for their generosity and their passion to keep this beautiful practice alive. Lastly, all the experiences of teaching and working with movement could only have been possible with the actors and students I have worked with.

This book is for them, and those that follow.

Movement is what happens between us.

2 First steps

The ball

Roundness! So high, so prodigal in losing
warmth of our hands that was not yours to spill!

(Rilke, 2004)

You throw a ball into the air, and it finds its own momentum.

The body speaks without words. Silence. There is always a reason to be silent. Stillness is also movement – as a pause is part of music. Stillness. Silence. All feelings and sensations move through our bodies.

In movement classes we work with stillness, or a suspension of activity which is usually silent. Lecoq's work on the still point, and the suspension in a 'swing', as I learned from Trish Arnold, communicates both what can't be said and what could happen next, and is part of the body of work I describe.

*

This chapter introduces some guiding principles of Actors' Movement through its history, and my own first steps encountering it, both as a practice and a pedagogy. Previously I mentioned the community of movement practice I am from, whose techniques were consciously researched and developed for teaching in drama schools. These techniques form part of a paradigm that changed drama school training and movement education in the early twentieth century. I look at how I first encountered these techniques as a child and young person, at school and at home, before I knew what they were. I started to teach movement because I was an actor, not because I was a movement practitioner. When I started teaching there were no qualifications for movement teaching in drama schools. In my case, I trained through an apprenticeship (which I describe below) and applied my experience as an actor, but I share the individuality of my journey with many movement teachers. I interviewed some of these teachers working today, to see how they had started, and they revealed equally circuitous routes as my own.

The response of Micaela Miranda, Head of Movement at London Academy of Music and Dramatic Art (LAMDA):

> [She knew] Intellectually nothing [about movement teaching]. Growing up in a house where lots of movement happened – I was a gymnast and then went into sport …. when I was 17 I integrated movement into acting training when I went to a vocational school to learn to be a professional actor to make money – the school I went to had teachers from Lecoq – Sandra Mladenovic who taught Neutral Mask – who were movement-driven actors. Then I went to Lecoq (after 2 years of working as an actress), which crystallized Theatre and Movement back into my body. (Micaela Miranda, 2022)

Marcin Rudy, Movement Tutor at East 15, also hadn't planned on being a Movement Teacher. He worked with 'Song of the Goat', whose work was influenced by Gardzienice Theatre, in turn influenced by Grotowski.

> Introduced to [Movement] by practising it with a master – Song of the Goat, Grzegorz Bral – [whose strength was] bringing together an interesting ensemble with everyone coming with some sort of skill – so not a traditional path. I moved to the Grotowski Centre – working every single day, learning things in action. I was the last person to teach in the company. I wanted to act not teach – [I had] an embodied knowledge – I had no idea what is taught in schools. (Marcin Rudy, 2022)

Early life in the theatre and in dance

My father, Wolfe Morris, was an actor – he had trained at RADA on a scholarship in the late 1930s. He was a second-generation immigrant from an Ashkenazi Jewish family. His parents were Yiddish speakers and had fled the pogroms in Eastern Europe to come to this country without papers. They remained stateless all their lives. A familiar story for many Jews. His origins weren't auspicious, but his passion for acting was. His father, Maury Steinberg, ran a greengrocer's shop in Portsmouth, where Wolfe continued to work when studying at RADA from 1939 to 1942, commuting by train to his classes. He showed me how to do voice exercises to the rhythm of the train – bubedy, bubedy, bebedy baaah – he was always full of flamboyant and entertaining information. My uncle Aubrey Morris also trained at RADA, on a scholarship. There were nine children; the daughters opened a dance school and were gifted singers and dancers. All my uncles were good singers, and Grandma Becky used to sing at Jewish weddings. Rumour had it my aunts opened their dance school because, as Jewesses, they weren't allowed to teach in the more established schools, so if you can't join them, beat them, figuratively speaking. Rumour, and humour, also has it that my grandfather – Maury Steinberg – sang in the Jewish music hall in the East End, until someone hit him on the head with a hammer. The hammer is probably a myth, but he did teach my uncles Jewish music hall songs, which I can testify, as they were passed on to me. So he sang in those halls, but clearly without success. He had many jobs, disappeared from the family, came back, opened and closed businesses, and had to go to court for several irregularities. Without papers, immigrant families live under the radar where stories about their origins proliferate and life is precarious. This was my father's story, and though he didn't often talk about it, there were enough stories and jokes in the family for it to affect me.

*

By the time I was born my father was what is known as a 'working actor'. He had made quite a few feature films and was an accomplished stage actor. I grew up in the theatre and spent a lot of time in dressing rooms watching my father prepare to go on stage, seeing the process of transformation with my own eyes. He was a nervous brilliant man, and I have vivid memories of him smoking intensely as he went over his lines or created his make-up for his 'character' roles, as they were then called. His transformations were wonderful. He worked meticulously on the physical details of his performances. So, I was shocked, crestfallen in fact, when a family friend who was an actor and teacher and director said he was referred to as 'the barrow boy' when he first started acting. This was because he had to carry vegetables from the market on a wheelbarrow to his father's shop every morning before commuting to RADA. I thought it dismissive snobbery, but it gives an insight into the British class system inherent in theatre at that time. As an actor from a working-class immigrant family, he was 'on licence', not quite 'one of them'. However, he was still considered not only a classical actor but a method actor. He loved Marlon Brando and Rod Steiger and 'lived' his roles. He had great admiration for American actors and the parts of 'the method' (as it was called then) which asked actors to research the previous circumstances of their characters. He spoke of his characters as if he knew them intimately. He gave me a copy of Harley Granville-Barker's *Prefaces to Shakespeare* when I was playing Ophelia, so I could see her as a real person, rather than a character in a play. I also understood that thinking about the life of your character meant finding who they were, physically and emotionally, and creating their backstory – not just speaking the words. But he also had a rigorous approach to text, its rhythms and the musicality of the language.

*

Theatre also came home. As well as going through his lines – Beckett, Marlowe, Shakespeare, Pinter and copious TV scripts – my father would do his voice and movement exercises. The movement was the strangest to me, like nothing I had ever seen – spine undulations, drops, whooshing sounds, swings. We were living in a one-bedroomed rented flat, and his study was my bedroom (my parents had a bed in the sitting room).

My parents didn't have any money behind them, they both came from poor working-class backgrounds and large families. My father dedicated his life to being an actor and gradually earned enough money to keep the wolf from the door, working in theatre, film and TV.

There was more culture than capital in our house and when he was unemployed (the slime to which all actors are doomed to return as Simon Callow once said) there was nothing to fall back on. Sometimes to get a free loaf of bread, my father would go on one knee and sing 'my yiddishe mama' to the lady in our local bread shop.

Both my parents were auto-didacts. Wolfe left school at 16 to go to RADA, and my mother, Eva, left school at 13 to support her family, but that didn't seem to limit their capacity to read or understand socialism (which was their other passion). I was also the first person in my family to go to university, along with my cousins, the children of their brothers and sisters. Social mobility after the Second World War, for my parents, meant I was expected to get a good education, and to stay at school until I was 18. I cannot overestimate what a radical idea this was for working-class families.

While I was at school, I went to the Phyllis Bedells ballet school on the Quex Road, and I loved the classes. I took all my exams and particularly loved the dance improvisations and character dances – which ranged from being butterflies to dancing the Mazurka. I wanted to be a ballet dancer, and I was probably in with a chance. I never stopped dancing. I would make up ballets and choreography, listening to the radio. My parents were not in favour and didn't support the proffered possibility of auditioning for the Royal Ballet School, for financial and educational reasons 'your career will be over by the time you are 30 and you'll have nothing to fall back on'. So, I danced at home and with my friend Rowan Wymark. 'The Nutcracker Suite' was a favourite, played on a portable turntable. My petticoat was a tutu (for 'The Dance of the Sugar Plum Fairy') and my wellingtons the boots for the 'Russian Dance'. Make-believe games were also vital to our inner lives (like lots of

Figure 1 Wolfe Morris in *Ill Met By Moonlight*, directed by Michael Powell and Emeric Pressburger in 1957.

children in the 1950s) and involved making little boats out of leaves and launching them onto streams on Hampstead Heath – for the fairies. My friend Rowan and I watched in the bushes as the fairies quietly found them, or so we thought.

Rowan Wymark lived up the road from me. Her father was the well-known shakespearean actor Patrick Wymark. She was scarily literate so we would compete with each other to learn two-handed scenes – she was Katherine, and I was Petruchio in the wooing scene from *The Taming of the Shrew* – or she was Puck and I the First Fairy – and subjected the actors at the Wymark's big Sunday lunches to our 'serious' acting, along with our dance interpretations of 'The Nutcracker Suite'. We usually got large crowds watching us, who laughed not exactly kindly at our attempts, and made drunken comments about our committed efforts. Years later my mother reminded me how Patrick Wymark as Bottom doing the burgomasker's dance in *A Midsummer Night's Dream*, bore quite a strong resemblance to our dances on Sunday afternoons. No wonder we always had an audience! We were creating comic material.

Growing up in the theatre in the 1950s and 1960s was not comfortable or secure. Though my father was an actor, it wasn't a salubrious or privileged existence and felt very much on the edge. So, these play-acting games reflected theatre at that time – tough and truthful. We were baby apprentices, but it gave me permission to immerse myself in these vivid transformations.

My mother was more practical, and used to say, 'over my dead body', when I said I wanted to be an actor – but she was a voracious reader. We would go to the library each week and dissect the books we'd read in great depth. The Brontës were a favourite, while Jane Austen was appreciated for her prose but not for her snobbery (as my mother saw it). I became an avid reader, in my turn, and started to adapt the books I liked into pieces of theatre when I was at Primary School – 'Havelock The Dane' (based on Hamlet) and 'Path Through The Woods' (about Camden School for Girls which I hoped to go to) – and got all my friends to act in them. I was on track to be an actor, but my parents were not behind that either. They both wanted me to be independent and have a career, because even in the early 1960s most women weren't in the workforce as they are today. They were always worried about money, and acting was a very insecure profession if you didn't have money behind you. I listened to their concerns about the need to earn money to be independent as a woman, but law (the profession my father was keen for me to follow) didn't interest me. Not a lot has changed about the need for financial support if you work in the arts: in fact, it has got worse.

Free dance and expressionism: The roots of Pure Movement: The body in the space

I first heard of Litz Pisk from my father as she taught him movement at RADA. My father's response to her movement classes was profound and influenced my understanding of theatre.

Litz Pisk was born in 1909 in Vienna and came to Britain in 1933 as a Jewish émigré from Vienna; she found work drawing caricatures for the *Evening Standard*, as well as teaching movement at RADA. She had been taught movement in Vienna by Elizabeth Duncan, the sister of Isadora Duncan,[1] to cure a scoliosis of the spine. She also studied at the Bauhaus where she went on to train with one of Max Reinhardt's designers. So began a connection between body, space and motion. She had a successful career in Vienna, where she was involved in the premiere of *The Rise and Fall of the City of Mahagonny* – working with Brecht, Kurt Weill and Lottie Lenya. This was the hinterland that she developed into Actors' Movement classes which she taught at RADA, the Old Vic Theatre School and then at Central School of Speech and Drama. Her movement was unique and informed by the

---

[1] Isadora Duncan, pioneering American-born dancer, who developed the art form of modern contemporary dance through freedom of movement, creating its form from the study of Greek art.

principles of Expressionism and the use of space.[2] An expressionism that when adapted to an actor became about freeing the individual. Her teaching convinced students that:

we had it in us to become more alive physically, more transformable and expressive.[3]

*

The movement exercises I described above were Pisk's exercises. My father then went on to teach them to me when I was still at school. I was curious, while he was unconvinced by ballet,[4] which he thought repressed natural responses, and didn't contribute to acting. I sensed how Pisk's exercises changed my movement, making it more expressive.

Physicality was an important part of my family life, and held the same importance in our family as singing round the piano might hold for other families. My mother used to go to Scottish Country Dancing once a week, and taught me the highland fling, and the elusive pas-de-basque. As a young boy, Wolfe was a boxing champion and an athlete. Boxing was one of the routes to success for Jewish families like my father's.[5] But once he went to the Portsmouth Grammar School he discovered poetry, which took him on his path to RADA. However, every day he would follow a physical regime: track running at the sports field, and outdoor swimming.

He was physically transformative as an actor, but the ideal for Shakespearean actors was more elegant and upright in the 1930s and 1940s – even in the 1950s with the advent of social realism. He viewed Shakespeare as the pinnacle of success, and played many Shakespearean roles, but never Hamlet or Benedick. In those days you still had to look a certain way for roles like that. His obituary described him as a 'protean' actor – or character actor, and physical transformation was part of how he approached his roles. So this radical form of physical expression from the heart of Central Europe had a powerful impact on someone like my father, whose background wasn't Anglo-Saxon, and by declension, on me.

Many of the movement teachers who had followed Pisk at RADA were part of this tradition. Madame Toshka, Ruth Ena Ronen, Joan Kemp, Jackie Snow and then of course me. The principles of expression in movement challenge more corrective practices, which look at the body as a problem to be solved – whereas expression looks at how and why a body moves.

For those of us whose bodies don't conform to an Anglo-Saxon norm, expressive movement with its lower centre of gravity, dynamism, as well as freedom to use the imagination (techniques I explore later) was very liberating. When I went to RADA in 2015, though this form of movement was recognized, it was less clear on its connection to acting, and there was little mention of the work of the teachers I mention above. Instead, there was a strong focus on alignment – the locus of which was usually shoulders that needed to drop, pelvises that needed to tuck, and heads which needed to pull back, producing a long silhouette. This is useful for breath and voice work but is not the only way to access sound. And it is

---

[2]This is Pure Movement, as taught to me by Trish Arnold. Pure Movement is also (as I mention frequently) part of a community of practice and comprises, as well, the work of Litz Pisk as taught to Sue Lefton.
[3]George Hall in *The Independent*, 29 March 1997.
[4]Both my parents would have liked me to have stopped my classes for financial reasons – which is probably one of the reasons I kept dancing, which thankfully they tolerated!
[5]A fact reflected in Clifford Odet's play *Golden Boy* – a part my father played.

essentially static, and upright – when actors need to move as much as they need to stand still. Students need agency if they are to learn. Self-education through understanding how the body moves, and why, rather than focusing on what needs to be 'corrected'.

For my father (and for me), expressionism, or expressive movement, also reaches into our heritage through Klezmer music, the Jewish music of exile, for dance and expression. A seminar on the origins of Klezmer at the University of London School of Oriental and African Studies, which I attended in 2023, charted a link between Klezmer music played at funerals and the physical responses of the musicians and mourners. The mourners expressed their grief in gesture, movements which reached upwards, and many of the violinists also moved when not playing. Musicians and mourners were 'dancing' their grief as they expressed their feelings. When I watched the movement, which the ethno-musicologists suggested evolved before the pogroms, it resembled expressionistic dance, which I describe below. There is clearly a connection between self-expression, cultural inclusion and self-education.

I met with Thomas Kampe, to discuss the displaced Jewish modern dancer and dance educator, Tile Rössler, who was dismissed from the Palucca Dance School in 1933 after Hitler came to power.[6,7] My focus here is on a particular humanist model of movement education, which many of the modern dance innovators initiated, described by Kampe as an 'organic' approach to teaching. Rössler aimed to:

> give all students the opportunity to be free and uninhibited in our lessons. (Kampe, 2025)

As a teacher of dance teachers, Rössler developed a 'reflexive model', where students would observe class and then discuss with each other dance problems they had witnessed, and exchange opinions. This was a process of self-education. The movement classes encouraged

> development of the senses, imagination, self-education and daily life experiment … [through] … Rhythmical movement practice.[8] (Kampe, 2025)

This shows how movement training, as it came to this country from Central Europe, was a liberating set of techniques, teaching actors how to express themselves without adhering to cultural norms and traditions. As I show, its development in Drama Schools relied on individual artist teachers developing these practices.

Teaching developments in movement and education

These teaching developments in movement that the free dance exponents from Central Europe pioneered emerged in state education, after the Second World War. At Fitzjohn's Primary School we did 'Movement with Music' played to us on the radio, in the assembly hall. We were encouraged to move freely to classical music, with just our imaginations

---

[6]April 1933 saw mass arrests, books were burnt, Jewish businesses were burnt and laws enacted to suspend Civil Liberties. The 7 April 1933 'Law for the Restoration of the Professional Civil Service' excluded Jews and political opponents from public positions. It was this climate that led to Rössler's sacking.
[7]Rössler continued dancing and writing about movement in Palestine/Israel – a displacement which made her both part of the Zionist project, and a victim of racism in her own country. Kampe writes about how reading her students' essays, written in 1944, 'full of hope in times of extermination, was shockingly breathtaking', and the discovery of drawings and photographs of 'a lost body of German Modern Dance'.
[8]Tile Rössler quoted by Thomas Kampe in 'Tracing Fertile Ground' (2025).

to guide us. I vividly remember enacting a bear to Mussorgsky's 'A Night on the Bare Mountain' – children and words! We also did country dancing in our black plimsoles, shorts and T-shirts, as part of Physical Education. These influences were part of the development of dance and movement education that had started in Central Europe and then also formed part of the post-war revival of interest in the folk culture of the working classes and pre-war interest in movement education.[9]

Later, when I was at Bristol University studying Drama, the dance educator Veronica Sherborne taught us movement. Her classes freed me both emotionally and physically and they struck a chord. 'You have a passion for movement, don't you?' Despite loving to move, I hadn't really grasped that there was a subject called movement. I found her classes revelatory with their emphasis on the body to create a narrative, and my reply was yes, and where could I go to study 'movement' further. She then suggested I go to Ecole Jacques Lecoq in Paris – which I had already heard of.

Sherborne exemplifies the journey of movement, from the British education system to drama schools, as part of the culture of renewal after the Second World War. In 1972 Sherborne was teaching at The Bristol Old Vic Theatre School and in the Drama Department, and I recall how many students in my year were dismissive of her work. She had impeccable credentials; she had studied with Laban and Lisa Ullman in the Art of Movement Studios in Manchester, and had worked with Laban on his book *Modern Education Dance: Pioneering Developmental Movement for Children*. Her emphasis was human expression, through movement and relationships – something that actors explore all the time – and she often did the movement on our productions in the Van Dyke Theatre. The un-showiness and authenticity of her work was unappreciated by young students of theatre and culture and my conclusion is that we prioritized the influence radical male practitioners had on theatre: Brook, Brecht, Grotowski and Artaud, which we could analyse intellectually, over the nitty-gritty of physicality which asked us to be in touch with our feelings and sensations. Many women contributed to these innovative practices and pedagogy but were overlooked, perhaps because the work depended on experience over theory. And possibly because of the importance they gave to educating young children, as well as artists.

> Through my own experience of teaching and observing human movement, I have come to the conclusion that all children have two basic needs: they need to feel at home in their own bodies, and to gain body mastery, and they need to be able to form relationships.[10]

These basic human needs that Sherbourne describes are the same for actors, who also need to feel physically at home, be in charge of their movement and create believable relationships on stage. I recall one class where she berated us for being intellectuals – 'you are all in your heads' – unable to find any impulses that were human! This is a constant dilemma – how to get thoughts and responses flowing through the body. It took me a lifetime to find this out.

---

[9] These classes owed much to Laban, and the dance and movement traditions pioneered by Margaret Morris, for health and fitness. Country dancing was part of Physical Education. Margaret Morris was a dance pioneer, who trained with Raymond Duncan (brother of Isadora Duncan). In 1925 she started to promote dancing as exercise and promoted the remedial aspects of movement.

[10] Veronica Sherborne Website, 2025. https://www.sherbornemovementuk.org/about/sherborne-developmental-movement/

From quite a young age, I was grappling with how different these experiences with 'movement' were to my ballet classes.

Physicality in theatre in 1969 in the UK

Litz Pisk

I first saw Pisk's theatre work when she staged the movement in *Peer Gynt* at Manchester 69 Theatre, directed by Michael Elliot. When I met the actors afterwards, they told me that Litz Pisk had also been their movement teacher at Central School of Speech and Drama. Movement was a new idea for me – and it clearly formed a direct line to movement directing. Litz Pisk, pioneered the impact movement teaching had on both theatre and training, and I describe the creative impact this production had on my thinking, below.

Steven Berkoff

I saw Steven Berkoff in *Metamorphosis* at the Hampstead Theatre club, also in 1969, and it was my first experience of how movement can be used as dramaturgy. Steven Berkoff's adaption of Franz Kafka's novel dramatized how '*In all of us there is a little Gregor Samsa beetle*' (Berkoff, 1999), showing the horror of Gregor Samsa waking up one morning transformed into a beetle. Berkoff describes his dramatization as a rejection of the '*barking at the social order by our angry young men*' which '*seemed to be so dated and irrelevant to me at the time*' (Berkoff, 1999).

Berkoff had been to Jacques Lecoq in Paris where he encountered the transformative training of modern mime, which he describes as physical action, which is suggestive, rather than mimetic. Berkoff applied this to *Metamorphosis* which asked the audience to engage their imaginations as he used movement to convey the nightmare of Gregor's giant beetle trapped in a small conventional flat (and family). He acted the beetle by crawling along the floor, his back legs sprawled behind 'like broken limbs' and his arms at 45-degree angles. He scuttled up scaffolding and suspended from the ceiling, sometimes dropping like a stone onto the ground. His family moved to a metronome, with white faces like Kabuki theatre, and the beetle kept pace with the rhythm, '*as if it was born out of the misery of the family's routines*' (Berkoff, 1999). The text was truthful, delivered naturalistically, but the movement expressed the masking of despair, and underlying political horror that lay at the heart of Kafka's story, much more powerfully for me, than many 'straight' plays I saw. The connection between movement, acting, scenography, lighting and intention was an entirely new way to work with physicality.

Jacques Lecoq and theatre

I had never heard of mime,[11] or Jacques Lecoq, but in the programme I read that Berkoff had trained at 'L'École de Mime, Mouvement et Théâtre' in Paris. By the time I went to Bristol

---

[11] Except for the pantomimic version I had learned for ballet exams.

University I had my dream of where to train professionally, if I could find the money. I would go to Paris to learn how to be animals, re-play ordinary life strangely, and make extraordinary theatre. Veronica Sherbourne's prompt gave me the courage to apply to Jacques Lecoq, and I was admitted to the course and received funding. The post-war Welfare State funded innovation of this kind, for many of its students. All my studies were state funded: my schooling was free; I didn't pay for university, and then I received a scholarship from the Inner London Education Authority (ILEA) to go to Lecoq. At my audition in 1972 the ILEA asked me how I would 'repay' them. I meant it when I said, 'I'll bring it back to this country and I'll share my knowledge'.

Training with Trish Arnold: Movement and education in drama schools

In 1996, after working professionally as an actor for nearly 20 years, I was offered the post of Head of Movement at Rose Bruford College. My brief was to create a movement syllabus for the BA Acting and Directing Courses, staff it and teach it. In 1996 movement teaching in drama schools was mainly handed on through transmission[12] and many of its pioneers continued to teach. Trish Arnold still worked at Guildhall. I approached her, to teach me her system and help me create a three-year syllabus in actor training. First, she auditioned me to see if I had 'an educated body' – as she put it. I passed that test easily and committed to training with her once a week for as long as was needed. This was for thirteen years as it turned out! It took some time though for her to be convinced by my stamina or commitment as a teacher. 'Won't you miss acting dear?' she kept on asking (I did and kept finding ways to keep it going, as well as my movement directing). I was doggedly committed to understanding her technique and how to teach it and eventually I became one of the people she passed on her work to.[13] I learned her work systematically and was only allowed to teach aspects of the syllabus (some exercises being more difficult than others) once I had embodied them fully. This helped me understand when I had embodied an exercise, and what I still needed to keep working on. It took me months to learn how to drop my weight in the leg swing, for instance.

To make the movement seem natural to me involved many hours of private practice. It was exhilarating – where most of my learning had been collective and with performance aims in mind, here I was learning movement in a very pure form. Pure Movement[14] gave me a technique that allowed me to be accurate and nuanced as I moved. Embodying the movement was like learning a role: going over the words, the intentions, the sensations, the rhythm of the text until one day you know the text completely. It was the same with Pure Movement. There is a moment where the swing drops with an impulse, when it is in your body.

I quickly recognized the privilege of learning Arnold's work firsthand. This was a whole system of movement training based on 'the swing' and its various pathways through space.

---

[12]Or delivered by movement teachers who had trained in Europe in modern dance. My point being it was hard to train in Movement Teaching as a subject.
[13]For further reference to her community of practice, see the DVD 'Tea with Trish'.
[14]There are some concerns about the term 'Pure Movement', which I discuss in Chapter 5 on Trish Arnold.

There was a consistent methodology and ethos and a calibrated approach to how to teach the work. It was a long, productive thirteen-year apprenticeship.

As I got deeper into the work, I became curious about its provenance. The work came from the dance practitioner Sigurd Leeder and I traced his connection to the dance movements of the Weimar Republic. The Weimar Republic (1918–1933) was Germany's first republic, established by a constitution drafted in Weimar. A period of innovative culture and also political instability.

Sigurd Leeder

Sigurd Leeder had danced with Kurt Jooss in Germany in the 1930s. Jooss and Leeder developed a pedagogy to teach modern dance – or dance theatre as they called it. Arnold explained to me its principles and how this freed the dancer's body and made it expressive. These principles were being researched and developed in the early twentieth century and were part of the revolutionary movements taking place in the Weimar Republic, before the rise of the Nazis.

Trish Arnold and free dance: Gravity and the natural world

There is a book by Jane Winearls called *Modern Dance: The Jooss-Leeder Method*, which describes the development of twentieth-century modern dance as an 'expressive style quite different from that of other forms' of dance.

The revolutionary dance practitioners of the early to mid-twentieth century[15] broke with the archaic form of ballet to research new ways of moving with 'ceaseless probing and experiment' (Winearls, 1958).

The link between these revolutionary practitioners was gravity, the analysis of the body in space, and an understanding of weight. This often led to an abstract expressionistic idea of the earth, the life force, harnessed in interpretations of myth, politics or personal expression. Reflected in the innovations of the jazz age, expressed through the music of Stravinsky or Shostakovich, but also through jazz itself. All these influences created many physical possibilities of how a body moves in response to forces both from the inside and the outside. Impulse and stimulus.

Described in this way, we can see the multiple possibilities for artistic and creative expression that flourished in the Weimar Republic.

Pure Movement: A synthesis

'Pure Movement' comes partly from this tradition and partly from the Michel Saint-Denis tradition and was developed specifically to reflect the pragmatic and text-based tradition of British actor training.[16] Its repertoire is taken from only a selection of the exercises described in Winearls' book – as the degree of technical complexity in the Jooss-Leeder method is not necessary for an actor.

---

[15] Martha Graham, Kurt Jooss, Rudolph Laban, among many others.
[16] It didn't encompass the more abstract ideas of 'the earth' or 'the life force', but rather, connected the work to plays, or characterization, or simply every day activities.

The fundamental principle of these modern systems of movement – a balance between tension and relaxation – is followed in 'Pure Movement' – as described below. The dynamic oscillation of movement that we can all tap into.

> The underlaying rhythmic cycle of all life forms is a waxing and waning of energy. Both are living forces and one is constantly flowing into the other. Relaxation in movement should be regarded as a living force out of which a climax of tension may be achieved steadily and harmoniously. It must be a consciously controlled diminishing of power rather than an uncontrolled collapse separating movements of aggressive tension.[17]

However, Arnold would never use language suggesting 'conscious control' and her approach was much simpler – exploratory and technical. In Chapter 4 I examine how conflating physical experiment with spirituality or even morality led to dance being used for social improvement, in ways that are extremely hard to countenance today.

However, what Arnold shared with the new dance experimenters, Jooss and Leeder, was the understanding of the need for a pedagogy and how movement can be broken down, often into a play of opposites.

In her book, Winearls shows how Jooss and Leeder adapted the methodology of their ballet training to their own movement techniques and disciplines. For instance, the first chapter 'Principles of Movement' is broken down into the descriptors:
Tension and relaxation
Weight and strength
Flow and guidance

Arnold and LAMDA

This is a brief description of how Arnold developed her training with Leeder as a practice for movement teaching in drama schools – what she utilized and what she left out.

From 1955 to 1964 Arnold was recruited by the Principal of LAMDA Michael McCowan who, alongside the Head of Movement Norman Ayrton and Head of Voice Iris Warren, was looking for a movement teacher in the 'Michel Saint-Denis' tradition.[18]

Iris Warren said to Arnold: 'I hope you won't do anything that interferes with their breath.' This is how movement was 'imported' to drama schools to support vocal technique. It also shows how movement practices are developed organically in relation to what is needed, that practice precedes theory: that practice is in fact empirical.

McCowan had been influenced by the impact of Michel Saint-Denis' school at the Old Vic, with the body key to the training of the actor. He wasn't an advocate of Free Dance, and owed more to the influence of Jacques Copeau, whose school in Paris had introduced many of the elements of how to train the actor in physicality that we take for granted today.[19]

Arnold was part of this new body-based tradition of training. She had trained with Leeder, rather than with Copeau or Michel Saint-Denis, and her practice was more linked

---

[17]*Modern Dance: The Jooss-Leeder Method* by Jane Winearls. Chapter 1, page 24 (Winearls, 1958).
[18]I explain this tradition in later chapters.
[19]Which I describe later.

to Expressionism. However, Arnold eventually embodied a synthesis between the two traditions of Expressionism and Lecoq, mentioned above, as she also went on to train with Lecoq.

In turn she was able to help me think how to adapt my understanding of Lecoq into the more psychologically based training the drama schools were intent on.[20]

*

I have described some of the historical background to some of the work I teach, and the ideas that considered physicality as expressive and communicative. There are already some concepts that are hard to grasp – the idea for instance that relaxation is 'a living force', or that moving from ease to tension ought to happen 'harmoniously'.

Actors respond to practical activities that can be taught. But the balance is, as soon as movement for actors becomes just a series of exercises – even good ones that strengthen the body and develop flexibility – their connection to acting is lost. Here are some thoughts that guided me, when putting together the syllabus I made; however, the depth and detail of these ideas are more fully explored in later chapters.

1 Moving and exercises that help us move freely

Exercises need to help actors transform – both by opening out their bodies and through the experience of how movement can change their bodies and their imaginations. The Gravity Swing[21] is excellent for actors, its momentum has its own energy and can't be controlled. You let go in the swing, and you breathe when you move. When you do a huge arc of movement, like a Gravity Swing,[22] you move through the dimensions of high, low, wide, narrow, forwards and backwards, harnessing your weight, balance, breath and physical power, which takes you into the space around you. The Gravity Swing demands physical technique and body awareness from the actor/mover. It is exciting to do, and requires an understanding of what the body is doing at any one time.

2 Movement in drama schools: How it is transmitted

Movement teaching in drama schools is a technique, delivered through structured classes. You can then rely on these techniques to give you options when you rehearse or perform. Movement is part of actor training that has been taught for decades: often broken down in Movement, Voice, Acting, Text, Singing and Scene Study. Movement classes are meant to connect to all the other classes. The classes are transmitted through the expertise of the practitioner who is the teacher.

---

[20] I also developed a lot of my thinking on this when working with Annie Tyson at Rose Bruford.
[21] I will come back to the Gravity Swing frequently.
[22] I describe the swing in Chapter 5 on Trish Arnold.

3 First steps teaching movement

I start with the body in front of me. Movement teaching is essential for all actors, but not all actors find moving easy. I am teaching a practice that is accessible for all professional actors, so I focus as much on the individual as I do on my practice. In a class I will swiftly assess how I need to adapt an exercise, if someone finds it too hard. Or I will stop the flow and break the exercise down for actors to explore together. This is how most teachers of any physical discipline make their classes accessible.

4 Is correction negative?

Movement training for actors helps them understand how their body functions and moves in any direction.[23] I give feedback that refers to the exercises I am teaching. Working with detail can change how the movement feels for an actor. Feedback and sensation are vital principles for teaching actors. But I don't want to give an overview in my classes of what an actor's problem might be – tight shoulders, hamstrings, etc. The work will gradually unravel this, and the actor isn't to blame if they have tight muscles.

The actor learns how to express themselves artistically and technically through their body. Movement is a physical activity: sports and dance and martial arts classes give feedback, so the body can function at its optimum capacity. This is the same spirit in which feedback is given for an actor's movement, only the feedback is also about the meaning or the story. Movement training allows actors to recall and replay physical actions and responses, consciously crafting them to create meaning. There is a technique to learn how to do this, and a sensibility to develop to inhabit this. Feedback is a yardstick that enables, and not a judgement of the actor's body.

*

Much of twentieth-century movement training in Drama Schools has focused technically on the following, delivered experientially and over a space of time.

1. Alignment
2. Availability – being ready
3. Changing old habits: posture, tension or 'blocks' that get in the way
4. Expressiveness and physicality for characterization
5. The use of the space

The neutral body as a trope in drama school training

How much do drama schools focus on the neutral body as a starting point from which to transform? The first three points above are to help the body be functional and creative, and

---

[23] When I worked at Stratford Festival Theatre, I was struck by how many of the actors could talk in detail about their spines, or their muscles and tendons, or why certain movements were unavailable to them. British actors are less educated about their own skeletal musculature systems.

could be seen as contributing to a 'neutral body'. It is easier to move if your body is free and 'softened' (or available), to make more deeply expressed choices. Tension can (for instance) block effective communication.

There have been concerns expressed about training actors to start with a neutral body.

Mark Evans in *Movement Training for the Modern Actor* has proposed that movement teachers working in drama schools in 2009 worked with the idea of a 'neutral body' and the 'natural body' and places me very much as one of its proponents, quoting me as saying:

> The neutral body isn't the perfect body. The neutral body is your neutral body, your body without tension, with alignment, that is physiologically possible for your body. (Evans, 2009)

My response describes physical availability – a process of discovery, and openness from which to build your physical choices as an actor. But he also makes a very interesting point that the idea of the 'natural' body connects to culture, and aesthetic, and there can be difficulties when the two are conflated and when one or the other is held as an ideal. I address the difficulties this can cause for actors in the next chapters, and how this can lead to training that is based on an ideology of the 'perfect body'. This is not my focus in any of the movement classes or body of work I teach.

*

It is true that there have been pressures on movement training in drama schools to address postural issues. Movement training needs to encompass the twin demands of voice and acting and actors need to discover vocal freedom to be able to be fully expressive vocally. The voice becomes trapped if the neck or larynx is tight, or the head pushing forwards and vocal power is harnessed by a deeper breath connection, which is easier when the spine is free and aligned, with the weight balanced. This is not aesthetic, but functional. How to get the body to support the voice? The implications of this, and how wide the feet are placed, which changes whether your weight is lifted or dropped, are considered in 'Stages of Reckoning' which I discuss later.

Neutral is not used in an aesthetic context, and I am not aware of it being used at all, except in relation to the 'Neutral Mask', which I also discuss later. I am not a proponent of the 'neutral' body, and even referring to 'natural' has normative connotations, suggesting the opposite, unnatural, is wrong. As can the word 'authentic', whose opposite 'inauthentic' can imply a judgement – and who gets to say what is authentic or not?

I don't use the term neutral, or natural, in my classes. The actor is learning how to move with expression and clarity of intention. Not a perfect body, nor prioritizing one body type over another – because there is no such thing. Theatre is for all bodies and features a cast of all bodies and equally an actor transforms into a body that is different from theirs – an elastic body, not a neutral body.

*

> Drama schools are repositories for significant knowledge and experience, but could they do more to provide … experiment and research? (Evans, 2009)

How does this relate to movement?

Many movement teachers, myself included, have been 'researching' throughout our careers how movement training can develop physicality and acting. In many cases the research has been unfunded, within the drama schools themselves, and quietly pursued in class or with our peers. However, there needs to be more research, and recorded reflections, as Evans suggests, and the drama schools could actively fund this, so that training remains contemporary.

The next chapters explore how this river of work continues, and how I have understood the exercises I teach – with the awareness that more research is certainly needed.

3 Transformation

Acting is transformation, movement is transformation, transformation as a part of social change, transformation of our drama schools.

I remember going backstage as a child. It would haunt me how, from the moment the play started, worlds changed. How was something so vital, not real?

'I feel like time stops in the theatre'. My father and I had walked onto the stage before the half-hour call.[1] The stage was eerily silent. The auditorium empty but poised for action. I could see myself 'out front' watching the performance as if I had jumped through time. My heart was skipping with anticipation.

My father agreed 'Yes, as soon as the play starts, the actor is in the same space as the audience, but time is different, more intense'.

*

Acting is transformation. You create something true, but you honour something constructed. The text you speak (on stage or film) might be a speech pattern you don't use, the actions you embody, not how you move, the relationships you have with others, outside your experience.

You need craft to do this, brought to life through your imagination. You learn *how* to do this as a preparation for performance, usually through training.

Movement and transformation

Movement is one of the key subjects you learn at a drama school that teaches us the art of transformation:

Acting – movement – transformation

The movement classes and syllabus I teach come from two twentieth-century innovative and radical (for their time) traditions. Body-based training gave actors techniques to embody craft and develop their imaginations, and to work as an ensemble. Transformation can also be social and political. My understanding of working with movement included this propulsion towards the social change it was also part of; and an appreciation of how important movement was to the post-war drama school project. Transformation in every sense.

---

[1] Actors are meant to be in their dressing rooms thirty-five minutes before curtain up, this is called 'the half'.

When I started teaching in 1989, it was still on the crest of the wave of these transformative traditions, which inspired me to want to teach and continue to develop an understanding of movement. But how do we continue this spirit of enquiry and radical transformation?

*

Jacques Lecoq opened his school in Paris in 1957. It was called L'École Internationale de Théâtre Jacques Lecoq – giving equal importance to mime, movement and theatre. *The Moving Body* (Lecoq, 2002 [1997]), which describes Lecoq's work, places Lecoq's journey with movement in a political context, both during the Nazi occupation, and after the Liberation of France 1944.[2] Lecoq set up a theatre troupe, 'Les Compagnons de la Saint-Jean' to stage festive events and mark the end of the war – such as re-enacting the arrival of a train carrying liberated prisoners. The company mimed and danced to thousands of people. The biographical note[3] at the beginning of *The Moving Body* also mentions how during the occupation Lecoq worked with a 'a group of enthusiasts' exploring gymnastics, mime, movement and dance as a form of resistance to the fascist ideology. After the war, Jean Dasté[4] invited Lecoq to join a new company, 'Les Comédiens de Grenoble', where he took responsibility for their physical training. Lecoq had trained in sports and extended this understanding of physical action to dramatic action.

> It was not a question of training athletes, but of training dramatic characters ... – a natural extension of the gestures acquired through sports.[5]

Lecoq credits Jean Dasté as introducing him to the expressive and non-naturalistic possibilities of masked performance and masks. This was both Japanese Noh Theatre and the 'noble mask', introduced in a performance of 'L'Exode', which Lecoq went on to develop into the neutral mask.[6] Lecoq's description of performing a Noh play called 'Sumida River' with mimed movements of the boat, while they vocalized the sounds of the river, connects to some of the experiments in expressionistic dance which I describe below. Jean Dasté was Copeau's son-in-law and had trained with him. The influence of Copeau was fundamental for Lecoq, especially the objectives of 'Les Copiaux', the theatre company he founded – to create theatre that is simple, direct and accessible. He says that *'Copeau became a reference point to my work'*.

*

The other tradition of Expressionism, Free Dance, was equally radical. I reflect further here on how its teachers encouraged students to express themselves[7] and delve into emotional life channelled into a physical life. Expressionism comes from a deep vein of movement pedagogy which started in Central Europe but was disseminated globally by dance teachers (frequently of Jewish heritage), many living in America or, if from Europe, often in conflict

---

[2]When France was liberated from the Nazis by the Allies (Britain, the United States and the Soviet Union).
[3]Jacques Lecoq, *The Moving Body*, (London: Methuen Drama, 2000).
[4]Jacques Copeau's son-in-law.
[5]Lecoq, *The Moving Body*.
[6]Discussed in Chapters 11 and 12.
[7]See Tile Rössler above.

with the Nazi regime. The common description for this movement was Free Dance[8] and it is striking how many women made up the teachers who left Vienna or Germany, or were from families from Eastern Europe fleeing because of the pogroms;[9] women whose politics, repertoire or race (as Jews) antagonized the Nazi regime.[10] The reach of these 'dance artists' was international and the slant of their work politically and socially aware. Their performances were often dangerous politically, as they looked at difficult and emotionally challenging subjects. Their observations on dance and gesture shared similarities to the developments in psychological acting at the time. Here is Nadia Chilkovsky expressing how we move differently in private from in public.

> Every time you move around when you are alone, you perform a soliloquy at a very intimate level. You would probably not use similar movements in public. Human movement reveals things about your personality that your tongue will never say.[11]

Anna Sokolow

Anna Sokolow was born in the United States, the daughter of Russian immigrants. She was a proponent of Free Dance and 'felt a deep social sense about what I wanted to express, and the things that affected me deeply (are) what I did and commented on' (Harris, 2021).

Her dances explored the Great Depression and the Holocaust, famously expressed in her dance 'Kaddish' in 1945. She collaborated with Elia Kazan at the famous Actor's Studio in New York, taking sessions with the actors – another example of how movement innovations connected to developments in psychological acting (Harris, 2021).

Hannah Berger

Hanna Berger was an Austrian dancer, choreographer and lifelong anti-Nazi and communist. She remained in Germany for some of the early part of the Nazi regime, but her dances and writings were fiercely anti-Nazi. She criticized Nazi cultural policy in an article 'About German Dance and its real contents'[12] and was involved in anti-communist resistance in Berlin. In 1942 she was arrested and sentenced to two years hard labour but escaped during her transfer to Ravensbrück concentration camp. All this time she was an expressionist dancer – one of her anti-war dances which she performed in 1937, 'Solo Krieger' to music by Ulrich Kessler, was banned by the Nazis.

---

[8]Laban, Mary Wigman, Martha Graham (the development of whose practice was informed by her German musical mentor Louis Horst), Dalcroze who was a forerunner of Free Dance but developed his own movement system and Yat Malgrem who developed Laban into a movement methodology for acting. And as previously stated Sigurd Leeder and Kurt Jooss.
[9]Nadia Chilkovsky and Miriam Belcher and Anna Sokolow were American, but their parents had fled the pogroms, as had my father's family.
[10]See my reference to Rössler below.
[11]Miriam Blecher co-founded the New Dance Group in New York with Nadia Chilkovsky in February 1932. A working-class organization for dance, advocating 'dance is a weapon in the class struggle' and offering classes for workers as 'enrichment'.
[12]Published in the Swiss Magazine *Der Buhnenkunstler*.

A famous piece she made after the Second World War, 'L'inconnue de la Seine', foresees Lecoq's work on identification with the elements. This showed Berger representing both the waters of the river Seine and the suicide of a woman who jumped into them, with much of the work improvised, to keep the artist connected to her impulses. This creative flow between embodying the river and the subject was an approach that Jacques Lecoq developed in his school through the identification with the elements and the Neutral Mask.

In all these examples, consider how alive and unfiltered these dancers were – the body expressively communicating in an empty space the intensity of their physical narrative, propelled through their passion and their imaginations – as much as their technique. Can you teach this technically and practically, inside the confines of a course or a drama school? Can this be adapted for actors to tap into empathetically and develop their physical imaginations?

In order to 'play' at being the river, the body becomes eloquent, embodying its rhythm, weight, tempo, dynamics. You could describe this as the body 'becoming' the story, the narrative. At Lecoq, these interpretive techniques would be researched in movement classes as a 'preparation': 'of the body, of the voice, of the art of collaboration (of which theatre is the most extreme artistic representation) and of the imagination'.[13]

The power of the body and physicality to transform is more than just learning a skill – a description often given to movement in drama schools. It is learning to move with the language of human expression, which is shared with other actors, and channelled into theatrical innovation.

Exercises as technique

The syllabus I developed is delivered as a series of classes broken down into a series of exercises to prepare the actor for performance. But the desire and design for the teaching is for the actor to find the full range of their expression, as described above.

All movement and dance classes share a similar approach – preparation, teaching of new exercises (which often consolidate the technique of older exercises already taught) and exploration or composition of dramatic themes to conclude the class. Movement is also acting, and the classes develop emotional and imaginative connection and the art of storytelling.

The classes in the syllabus I developed come under two separate headings, delivered as two separate strands:

1. **Pure Movement** (technical movement):
2. **Expressive Movement** (creative expression, using a movement vocabulary).

This followed Lecoq's structure of 'Analyse de Mouvement' and 'Préparation Corporelle' (technical preparation, which could be Pure Movement); and the Improvisation and Autocours classes for students that explored creative expression (Expressive Movement); I was guided by Trish Arnold in how to do this, as I describe in Chapter 5. The principles that lie behind the skills and techniques taught, are creatively adapted from the movement forms, described above.

---

[13]Simon McBurney: Introduction to *The Moving Body* (Lecoq, 2002 [1997]).

Pure Movement and the Gravity Swing

I taught Pure Movement and its tenets and principles in drama schools without needing to explain its purpose. It spoke for itself, and I explained to students that the work was experiential. I approached the work physically, not theoretically – the exercises were incremental, and I kept the classes playful and creative. Underneath all my teaching lay an understanding that, as the actor grows and develops physically, their capacity to work with greater emotional and expressive freedom also develops. This is an organic approach to teaching, which I discuss later, and came from my understanding of the effectiveness of the Gravity Swing – how it transformed expression and movement.

The Gravity Swing makes up most of the exercises in Pure Movement and has been sequestered from the explorations of Free Dance and Laban, so that actors experience the sensation of moving with an impulse.

Modern dance class also uses swings and the momentum of gravity for propulsion. For in dance the 'swing' is used in an abstract or expressive way – to propel you through space or spiral you from one direction to another. In Pure Movement, the Gravity Swing is delivered unadorned, and focuses on the simplicity of its components. Each moment has potential for the actor. The body starts in stillness and silence, from one of the key starting points in space – wide, or high, or on the diagonal.[14] The journey to the starting point will also be dramatic and expressive – opening your arms to greet someone, reaching up high as a preparation to dive.

> The principles of a swing are:
> Preparation
> Drop
> Swing
> Suspension.

You lift your arm or leg, and you drop the weight, to let it go into momentum. This develops into a swing, as the body falls through space (in the opposite direction to where it started), to complete its journey and hover in a suspension (like a musical pause) to return through the same arc.

This discovery of the dynamic momentum of the swing introduces unpredictability and 'surprise' into movement. But freedom in movement is equally important – freedom in movement is liberty.

Trish Arnold would say, not only does the swing improve functional movement, as in balance, walking, being able to sit, stand, but it also makes dancing better (if you are a dancer).

> The swing works with gravity, harnessing your own natural weight into a movement that is free, and where it finishes in space, is natural, inevitable – not placed.[15]

The harnessing of energy for both acting and dance allows the body to respond, travel and be still, in the performance space. Expressive. Uncensored.

---

[14] These are starting points in dimensional space, which I introduce later.
[15] Taken from my notes when learning with Trish Arnold.

Expressive movement: Dance and play

Expressive Movement (as I developed it) was based on two very simple principles – play and dance, as they *relate to the craft of acting*.

Dance

The principles for acting taken from dance derive from either traditional dance forms, or modern dance forms like Free Dance.

Play

Play shares some principles or techniques taken from Mime or Physical Theatre, but the focus is to develop observation, reciprocity and transformation, so you move expressively, create a story and work as part of an ensemble.

Play is also a response to the world we live in, but as observation and re-playing the world around us.

Dance principles for actors

- Rhythm, tempo, use of space, connection to others, patterns
- An extended form of movement or a phrase of movement; broken down into movement qualities, tension and energy to express physical responses to internal stimuli – joy, fear, love, relationships
- Expression of myths, stories, ceremonies, rites of passage – through rhythm and patterns
- The language of modern dance, connected to inner tempo, and physical use of space to express intention, or character, inner life, or outer expression
- Sometimes supported with music and rhythm.

Play and its principles for actors

- Play as in taking on the physical attributes of other people, or nature, or animals, in dynamic and movement qualities, and inhabiting them fully
- Play as in playing with three-dimensional space, or playing through space
- Play as in playing, as children play, or young animals play, to interpret and understand the world around them
- Play as in re-playing life
- Exploring dynamics, the variety of speed and tempo of the natural world, and then of the people or places you are playing or in
- Play as in the stopping and starting of everyday physical actions
- Play as in reciprocity, response and physical listening.

The combination of both when training actors is to help the actor find a deeper, more expressive form of physicality for stage or screen, and to enable them to work in three-dimensional space. Both are linked by the actor using breath freely and intelligently when they move. Breath also connects to transformation and physical action.

Breath forms a key part of actor movement training

The sense of time is compressed when acting – an intensity which is felt in the body. Sometimes this takes the actor away from their capacity to use their breath effectively. The adrenalin from standing on stage speeds up the heartbeat, quickens the breath – almost a fight/flight sensation. This is before you start to move. Covering distance onstage, or climbing levels, fighting, dancing, or connecting to emotional extremes, demand a deeper connection to the breath, which the actor has to learn to access. This is a paradox because in any high stakes situations in real life, we will usually find the breath or energy we need, but we might pay for it later. Our voice might be ragged if we've partied too much: our body might be tired if we've run a marathon. But the actor trains to mitigate against these 'real-life effects', so they can perform them effectively, and use the breath properly so as not to work with such extreme levels of tension, as in real life. Breathing techniques help open the body and maintain the actor's awareness of their instrument, to work efficiently. Like all Actors' Movement, they also help the body to make meaning in the space.

The journeys of the breath

Try these experiences with breathing.

Breathe in and breathe out – this could be described as a suspension followed by action. Breathing in can be a preparation to move, and when you breathe out there is movement.

Breathing in can also be a gathering inward (or contraction), with the breath out a release or floating free. Inwards to outwards, or downwards to upwards. Contract, expand. Compress, surge upwards.

Or the opposite.

Breathing in can be an inflation, an expansion, with the breath out, a release into movement.

A breath in can be a lifting up and away from gravity: a breath out, a dropping and letting go, as you give into gravity.

Breathing with a Gravity Swing

Breathing in as a preparation, and releasing the breath into a swing, creates the dynamic of the Gravity Swing.

At the end of the swing is a suspension – and another breath, as it returns to the body.

These approaches are also linked to the spine: how to move from the centre of your body out into space.

All movement starts with a breath and moves through the spine

Everything starts with a breath, and everything ends with an action.

The spine is a scaffold for the torso, from where action is generated.

The added physical sensation from working from breath into impulse is release, and the change of weight as you shift or travel through space.

Movement Equation

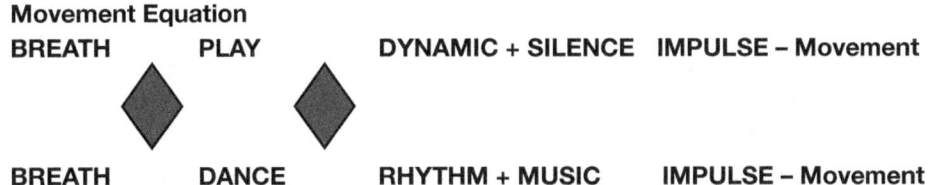

BREATH   PLAY   DYNAMIC + SILENCE   IMPULSE – Movement

BREATH   DANCE   RHYTHM + MUSIC   IMPULSE – Movement

Whether you move in silence or to music, your body finds meaning and expression without words.

The use of the breath in the principles of 'play' and 'dance' (for actors) creates an impulse which, when followed, releases into movement. Release means letting go: let the movement or the response happen and release muscular tension as you 'swing' or move. All movement changes the body.

Actors' Movement is human expression, and the technical skills acquired help actors effectively communicate action and intention during rehearsal and performance.

Radical and feminist movement

Movement practice helps an actor transform physically, to play many parts. But in whose body? The exercises are meant for everybody, to adapt to suit their own physicality. But does our identity influence the art of physical transformation, or impede our opportunities creatively?

Women playing Shakespearean roles is no longer seen as unusual or radical and could be described as part of a renaissance in the exciting reimagining of Shakespearean plays taking place on our stages today. In 2019 Lynette Linton directed *Richard II* with Adjoa Andoh and an all-women cast of colour. Michael Billington's review in *The Guardian* praised the actors for their detailed characterization with Andoh's expressive performance, described as 'a brilliant study of a whimsical tyrant wreathed in the luxury of inherited power'.[16]

But though this had been evolving for several years it was Phyllida Lloyd's Shakespearean Trilogy at the Donmar Warehouse, with Harriet Walter at the helm, that definitively showed how women had the dramatic power and range to tackle Shakespeare in these all-female visceral productions.[17] The trilogy first performed at the Donmar Warehouse in 2008 and was revived in 2016. Suzanna Clapp called it 'one of the most important events of the past 20 years' and asks what makes a bigger difference in theatre: 'the use of new skills or the unearthing of forgotten resources' (Clapp, 2016). All-female productions of Shakespeare plays do both. They expand the range of skills women need to take on roles that are proactive and powerful; while their innate resources are brought to the surface, tapping into their prodigious creativity and expression to make it visible. Women want to tackle the big Shakespearean roles because they are often more interesting, and a more honest reflection

---

[16]Michael Billington, *The Guardian*, 7 March 2019.
[17]Brigid Larmour, when she was directing for Playmobile at The National Theatre, cast women to play Prospero in her two productions of *The Tempest* in the 1990s.

of women's lives today, no longer confined to spousing, childbearing or housework, or charged with being someone's muse (an essentially passive role).

When I was a young actor in the 1970s, there were many feminist theatre companies flourishing in spaces that were exclusively for women, or which foregrounded women's stories.[18,19] Some of these explored a feminist aesthetic, other plays and subjects looking at history through the lens of feminism, like *Vinegar Tom* (by Caryl Churchill) for Monstrous Regiment, repositioning witchcraft as wise women.[20] But these opportunities were exceptional, rather than assumed, and by no means mainstream. It was one of the reasons I came to teach movement, as it was still very hard to get work as a female actor – particularly if you wanted to play a wide range of roles which would develop or deepen your craft.

*

The tsunami in drama schools in 2020 changed my perspective of myself as a woman and a teacher. Feminism, and being female, wasn't considered enough to help my understanding of diversity. I was asked to position my teaching within a different theoretical lens, to determine an understanding of racism, ableism, transphobia and classism. But the answer could also have extended to practical research, rather than theoretical understanding.

When you work physically, it is not enough to have read a book or to discuss its principles. Reflections to do with the body are based on what the practitioner physically understands, alongside what is technically possible to achieve – practice-based research. Instead, we were asked to write down how we proposed to implement change in our practices.

However, I couldn't ignore my own identity as a woman in theatre in the 1970s and 1980s – the struggles I'd had when starting in the theatre in the 1970s and the path I had taken into teaching movement, consequently.

*

Here are some interesting facts about being female in the 1960s and 1970s when I trained and went to school.

- Women were only allowed to open a bank account in their own name in 1975
- It was only in 1965 that you could apply for a no-fault divorce
- Abortion was only legalized in 1968 but still required the signature of a man
- In the 1970s there were three times as many men as women enrolled to study for graduate degrees[21]
- In 1988 Thatcher's government passed clause 28 prohibiting 'the promotion of homosexuality in schools', which had a direct effect on sex education in schools and self-censorship[22]
- It wasn't until 1991 that rape within marriage was criminalized.

---

[18]Female playwrights like Bryony Lavery, Sarah Daniels.
[19]Women's theatre companies, like Cunning Stunts, Blood Group and Monstrous Regiment.
[20]Interestingly, Wise Women are now being researched for stories of how many of them were fraudsters, rather than experts in sympathetic magic.
[21]That was when I was at university.
[22]The Abortion Act was passed in 1967, making abortion legal up to 12 weeks (but not in Northern Ireland), and there have been constant attempts to reverse this in the House of Commons. In 1967 homosexuality was decriminalized, but not all homosexual acts were decriminalized, though homosexuality is now a protected characteristic. I am not sure if the right to abortion is now considered a human right.

Sexual orientation, reproductive rights, access to further education and financial independence (or the lack of them) were all circumscribed as to how women functioned in the workplace, especially one as precarious as the theatre, if you didn't have money behind you, or didn't want to be supported by a husband, or get married.

*

In 1972 a group of women from the second wave Women's Liberation Movement visited my school, during a Domestic Science lesson.[23] They showed us models of the female reproductive system and talked to us about contraception and taking charge of our bodies.[24] They educated us on consent and how to navigate going out with boys, by not being subservient to them. They brilliantly de-constructed the 'wolf whistle' as a tool of female sexual oppression.[25] These discussions were eye-opening and politically transformative. Instead of accepting ourselves as objects to be defined by men, we were being invited to make ourselves the subjects of our own lives and develop critical thinking about our role as women. They didn't mention same sex attraction or homosexuality, though it was implied in much of what was covered. These discussions were necessary in 1972. They were 'consciousness raising sessions' which helped me understand that I didn't need to comply with what society expected of me as a woman.

We were at a school whose badge was the suffragette colours and were expected to excel academically and make up that one-third of women going to university.[26] However, the careers advice many of us received (me included) only suggested the traditional roles of teaching, nursing and social work, not leadership roles or creative paths, and as for marriage and children – it was still expected that women would put their family first. Though I was educated, it was still the exception for women to break into the male-dominated professions.

In 1972 I read *Our Bodies, Ourselves*, published by the Boston Women's Health Book collective. It is a fascinating insight into how women's lives and their bodies were controlled by the patriarchal attitudes of the medical profession and education, particularly in sexual health, abortions and sexual orientation, at that time. There are beautifully clear drawings and frank descriptions, which were researched by the contributors, who were not medical professionals:

Not having the information we needed we decided to find it on our own. (Collective, 1968)

This book helped me realize that knowing something wasn't the same as doing it. For any group of people to feel free and be understood, this must be supported by society, by the laws that govern us, and by our schools and teachers. In other words, the institutions must open the doors to all, without which very few people can ever pass the

---

[23]This was a subject most girls' schools taught: where you learned how to cook, sew and plan meals for your family.
[24]You need parental consent to go on the Pill.
[25]A wolf whistle was when you walked down the street, and a man or boy whistled in appreciation of how you looked: cat-calls were another phenomenon, with men shouting out their approval, or annoyance (if you didn't respond).
[26]It was a state school.

threshold. But it also helped me see that, if the template didn't exist, you had to make it for yourself.

*

I left Lecoq in 1978 and went back to the UK to start acting professionally but the focus was on the text, and not on the body. And most of the words were said by men and were usually played by men. Women's roles were less interesting, and most of them had fewer words to speak – so less to do. The roles I was cast in often required me to mask my energy, and 'play' at femininity. I often ran the warm-ups and started to do movement on some of the shows I was part of – which was one way to stay in the conversation about how to make theatre.

However, what fascinated me at the age of 23 was the synthesis between movement and text to create a theatre, that was political and innovative, by using the body as a starting point. Apart from Ariane Mnouchkine in Paris,[27] who had started the Théâtre du Soleil, most of the role models in the 1970s or 1980s working with the body in theatre in Britain were men – particularly in the Lecoq-based theatre troupes[28] – such as Toby Sedgewick from The Moving Picture Mime Show and Simon McBurney from Théâtre de Complicité.[29] In playwriting, the work of Caryl Churchill, and later Sarah Kane, were ground-breaking in how they explored form and content. However, women directors making theatre, using the body and physicality as a starting point, were rare when I came back from Lecoq in 1978.[30]

*

So, I very happily worked as an actor, every so often earning my living when not acting, by teaching movement. But all the time I searched for companies or role models where the narrative starts *with* the body, to combine text with action, thought, character and situation. Nor did I want to work just with women, but instead with cross-cultural references that were European. I wanted to shape the narrative as a woman working in theatre, working with the physical innovations I had trained in.

In the end I found this when I started to teach movement. This decision was partly determined when I could no longer go on tour as an actor, after my son started school. But I was genuinely excited to have found a way to explore the body, the text and ideas, through movement teaching. All the above charts how my teaching of movement was determined by my gender. Perhaps this isn't fashionable, but it is a fact.

Women movement teachers in drama schools

Drama schools offered women movement teachers an opportunity to develop new practices. My experience of why I taught movement and how I taught it was in direct relation to my experience as a woman. I felt I had direct experience of feeling marginalized and I could work with the body in the theatre space, helping actors move with creativity, unfiltered by

---

[27] See below.
[28] Joan Littlewood was the exception to this. I discuss her impact below.
[29] Simon McBurney, and Marcello Magni and Annabel Arden founded Complicité.
[30] Anna Furse started Blood Group and then went on to run Paines Plough.

socialization. My understanding as a feminist contributed to this. I brought my political understanding to my desire to teach. I saw the students I taught not as conforming to social norms. I believed working like this, the material, the way of playing, the action on stage would be different. Movement colleagues frequently said we were teaching theatre to change theatre.

I was often reminded of the last thing Lecoq said to us, before we graduated. He was a conduit for 'our' creativity, not its determinate. Our learning travelled through him, and out into the theatre. McBurney quotes him in the introduction to *The Moving Body*:

> I am nobody. I am a neutral point through which you must pass in order to better articulate your own theatrical voice.[31]

Teaching movement, I believed, would give actors the ability to transform theatre and transform themselves. When I started to teach movement, I saw it as a catalyst for change. It was the students' work, not mine.

Women teachers in drama schools as pioneers

When I started teaching, movement teachers were pioneers. 'Movement' was both radical in the classrooms, and, paradoxically, the poor relation in the heirarchy of drama schools and theatre making. For example we weren't often consulted on what plays would be chosen that could showcase the physical skills the students were developing. And we were frequently expected to defer to the directors or acting teachers about the students' acting talent. All the movement teachers I came across in the UK at that time were women, so this phenomenon was very gendered.[32] But excitingly, as teachers and movement directors, the teaching of movement gave us a sphere of influence in our classes that bypassed the mainly male-dominated professions of theatre directors and writers. However, while we held sway in the classrooms, we were expected to be silent in the rehearsal space. This meant that I judicially restrained the vibrancy with which I experimented in the classroom, when working with the directors on their productions. But together, as movement teachers, we explored some exciting ideas and ways of working. I therefore understood there was much more potential held within movement than just skill-based classes, as I show below when discussing my theatrical influences in Paris – but I was realistic about what was needed for professional theatre in the UK, as defined by British Actors' Equity, and the Arts Council and Higher Education Funding Council (HEFC).

However, I had the artistic freedom to develop my craft of movement teaching, connecting physical technique to making theatre, unencumbered, because, as a woman, I flew under the radar. I was an outlier, but the benefits were that I had space to experiment. Though much of what I taught in the drama schools never made it into productions, the

---

[31] McBurney, in Lecoq, *The Moving Body*.
[32] Sue Lefton had taught at Guildhall and was the Head of Movement at the Royal Shakespeare Company. Jane Gibson had taught at LAMDA and was the Head of Movement at The National Theatre. Sara Van Beers and Lorna Marshall had been Head of Movement at Rose Bruford, respectively. Wendy Allnut was Head of Movement at Guildhall and Jackie Snow was Movement Teacher at Guildhall and then went on to be Head of Movement at RADA. Lliana Nuquist was Head of Movement at Drama Centre. The exception was Danny McGrath, who became Head of Movement at Guildhall.

schools themselves were positive about the opportunities for educational development and expression it gave actors. A tactical compromise.

Few women were in the spotlight as directors or writers at that time, and I didn't look for recognition in my own profession, just freedom to explore the work. I admit I was more interested in developing the work I was teaching, than considering my political position as a woman, within the industry.

My influences: Paris, 1970s

However, the work I was seeking to develop was different to British Theatre. It was hard to ignore the traces that watching theatre in 1970s Paris left on my imagination, giving me ideas for movement direction and for movement teaching. I only mention a few here, but the experience was very different to British Theatre, and though its practices had not yet reached British drama schools in the 1980s and early 1990s, they certainly influenced my teaching.

Peter Brook

Peter Brook's theatre company was situated at the Théâtre des Bouffes Du Nord in the north of Paris quite close to Lecoq. Our movement teacher, Monika Pagneux, worked with Brook on creating movement for *The Conference of the Bird*s, and many of the actors came to watch our work at the school. Before we even saw the plays there, we felt connected to its work and its actors.

Brook had created the 'International Centre for Theatrical Research'. This was an international group of actors gathered from Mali, Iran, Greece, Spain, Morocco, Japan and the United States, who had travelled round the world researching theatre, and how to make any space you perform in, theatrical.[33] I went to see every single production at the Bouffes Du Nord to witness how actors changed spaces (scenes) and created the narrative by the simplest of means. I saw how physicality and an openness/readiness (as we called it at Lecoq) created an artlessness in their contact with the audience. I saw the diversity of the performers, and the richness of their individuality.

Ariane Mnouchkine

Ariane Mnouchkine was the artistic director of the Théâtre du Soleil. Her production of *L'Age d'Or* used the comic masks (from the Commedia dell'Arte) to tell heartbreaking stories about migration and exploitation. These contemporary events with a politic, even when performing in a playful register, led by the body and a physicality that was emotional, made their socially critical themes immediate and accessible and poetic. As a student of the physical in theatre – the craft of the actors as they ran up walls or created images of riding motorcycles, through flapping their clothes as if the wind was whipping past them, was phantasmagorical and brilliantly played. I longed to see theatre like this in Britain. In my

---

[33]See *The Empty Space* by Peter Brook.

opinion, it has yet to appear. Such work can only occur through ensemble-based production, visionaries and funding.

Tadeus Kantor

The Polish painter/director Tadeus Kantor brought *Dead Class* to the Hotel de Ville. This was a macabre and eerie circus-like séance. An expression of death, where old people, haunted by their childhood, carry the effigies of themselves strapped to their backs. A visceral embodiment of the burden of the past. Their physical presences a ghostly amalgam of young and old, as they sat in the schoolroom and craned to hear the teacher or raised their hands – all conducted without words, to music. All from an acting impulse, rather than the codification of dance. Strange characters emerging from a cycle of waltz music, imagery, repetition and rhythm. Kantor conducted the action on stage, adding to its intensity. The production expanded the possibilities of dramaturgy that bodies can offer. The first time I saw this, the hairs on my head stood up with fear and awe.

*

It is hard to convey the shock of the new these performances had for me. Watching these productions was to see the world as strange, and as such, helped me to understand it and have compassion for people and situations outside my experience. I was transformed and educated by the radical possibilities of what you can do with theatre, with the body as the starting point. I witnessed the magic of an ensemble creating narrative, ideas and emotion through movement, with the individuality of the performers at the heart. When I taught movement in the drama schools, I didn't seek to recreate this, but it would serve to remind me of the power of physicality, and I would use some of the images I had witnessed as a stimulus for me to teach.

Movement training no longer seen as radical and in need of reform

Considering these opportunities and the difficulties working with movement as a woman led me to this conclusion. I had found space to develop a body of work, outside of the mainstream, but I could no longer assume that the radical origins of the movement practice that shaped my thinking and my practice were enough to accommodate all bodies in all spaces, as it had previously done. Besides, as I have explained, I had accepted the need to compromise some of my training, if I was to work collegiately with the drama schools I taught in. There is a new politic today but, although the movement I taught wasn't rejected by the students, it is not understood or trusted by those running the drama schools anymore, particularly the radical part of its provenance.

In 2020, when the big questions about how we teach in drama schools and what we teach started to be considered nationally, it became clear how little the institutions knew about Actors' Movement. To change something, we must first understand it. But was there a desire to ask us what we had done and why? And more importantly – who we were?

*

The inaugural speech of Josette Bushell-Mingo, when she took up her post of Principal of the Royal Central School of Speech and Drama in 2022, was quoted when she was interviewed in *The Stage* newspaper by Orla O'Loughlin.[34] The article argues the need to reform actor training to reflect a broader range of cultures and pedagogical practices. The view is that teaching in drama schools has been secretive and unresponsive to the students, and to the industry, with the pedagogy and practice not inclusive, and arcane.

> Actor training generally happened behind closed doors. (O'Loughlin, 2024)

> It is no longer possible to look at drama or arts training held by one teacher who has the final word without taking account of the student voice. (Bushell-Mingo, 2024)

However, theatre is a collaborative art and in drama schools members of faculty had always collaborated. Voice and acting teachers would often apply our movement exercises in their classes and at RADA, both the Director of Training and the Principal regularly watched our work. The idea that the training is only held by 'one teacher' is also not true. Movement in drama schools, for instance, was part of a community of practice. Many of us, shared exercises, watched each other's classes, and were trained by the same teachers. We often stepped in for each other, if we were working elsewhere, or not well.

There have always been mechanisms for students to feedback their responses to their courses and their teaching and their teachers, to Faculty – termly and annually. Changes were frequently made on the back of student feedback, with teachers asked to modify delivery and develop course content. Students had more say on course content, opportunities for development, and even who might direct them, than they ever would have as actors working in theatre, TV and film.

A vital part of training an actor is to give students the ability to make their own choices, through teaching them a calibrated technique. However, clearly, we hadn't developed the pedagogy in ways that resonated with management or students. Bushell-Mingo and O'Loughlin desire a new pedagogy to reflect different cultural voices in the teaching space as well as the acting space. Actors' Movement is designed for transformation – but the identities that pioneered it are European, or Eastern European (arguably outside of the EU) and many of them were women. Is the identity of the teacher more important to its delivery and its content? Particularly if the core principles of that pedagogy were always about the body transforming in a social and cultural context? Or do we need to change the repertoire and content of what is taught, entirely? As well as replace the teachers?

This is the heart of the tension between what is taught and who teaches it. But the question remains, where do these new techniques come from? And who develops them?

*

My own experience of learning was that there were very few women directors, few women teachers at Lecoq, whereas they were all women teachers at the ballet school I attended, and all my mentors were women movement teachers. And none of these teachers ever openly declared when they were of Jewish heritage. Movement and women were connected, and these were my role models. Movement in theatre, as I had encountered

---

[34]Vice Principle of Guildhall. The article is from The Stage, written by Orla O'Loughlin February 28 2024. https://www.thestage.co.uk/opinion/guildhall-vice-principal-orla-oloughlin-drama-schools-can-radically-reimagine-theatres-future

it, was inspirational, and this was my guide. But the reference to heritage is important, as maybe there were already voices from different cultures teaching in the schools, which hadn't been noticed?

*

In 1982 when I was in the acting company at Manchester Contact Theatre, I directed a lunchtime production of *Thermidor* by Howard Brenton. The artistic director Richard Williams then offered me the option of working as a director at the theatre, which I turned down. I am not naïve about the boundaries that hold people back, these can be internal as well as external. I respect Bushell-Mingo's observations. Richard Williams offered a transformative opportunity which I didn't believe I could fulfil.

How much did my social conditioning play a part? How should we adapt training to accommodate all these biases and restrictions? How important is identity? Internalized racism? Or misogyny? How do we nurture the new practitioners looking for new techniques to train young actors?

Who shares this view?

Movement training, then and now

Mark Evans has been an articulate advocate of movement training.[35] His book *Movement Training for the Modern Actor* charts the development of movement training up until I went to teach at Drama Centre (Evans, 2009).

When I asked Evans why, if the post-war project of training in drama schools was radical, was it floundering now?, he turned to the body as a starting point.[36]

> Not simply that our bodies are different, but that our experiences of our bodies are different – in terms of gender, race, disability for example.[37]
>
> Our appreciation of difference has changed and there is now a tension between what might have been seen as easily accessible – i.e. cultural assimilation and inclusion – with the power structures that won't shift.

As teachers, we were of course addressing this as best we could, but there was no road map to decolonize the body in the teaching of Actors' Movement, or research into how to update the pedagogy. And equally it was true that many students had pinpointed how managements had failed to respond adequately prior to 2020, to the need for anti-racist training in their institutions.

Evans suggested that what was considered (optimistically or with limited political awareness) multiculturalism in the 1980s and 1990s hasn't dealt with racism, and he challenged whether the structures that sustained this have been sufficiently dismantled in drama schools. He was also keen to discuss the sociological impact of post-war theatre training as

---

[35]One of the few theatre educators consistently writing about movement training.
[36]The other concerns were the classical canon plays (to quote the SAP) taken from the work of dead white men: Chekhov, Shakespeare, Congreve, Williams, Shaw and a Eurocentric teaching syllabus and bias.
[37]To this I would also add sex, and sex and gender are different.

germane to the current conversation. Who was being trained in the post-war 'drama school project' and what values did the schools reflect and who were its teachers? These questions relating to that time are still relevant today.

Evans considered with me how, before the Second World War, drama schools were training young people for an existing world and theatre, not trying to change theatre or the world. He referenced both RADA and Central (schools I knew well) as examples. Before the war there was no public funding for students in Higher Education – though there were scholarships, as my father's training attested. Even after the Second World War, post 1945, with the founding of the Welfare State and free education, and grants for university, grants for drama school were discretionary.[38]

So even though the content of drama school training shifted radically after the Second World War, introducing curricula with more body-based approaches, accessibility was still an issue, particularly for working-class students, and students from the Black and Global Majority. The training had a revolutionary ethos and was committed to changing theatre – but accessibility to its training was still limited.[39]

Part of this was due to how Higher Education viewed drama schools. Its remit didn't automatically extend to drama schools, making it harder for working class students to attend,[40] because grants were discretionary, dependent on local education authorities. Many working-class students would succeed in their auditions for drama school, and then 'fail' an audition with the local authority, and so not have funding. The casting of Classical plays still lacked flexibility when considering how to place actors from different ethnic backgrounds.[41,42] Roles for women also rarely extended beyond the gender-specific characters written by mainly male playwrights.

I was interested in the modernist European sensibility that Michel Saint-Denis introduced, when he moved from France to Britain to teach at the Old Vic Theatre School. Michel Saint-Denis had been trained by Jacques Copeau,[43] whose preference lay in preparing the creative performer through developing the craft of the actor, rather than equipping them for the commercial theatre, which he saw as moribund. Evans agreed that this approach was radical, particularly as it brought an embodied and socially aware understanding of acting, through the introduction of new subjects. For instance, Improvisation, which was called

---

[38]Candidates would audition twice to get funding – first for the drama school to gain a place and then for the Local Education Authority.
[39]There were exceptions, as Lee Montague's description of how he got a grant to go to The Old Vic Theatre School shows.
[40]There is a separate book to be researched on the impact funding for drama schools has had on what and how they teach. But the introduction of teacher training courses at drama schools ensured funding for students. Rose Bruford College was the first drama school to offer a BA in Acting, and students could get full grants to attend.
[41]My father often played 'foreigners' and 'exotics' in the bread-and-butter work of TV and Film. I mentioned previously that he didn't often play quintessential Englishmen. In the 1960s, 1970s, 1980s and 1990s, this limited how someone was cast.
[42]It is worth remembering that in the 1930s, 1940s and 1950s many Jewish students were first- or second-generation immigrants, and many were also working class, from homes whose first language might not always be English.
[43]See below more detail about Jacques Copeau's company and innovations.

'Mime and Silent Improvisation' developed the idea of the ensemble. Movement training was introduced to teach actors about the body and physical expression. Rudolph Laban also contributed to the establishment of movement teaching in the UK, through his former students, Jean Newlove[44] and Geraldine Stephenson. This was in addition to Litz Pisk, who, as mentioned above, had already been teaching at RADA. We can see that by the 1940s, movement teachers were already part of new ways of thinking about acting and training in Drama Schools. Movement was also taught by acting teachers, with an equal status to the other subjects – in fact movement and acting were interchangeable.[45] Students were sent out to observe the world around them and re-enact what they saw, which in turn affected plays and productions.[46] Many of the social realist plays from the 1950s onwards involved acute observations of real life that investigated what it was like to live in Britain in the post-war years – real people's lives, and their problems. The ethos of the Old Vic Theatre School was to train actors to be *artists living in society*.[47] The developments in the craft of acting were seen as ways to train actors for a theatre that didn't exist who would act in the new naturalistic plays being written, that reflected modern society. Movement training could contribute to a vocabulary to make new theatre and *reflect the world as it is*.

Mark Evans remarked on the paradox that, although the training of post-war drama schools *wasn't* elitist, access to that training was. In terms of casting, this was also a reflection of the prejudices and social mores of the time.

Is this the debate that Bushell-Mingo and O'Loughlin wanted to initiate? Or is the debate more about changing the curriculum and bringing in new teachers?

My understanding of Bushell-Mingo and O'Loughlin's concerns is that the actor and the training-in-the-work need to meet. In the past the industry, in my experience, found it hard to open the door to all its trained actors equally, especially in the realm of classical theatre, however innovative its training methods.[48]

The shadow

Evans agreed with me that there was a modernist, post-war project in drama school training. Post-war society (austerity and the fog-ridden 1950s which I remember, along with no heating, rose-hip syrup and ration cards) was part of the common European project of renewal post-Second World War: people were trying to rebuild after the war, transforming their lives, to move away from their class or their background through social mobility and education.

I mention this because I lived it. I lived in North London where there was a large Jewish émigré population, some of whom were my parents' friends. My parents, and those of my school friends had all fought in the Second World War. But it was rarely spoken of. I

---

[44]Jean Newlove worked with Joan Littlewood, see below, and wrote several books on movement (Newlove, 1993).
[45]See my description of Michel Saint-Denis and animal study in Chapter 10. And at Drama Centre, Yat Malgrem's movement work on Movement Psychology was fundamental to the acting training.
[46]See below for further details.
[47]My italics.
[48]The exception to this is Joan Littlewood's Theatre Workshop at Stratford East, and her training methods at E15, with Jean Newlove teaching Laban as a way to work with improvisation.

understand now that this might have been trauma: keep silent, move on. For my parents the war had not been glorious at all, it had marked them. Silence.

Our conversation linked the body to post-war renewal. Post-war was not only about renewal socially and educationally. After the war, there was a renewed interest in mime, and research to develop the art form in radical ways. Mark Evans and Simon Murray's book, *Mime into Physical Theatre* (Murray and Evans, 2023), suggests it was a reaction to the trauma of war – 'an empty silent space, which recognizes the inadequacy of words to deal with the most profound experiences'.[49] This quote deeply moves me. A whole generation of young people had been marked by their wartime experiences. There was indeed 'an empty silent space' all around us, which I recalled when talking to Evans. My mother appears to have gone through the ATS in a state of physical hunger and was carpet-bombed in her billet in Coventry; my father had experienced antisemitism in the armed forces, which confirmed for him a need to not draw attention to his heritage. The compulsion to move on, not dwell on the past, was almost reptilian, but also full of hope that nothing like that would ever happen again. But the traces remained. And the wars continue.

Drama schools still have rigid hierarchies, and levels of bureaucracy that implement the employment structures of universities. However, what struck me, forcibly, when discussing the post-war 'project' of drama school training for actors, was that the vision of what the training could be was determined by artists who were also teachers. Many of these teachers, myself included, also had a politic and a vision for a new theatre. A teacher in a drama school is as much at the mercy of social and political forces as their students. The compulsion to reshape those forces needs to be shared, and for that we need a common language.

Movement is not just what you do, but how you do it

Movement could be taught for any actor and any play-text and by anyone trained to teach movement. This had been my belief.

Consider the stage direction from Bertolt Brecht's *The Mother* from the first scene 'Vlasovas of all countries'. Set in pre-revolutionary Russia, Pelageya Vlasova is a widow, whose son is involved with revolutionary workers. The play charts her journey into activism, from her experience of poverty and deprivation. The first scene tells this story, by showing how there isn't enough to eat, and how poor the quality of the soup is that she has made for her son.

> She carries a tray with soup on it over to her son. When she gets back, she watches as the son, without looking up from his book, lifts the lid from the bowl, sniffs at the soup, then replaces the lid and pushes the bowl away. (Brecht, 1978)

There are two figures in this scene, a mother and a son. The action is pared down to the essentials. The actors aren't defined by race, colour, age – but only by class or gender. The stage directions tell a specific story, about soup, poor ingredients, the revolutionary who rejects the soup and the mother who serves it. The physical action as written is clear, clean, the gestures economical, the characterizations unemotional. The impact of the story, the

---

[49]Conversation with Mark Evans.

event, arrives through the action: what is done and how simply it is communicated – movement. The politics of the scene are 'shown' in this simple physical text; the identities and points of view of the 'actors' in the scene, determined by what they are doing.

You could set this scene anywhere and at any time. Your movement and your relationships with the props and the 'world' would communicate the essence of the scene, the casting dependent on the demographic of where you choose to set the production. I won't be so simplistic as to suggest where or what conflict. Our imagination and our empathy can decide a context and play the scene. Every gesture tells a story. Every gesture is political.

4   The need for a system and how to place that system in a contemporary context: The traces that matter

"Die aus verliessen" Those who left us

This is from a biographical note translated from a catalogue of an exhibition in Vienna 1980 of Litz Pisk's drawings held at Oesterreichische Galerie at The Belvedere. Her drawings showed 'a basic connection between the possibility of expression and choreography'. The note is held in Litz Pisks' archive.[1,2]

Who left us? Possibly the Viennese artists forced to flee in the 1930s? The quote haunts me.

Legacy and provenance, can we escape its political context?

The vitality of Expressive Dance, *Ausdruckstanz*,[3] is non-conformist, and multidisciplinary.[4] Litz Pisk, for instance, trained at the Bauhaus in the 1930s. Her training in architecture gave her insight into the connection between physicality and the spaces we inhabit. Her sensibility was gestural, kinetic and sociological. Here are some thoughts, lodged in the archive, that she wrote about social dance during the First and Second World Wars. She illustrated her thoughts with line drawings, which remarkably, convey the feelings of the dance spaces as well as the movements.

Doodles on the dance-floors

After the First World War limbs began to loosen and turn inward to the syncopated rhythms of Jazz. The steps drew criss-cross patterns of interlocking squares on the dance floors.

Very small square

During and after the Second World War dancers went underground and crowded into the small, dark, cellar-like dives.

Loose limbs, syncopated, the impact of an industrialized war on bodies: hiding in dark cellars, from air-raids, or soldiers. The images and the space express the shadows of the

---

[1] Free Dance is different to German Dance. Free Dance and Expressive Dance is what Litz Pisk encountered in Vienna, when she was taught by Isadora Duncan's sister.
[2] Litz Pisk's Archive at the Royal Central School of Speech and Drama.
[3] Also Free Dance.
[4] There are also more troubling aspects to it, as I show below.

physical and emotional experience of two world wars. In an interview in *Arts Guardian* in 1975 Pisk comments on the link between movement and the self. The individual actor as an artist and their body as an instrument. How feeling comes from the core of a person and flows out into the space through movement. Pisk is taking the experiment of the dance artists I refer to in the last chapter, and applying this to an actor's body.

> The actor must penetrate to a central part of the body … and work from the centre to change the periphery … the mental and physical processes go together – to find your identity you've got to start with the body. I always try to find the total understanding of the person; but I start with the body.[5]

For Pisk, the first task in teaching is to help the soften the body 'like clay'. She starts with the body in front of her. We are individuals and there is a connection from inside to outside: the feeling and sensation, that channels itself into movement. Once the body is loosened and freed, then you begin to string the instrument 'by swinging'.

> By swinging you have something like a physical acoustics starting. You link up and down, high and low, near and far: it goes towards you and away from you. You lengthen the ligaments, you make the movement go farther. You enlarge the scale of movement in the body. (*Guardian*, 1975)

You move more in a class, than you might in life, and for Pisk this was part of an artistic process, the art of making anything, where you stretch the material as far as you can, to then distil it to what you mean to say. The body is the material. Like all the dancers, and movement specialists that came from the Central European tradition, movement is in space, and how you move in the space comes from who you are and your feelings or impulses.

> In all art you do an enormous amount in order to forget it and throw it away.
> Something will remain, some trace, and it's that something that matters. (Guardian, 1975)

Pisk captures movement in language, helping us see it as 'the quality of silent poetry' (Pisk, 1975). Is this understanding of the power of movement, still relevant?

Pisk and Arnold taught students to help them find their creative expression. I wish to look at the 'trace' Pisk mentions and ask why a radical practice that teaches expression in the body and was eminently suitable to teach actors how to move has been left unsung in the current debate, despite its emphasis on identity and personal connection and innovation.

Let us start, as Pisk said, with the body, the person, the individual.

They stand, they reach up, with both hands stretching. Already a big movement. They drop their centre, soften their knees and squat, their upper spine rounded. They unfurl through the spine and stand again. They have gone on a journey. There are no codified positions to get to, but the softer the sinews and ligaments and the freer the joints, the easier for you. Let us call it expressive ease.

Teaching the expressive in movement is delivered through a body of exercises repeated over time. Repetition. Not learning by rote but exploring through sensation. Revisiting the

---

[5]*Arts Guardian*, 22 July 1975.

exercises is part of the process, as they go deeper and deeper. A spiral of learning that starts on the outside and spirals inward to the central core of the learner. Students in training are working on many levels, cognitive, physical, emotional – deepening their understanding of self, who they are in the world. They might take time to respond, perhaps only appreciating the work as it comes into a production. Before that the teacher uses their skills to expand their expression. Maybe the classes are oases of creative discovery. The teacher will wait. Movement training allows for different rates of growth. When I was at Drama Centre, we used the image of a garden, letting the plants grow, with tending – nurturing, not forcing.

My training with Trish Arnold[6] gave me a physical language to explore the space around me and inside me. This exploration of movement starts from relaxation, to create a place of emptiness or readiness that stops what Pisk calls 'the quarrel with the body'. Winearls, Arnold, Pisk and Lecoq all share an understanding that movement is a balance, or pendulum, between tension and relaxation, inactivity and activity, freeing yourself from the limitation that the weight of your body can impose. A balance between doing and 'letting be done'.

These might be abstract ideas, but they flow into the many exercises we explore with Pure Movement and are part of a language of expression that makes up movement studies for actors.

- Swings
- Weight
- Flow
- Use of space
- Spine work
- Floor work
- Use of the dimensions
- Working with opposite forces i.e.: rising/falling, pressing/pulling, bending/reaching
- Use of the breath
- Placement
- Alignment
- Softness and strength

When students can't connect

Many students come to movement from sport or dance. Or sadly, with greater frequency, from the sofa or their bedrooms. Some will have never moved at all, and fewer will have moved creatively or imaginatively today, as I describe many of my generation did in the 1960s through movement to music classes in their primary schools. They might come with circumscribed understandings of physicality – rules, steps, shapes. Actor's Movement is an expressive subject. It has content and feeling – a pedagogy, designed to help the actor to find *their own way of moving*. There is a technique – feet, spine, torso, space – and there is a grammar to work with – the essential components we need to move and play. How do students relate to a subject that is artistic and creative, based on sensation, or story, not on

---

[6]Which I explore in greater depth in Chapter 5.

aesthetic? The current discourse in drama schools is that we haven't taken our students' experience of life into account, and our practice isn't inclusive. But the feeling of unease about movement teaching is not new. I want to consider pedagogy as exemplified in the teacher, and the traces their background will bring to their classes.

Madame Toshka who is she? The movement teacher as shadow

Madame Toshka taught movement when many of my colleagues were at RADA in the 1970s and 1980s. They mentioned her name often, though few could describe in detail what she did, or even where she came from. She was a chameleon. She was a force of nature. Rootless. Russian, German, tiny, fierce, terrifying, dramatic. A shape-shifter of memory. According to one actor, she had danced with the Ballet Russe in the early 1900s and was 'the first dancer to take off her shoes'. The consensus may have been she was brilliant, but no one went to her classes. The Principal wouldn't hear a word against her, but the point of her pedagogy was never explained.

The movement teacher Jane Winearls, the author of the book on the Jooss-Leeder method,[7] taught at Birmingham University in 1967. She was also teaching movement from the Central European tradition, but to university drama students. Litz Pisk also taught movement at Bath University in the 1950s.[8] Teaching movement in university settings was beginning to take root after the war.

Winearls lived alone, in a little dusty flat on campus, a movement academic. A colleague of mine was taught by Winearls and confided how odd she found the exercises. 'No one had encountered them before' with some of the more working-class male students rejecting the movement.[9] However, the memory was clearly still in the body. As my colleague was compelled to re-enact one of the 'stranger exercises', her words spooled like an incantation. Students would walk in a circle, with Winearls beating a drum intoning: 'This is the passage of time … drum … drum … walk in a circle to the beat.'[10] The drumming would increase in tempo, whereupon the students would whirl round and round. This and other exercises are clearly part of the repertoire of Expressionism: levels, dimensions, curled up low on the ground, growing like trees.

I asked my colleague if Winearls had connected the exercises to acting, but like Madame Toshka, 'We didn't talk about how movement connects to acting'.[11] My colleague is a director and acting teacher, with whom I often collaborate as a movement director. Notwithstanding I was struck by how she had found it hard to see the relevance of these formative classes in movement.[12] The one series of exercises that struck a chord were 'Etudes'. 'A day in a park in New York' was a movement piece created from the music of Gershwin, all crafted to the beat. This made sense to her. It also mirrors the exercises Lecoq

---

[7]See below.
[8]There were many more women movement teachers in drama schools and universities at that time from this tradition.
[9]My colleague came from a working-class background herself, so the description of her peers as working class was factual, not judgemental.
[10]Quoted from my conversation with my colleague.
[11]Ibid.
[12]My colleague went on to train at a drama school, where they continued to learn movement.

set us at his school in the 1970s, where we had to capture the essence of a 'space' in movement but done without music.

As she spoke, I was aware of a depth to these experiences. Wasn't there a skill in working with rhythm in this way? The movement of walking in a circle sped up effortlessly to running surely showed Winearls' musicality to accelerate a beat from slow to fast? Yes, she agreed, but what resonated more, was the impact of Winearls' personality. She described her as a short, dynamic woman, with a drum and a very deep passionate voice. Reports of the dance experimenters and educators from this tradition also remark on their singularity and force of personality. Here is Sol Hurok's[13] account of meeting Mary Wigman as she docked at New York in 1930:

> I greeted a middle-aged muscular Amazon, a rather scruffy appearing Teutonic Amazon, wearing a beaver coat of dubious age, and a hat that had seen better days. But what struck me more forcibly than the plainness of her apparel was the woman herself.[14]

The experimental and experiential nature of the exercises had left inexplicable traces for my colleague, alongside total recall of the instructions. Lying on the ground 'listening to yourself'. 'Imagine your spine stretching and becoming more elongated'. Everything 'emanates from your stomach'. She told me that she liked her body much more by the end of the class, feeling freer and empowered. Winearls' interest in her was also a new experience, asking her what she thought about the world, art, theatre.

> No one had taken an interest in me as a woman, finding out what it was like to be me and my inner life and she was really funny about the male students.

These singular older women were outliers – working with the body in essentialist ways, in establishment institutions. But their movement catalysed visceral responses that lived in memory and in bodies, despite how alien the cultural context these women represented, and how irrelevant they seemed to an actor's process.

However, by contrast, Trish Arnold and Litz Pisk managed to succeed in aligning and adapting their movement and dance training with the artistic method of drama schools.[15] They persuaded the mainly male-dominated institutions and theatres that ran post-war Britain to consider the value of emotional and physical expression. Litz Pisk even communicated the importance of movement in drama to local education authorities. Here is an extract from a rather stuffy report written by a Mr Male, of a talk she gave in 1969 about Movement and Drama.

> Movement in Drama was concerned with communicating via a character, thoughts and emotions, so they were both articulate and observable to the observer.[16]

---

[13]Dance producer in New York in the 1930s.
[14]Quoted from Mary Wigman written by Sol Hurok in 'S. Hurok Presents 1953', included in *Reading Dance*, edited by Robert Gottlieb, Pantheon Books, 2008.
[15]The Archive testifies how often Pisk left the schools as well, in possession of an excellent reference.
[16]Notes from Litz Pisk's lecture 'Movement in Drama' at Kent Schools' Speech and Drama Associations by Mr Male, 6 June 1969.

Notwithstanding the impact of these seminal artist–teachers' work, their influence still remains shadowy – only those of us that teach movement seem to understand its depth. To survive and thrive, we need advocates, and for this we need to change the narrative.

Young voices and drama schools and nineteenth- and early twentieth-century practices

In 2020 students questioned their training and sought to curate it and urged us to update it. They weren't and aren't interested in the provenance – good or bad – of the work, so long as it speaks for them and to them. I believe they were the first generation of drama school students to have actively brought about systemic change within the schools – curriculum, social and pedagogical change. They sacrificed the continuity of their own training to bring this about. Classes were disrupted, teachers left (for various reasons), the curriculum was changed, senior management changed and then changed again: we were in the definition of revolution. Student dissent, disruption and rebellion are not new: but what is different is that the students made change happen to their own training, in response to the social and political context in which we taught them. In 1997 at Rose Bruford, something similar occurred, but for very different reasons. The students occupied the ramshackle premises in Deptford, where the BA Acting course was taught, to support tutors against whom the management were implementing disciplinary proceedings. The occupation was to show solidarity and send a message to management that they had confidence in their training. In 2020, the students were actively criticizing their training and many of their tutors, aligning themselves with the Social Justice movements, and anti-racism, even if it meant altering the syllabus, or changing tutors or pedagogies.

*

The 1970s was a time of change, but as a student at RADA at the time remarked to me, none of the experiments she saw from directors like Charles Marowitz at The Open Space, or Mnouchkine's production of *1789* at The Roundhouse, ever permeated its doors.[17] The change my colleague referred to in the 1970s was the radical and new ways to make theatre. Social change was part of this, but my colleague was as much frustrated by the conservatism of the training, and the lack of curiosity about new work. No doubt my frustration, had I trained there, would have made it hard for me to focus on the classical training it offered. However, today young actors don't just feel aggrieved about a training that feels stuck in a different era; in 2020 they challenged us to find systems and a pedagogy that foregrounds the individual and their identity, over what they saw as the tutors asking them to follow a body of work uncritically.

*

It is interesting to look back to the 1960s, to see how the Arts and universities played their part in student rebellions. The 1960s saw students take part in unrest over the war in Vietnam, the Sexual Revolution, the Civil Rights Movements, the Anti-Apartheid Movement,

---

[17]Drama Centre under Yat Malgrem and Christopher Fettes offered a different approach.

and revolutionary groups like the Baader-Meinhof Group[18] and the Red Guard. A list will never do justice to the turbulence, the vitality and jeopardy[19] of the times, pressurizing the older generation. The new order that came out of the Second World War was still patriarchal, and traditional. But many of the protests had poets and musicians warning that change was inevitable.

> Your sons and your daughters are beyond your command
> And your old world is rapidly ageing[20]

But what was the demographic of many of the protesters? Chrissie Hynde interviewed in the *Guardian* reflected on the class- and race-biased privilege of radical politics in the 1960s and 1970s. In response to a question about her presence on the tragic anti-Vietnam demonstration at Kent University where the National Guard shot and killed four students:

> my lasting thoughts …. (are) that all of us hippies were conned … by the peace and love thing. During the Vietnam war there was a draft system, and if you were in university you didn't get drafted. My dad had been a marine in the war, we were in the university but the kids whose parents couldn't put them there were in Vietnam.
>
> That is what us hippies didn't see. We'd seen Green Berets coming back from Vietnam, you know, and we'd be shouting and giving them the finger …
>
> Now I'm ashamed …. Those kids were 19 like me, but they didn't have a choice.
>
> Looking back, I realise I was conned and got it wrong. No politicians sent their kids to Vietnam. (*Guardian*, 2023)[21]

Chrissie Hynde sees the paradox in radical politics. One of her friends was murdered by the National Guard, yet she grasps the danger of blaming the young soldiers drafted for a war, they had no choice but to fight. Hynde points out the hippies' intolerance towards anyone who didn't share their values – even when they were working class. Many people don't have a choice, ethnically, geopolitically, historically. Revolutionary movements often behave as if we all have that privilege to make the right choice. Training in drama schools, honourably, in my view, has always sought to train students, not their political viewpoints. This has been an ethical position fiercely held by most teachers. At Rose Bruford I doggedly turned up to teach my movement classes during their occupation of the college, to crumpled students rolling up their sleeping bags, and quickly taking showers before we started our work. It was hard not to get involved, as the students were supporting colleagues, but it felt extremely important to focus on the work and to say as little as possible. I also remember the delicacy of navigating the election of Donald Trump in 2016 with the American students,[22] some of whom had voted for him, and some of whom hadn't. We were told, categorically, by our Director of Training, not to discuss our own views on the election, and to make sure if students wanted to discuss it, that we were fair and balanced in holding space for them.

---

[18]The Baader-Meinhof group were a West German far-left militant group founded in the 1960s. They declared themselves against the United States as an imperialist power, and the West German Government as a remnant of Fascism. They conducted a series of bombing campaigns and assassinations, funded from bank robberies.
[19]May '68 almost brought down De Gaulle's government.
[20]Bob Dylan, 'The Times Are A-Changing'.
[21]Punk rock singer and founder of 'The Pretenders'.
[22]At RADA.

As educators, these questions continue to play out with ever-increasing intensity in our classrooms and studios. Where is the line between political extremism and self-expression and free speech? When are we able to see the dubious ideologies of practices and teachers, that might existentially threaten one group, while advancing another? Teachers prefer to focus on the 'work', rather than the issues that surround the work.[23] But the landscape has changed. Before, in the theatre, you would leave your politics at the door of the rehearsal room. Now it is not unusual for theatres to be put under pressure to refuse funding for political and ideological reasons, actively supported by actors and artists, willing to diminish artistic output by forcing theatres to make the right moral decision.[24]

*

During the student demonstrations of May '68 in Paris, Jean-Louis Barrault,[25] in his beautiful book 'Memories for Tomorrow', describes the student occupation of the Comédie-Française and his complicated responses to it. May '68 started as a student revolt in a suburb of Paris and escalated into a General Strike and occupations throughout May. The revolt was triggered by restrictions against dormitory visits preventing male and female students sleeping together, responding to an entrenched and patriarchal society. As one of the female protestors at the time said:

> You couldn't go out with friends, and never with boys … You had to obey orders, in the factories, in the schools. We were suffocating.[26]

Jean-Louis Barrault was the artistic director of the Comédie-Française and was forced to confront the generational differences between his own political understanding, forged by the Resistance and the Second World War, and those of the post-war 'revolutionaries'. He invited the 'Living Theatre' to the International Festival, which he had set up, imagining they were political friends, fellow travellers, but when they instigated the occupation of his theatre, protesting what it represented, he realized that 'the "young" must have seen us in a different light. I had yet to learn that what is called "the conflict of generations" does not necessarily come from the behaviour of older people, but from rejection by the younger' (Barrault, 1972).

Barrault's experience in 1968 testifies to the inherent tensions between the post-war generation and their artistic predecessors.

*

We have similar issues confronting those of us teaching in drama schools today. The tsunami at RADA in 2020 caused me to re-evaluate practices and their systems that I had accepted all my professional life. I saw hidden beneath the liberal and creative values in

---

[23]Social media, and fake news: the impact of wars, race, gender make this increasingly difficult.

[24]On 6 June 2025 Caryl Churchill pulled her play from the Donmar Warehouse theatre, because of sponsorship from Barclays Bank. The theatre lost its funding from the Arts Council, so its dependence on philanthropy is critical.

[25]Jean-Louis Barrault, French actor and mime artist, featured in the film *Les Enfants Du Paradis*, made in 1947.

[26]Josette Preud'homme reported in Le Monde.

drama schools, troubling shadows – subjects – which pre-dated the Second World War, and had embedded themselves in drama schools as an unexamined part of the curriculum. There is a paradox: the techniques which had taken root were refracted discordant theories that led to shadowy alleyways of quasi scientific theory, and unproven claims for development and healing – but the students themselves were happy with them. As the Student Action Plan testifies, their focus was on the written texts, and the acting systems they were taught and the systemic racism in their drama schools, often allegedly expressed by their tutors; but they were uncritical, and unaware, of the racism inherent in some of their movement systems. There is a text in these movement systems – a silent text, and I believe their traces remain.

The Alexander Technique has long been used as a corrective to postural alignment in drama schools.[27] 'Corrected' posture can help in the teaching of Voice, Acting and Singing classes.[28] But its founder F. M. Alexander has been accused of racism and supporting eugenics, which its own professional body has acknowledged since 2020. STAT[29] issued a statement supporting diversity and opposing racism and wrote that they 'stand apart from any and all prejudicial passages' in any of Alexander's writings which don't 'define or expound the body of practice and theory that *has come to be known as The Alexander Technique*'.[30]

However, the technique itself is based on a premise that is worth parsing to fully appreciate what is being asked of a student of Alexander. The 'therapeutic' change in posture the Alexander Technique promotes requires the student to say 'no' to 'bad habits' – which Alexander referred to as a 'poor use of the self', leading to 'psychophysical degeneration'.

Slouching, tension in the shoulders, 'bad' posture, a lack of physical organization, are to be 'consciously' controlled and altered, by directing the energy up and outwards through the spine. As one actor who had Alexander training at their drama school described to me – so persuasive is the technique, that she would hand in her library books, conscious of leaning forwards at a right-angle, through the spine, and lengthening her arm from its centre.

What are bad habits? Are they purely physical? Or does physicality reflect something intrinsic, potentially negative, about the essence of an individual?

As a student of Alexander, I was less compliant than my colleague. Because the technique restricted my natural desire to use my spine with fluidity, my pelvis with freedom, my legs or my arms expressively. I felt my instinctive way of moving was wrong. The Alexander teacher attuned and corrected me, lying on the 'table' by adjusting me and reminding me to say 'no'. When I was in my fifties, one Alexander teacher I visited suggested that directing my thoughts up through my sitting bones and out through the top of my head, as I sat

---

[27]RADA, LAMDA had Alexander as part of their curriculum up until the 2020s. When I taught at Drama Centre London, Alexander was taught there, and for a while it was also taught at Guildhall. When it wasn't taught, many of its tenets and definition of alignment were referred to.

[28]It doesn't help with movement classes as alignment arrives through dynamic exercises, and an emphasis on expanding the muscles in the back. Movement classes are also not built on inhibiting natural responses, nor are dance classes, but instead on body awareness to shift patterns and habits, through changes of weight, and the opening out of physical tension, through working proactively with the breath and with gravity, which is understood by the actor's own body awareness. Agency over physical control.

[29]The Society of Teachers of the Alexander Technique.

[30]My italics.

immobile in a chair, would open me up and help me to look at the world with the innocent eyes of a child. But I was a mother, and innocence was far from what I needed to live my life with ease. These comments, though well-meaning, deny the body its history, and idiosyncrasies. Saying 'no' doesn't align with acting, intention, or impulse, or human expression which is messy and complex.

The Alexander Technique has been an intrinsic part of the curriculum in many drama schools for many years, though held within it are value judgements about how an individual needs to respond to instruction. To 'say no' to 'bad habits' is to apply 'conscious control', which Alexander saw as a 'good use of the self'. Not being able to exercise this control is a 'bad use of the self', stemming from 'instinctual' behaviour, which is a very problematic judgement. John Austin, in an online article on the 'dark hidden origins' of the Alexander Technique, proposes that 'conscious control' would help 'man' change his habits, and thus ensure the next generation are born healthy.

> Alexander's ideas related to eugenics boil down to: if you help people change their habits, they can have better children. (Austin, 2022)

This aspect of Alexander's teachings shares similarities to the racialized ideals promoted by the Nazis, of how a healthy body can purify the mind and the soul – and the race. Many of these ideas were endorsed by Laban and Mary Wigman's modernization of Dance, and their compliance with the Nazi regime.[31]

> National Socialism has pulled young Germans out of the dull caves of unnecessary scholarliness and has put them in the strong, wind, into rain and sunshine and this almighty steam of nature.[32]

This ideal of the beautiful body derived from classical antiquity and contributed to racial ideas of beauty and racial cleanliness and physical fitness. A striking example of this is when Leni Rieifenstahl discussed her film *Olympia*, made in 1936, to record the Olympic Games, claiming it was 'an ode to the beautiful body'. The idealized movement of the bodies filmed at the beginning of *Olympia* (on the Curonian Spit in Lithuania) refers directly to the Greek ideal – exemplified in the Discus thrower in Figure 2.

In the book *Hitler's Dancers* (Karina and Kant, 2004), Marion Kant and Lilian Karina locate how Goebbels (the Minister of Propaganda) and the Third Reich took the revolution of modern Expressive dance, and transformed it into German Dance, to promote Nazi ideology. Both Wigman and Laban became the main proponents of German Dance (as it came to be known). The innovative expression, and individual artists I described earlier, were not part of this journey, and many have uncertain legacies, sediments from the Weimar republic, or fled the country.

*

One of the aspects that derive from Modern Dance, at that time, is the idea of 'dance for dance's sake', which suggested that training an artists' body for theatrical expression was

---

[31] I discuss this later in this chapter.
[32] Rudolf Bode, cited by Kant (Karina and Kant, 2003). Rudolf Bode – founder of expressive gymnastics, actively supported the Nazis, and believed that rhythmic gymnastics connected the body to the soul.

Figure 2 *Discus Thrower in Classical Pose*, Olympia Part 1 Festival of the Peoples 1936, directed by Leni Riefenstahl. Getty.

not its main aim.[33] When I first went to the Stratford Festival Theatre in Canada, one of the actors confessed that he had always been suspicious of movement as a practice – and was relieved that I didn't arrive with incense, floaty scarves and gongs. This gives an insight into the difficulty when movement is seen as abstract or offering dubious psycho-physical results for well-being or a connection between body and soul. I understand and appreciate that somatic practices are more complex than this, and I also accept that there are links between physical action and psychological responses, but my focus is on the development of a physical technique that trained actors in the craft of movement for theatre and acting.

My argument here is to differentiate between the abstract and the specific. The difference between what is ideological and what is craft based and artistic. The movement training which evolved out of the innovative experiments that Wigman and Laban developed has been adapted for actor movement training in drama schools, but has troubling connections.

---

[33]This was also a difference between Laban and Kurt Jooss and Sigurd Leeder, who adapted Laban's innovations into a dance pedagogy for theatre dance and training for dancers.

About one thing there can be no doubt: the great creative figures in German dance admired and accepted Hitler and his ideas. (Karina and Kant, 2004)

Hitler's Dancers proposes that German Dance was taken up as part of the Nazi vanguard and examines how its influential dance artists actively collaborated with the Nazis to develop and promote German Dance to exemplify the ideology of the Third Reich. Nazis offered rewards and funding and employment to compliant 'Aryan' institutions who inculcated these physical values. For the Laban and Mary Wigman inspired dance companies, this led to the building and defining of German Dance to promote the Third Reich, and in particular, the sacking of Jewish dancers.[34] Kant and Karina both suggest that the developments of modern dance in Germany from 1933 to 1945 were directly in response to the aesthetic and ideology of building a master race.

*

Numerous movement cultures joined Nazi organizations during the Third Reich, with dance and gymnastics developed as a 'deliberate part of the Nazi aesthetic' (Karina and Kant, 2004). Rudolph Bode, for instance, was a German educator and founder of expressive gymnastics, and joined the Nazi Party in 1932. Bode developed special gymnastics for the Minister of Agriculture. He also supported German Dance, believing it expressed 'the healthy energy of the people'. This demonstrates the ideological link between German Dance and expressive gymnastics. In an article in *Der Tanz* in 1933, he described it as a bodily and spiritual truth, and described elements of the abstract dance forms that Laban developed in a quasi-spiritual ritualized language.[35] One form of movement, described as 'expressive', he called 'streaming binding':

> Expresses the outlet of swinging movements. Their deeper rootedness in the rhythmic circulation of all life forms manifests itself in free soaring movements.[36]

In 1933, Fritz Bohme wrote to Goebbels describing German Dance as a fully established modern art form, on the grounds that it was the perfect example of dance for an Aryan race:

> Dance is a race question. There is no supra-racial dance form.[37]

Bohme's letter also advocates Laban to lead a special department for Dance and actively recruits language that can only be described as anti-Semitic and racist to promote his argument:

> Dance could function as a constructive and formative force. It could defend racial values and ward off the influx of alien movements and gestures, which are confusing to the German character and are undermining the German attitude.[38]

Dance is a race question, which the techniques of modern dance, or German Dance, embody and promoted, with its advocates looking to Laban to be its interlocutor.

*

---

[34]See Kampe above, and clarification of this below.
[35]Rudolf Bode in *Der Tanz*, quoted in *Hitler's Dancers*.
[36]Ibid.
[37]Letter from Fritz Bohme to Reich Minister 8 November 1933, cited in *Hitler's Dancers*.
[38]Ibid.

To conclude this conversation about Alexander in particular, I understand that current Alexander Technique teachers work beneficially with their students, who value their one-to-one teaching and care. I also appreciate that today its teachers work therapeutically in a contemporary context with students, incorporating, as they did at RADA, training and knowledge about dyspraxia and hyper-mobility to help actors with proprioception[39] and organization. Alexander technique is now also effectively used as a useful relaxation technique as I witnessed at the Stratford Festival Theatre. The incumbent Alexander teacher there, Kelly McKevenue, adapted her approach for actors in a demanding repertory system. But, given the compelling reasons to update movement training, the premise of eugenics within the practice itself remains, and needs consideration; alongside the similar traces that come from Laban and Wigman's collaboration with the Nazis – where the body was a site of purification from which to build a master race. These 'traces' remain.

*

I have mentioned earlier that 'neutral' is not a term I use when teaching movement. But it appears that 'neutral' has been used to address or correct posture in ways that are both oppressive and racialized.[40] In *The Stages of Reckoning* (Ginther, 2023),[41] Alicia Richardson discusses the term 'neutral' in relation to the body for voice practice. Richardson is a voice teacher from the Black and Global Majority. Commenting on how she was taught voice to learn how to be a voice teacher, she rejects having to adopt a physical stance that wasn't natural to her body. This made her 'teach in a voice and body that wasn't mine' (Ginther, 2023).

> I tried to model the 'neutral stance' concept I learned from studying the teachings of F.M. Alexander and Kristin Linklater: feet hip-distance apart, an elongated spine with energy moving upward and arms that relaxed by my side with 'ease'. (Ginther, 2023)

Attempts to 'neutralize' her stance made her physically stiff and behave unnaturally, but by contrast, as soon as she listened to her own body, her centre of gravity lowered and found its natural placement. This meant that her stance would widen, and she could use her body more freely – she could use her arms, and her voice was more expressive. This stance also helped her connect to and teach students from the Black and Global Majority more effectively.

I am struck by how she was asked to change her own centre of gravity and the suggestion that leaving her arms by her sides would result in relaxation 'with ease'. To insist we stand in parallel lines from top to toe misunderstands human behaviour, and suggests there is a normative stance. When an actor uses their arms, it is a gesture to express an action or inner life. Nor is it wrong to move with text, or be expressive, or indeed 'overly' expressive. The reference to F. M. Alexander and its connection to Linklater privileges a certain body type and cultural point of view. Is this from Trish Arnold's input to Linklater?[42] I don't subscribe to an insistence of feet hip-width apart as the only starting point for movement or alignment. We find a position with our feet, where we feel balanced and grounded. This will

---

[39]Proprioception is located in sensory receptors in muscles and tendons: helps us determine where we are in space, and how we are moving. Also helps us co-ordinate, and find centre and stability.
[40]Lecoq's use of the word 'Neutral' in 'Neutral Mask' is not about posture or control, but about finding an openness and simplicity of physical response. I discuss this in greater depth in Chapter 12.
[41]See Preface for reference.
[42]See below how Arnold worked with Linklater.

be different for everyone. We are not 'neutral', but 'ready' and our point of readiness varies, depending on each individual body.

Richardson's account of feeling forced to narrow her stance shows the cultural and expressive limitations of privileging one specific posture, which inhibits rather than liberates the artist. The creative exploratory work of both Voice and Movement has ingested some troubling influences that need considering.

*

Vanessa Ewan[43] and I set up Conservatoire Conversations in Movement 2021, during the pandemic, to provide a space for movement teachers to meet and discuss their practices.

This was in response to how the pandemic had radically changed our pedagogies. Fear of the body as a site of infection, social isolation for students and teachers, pivoting from studio to online teaching – this mutual support offered opportunities to assess these changes. Meetings were monthly and open-ended, and covered several topics. Frequent themes were the loss of touch for teaching, student experience and student well-being. Conversations focused on the educational landscape we were in, but it was hard to ignore the political upheavals in drama schools. We spoke about the systems we taught, and what support we needed to update our teaching.

In July 2023 Conservatoire Conversations in Movement hosted a 'Movement Symposium'. Our mission statement invited delegates to discuss the challenges of teaching movement:

> Post pandemic through a cost of-living-crisis incorporating the challenges facing our students in an uncertain world for an industry that is also changing rapidly thanks to the energy of #MeToo and the urgencies of anti-racism.

The symposium in July 2023 was the first time we met in person and addressed a 'political' question. The title was: 'Movement Pedagogies as a Framework for Change'. How could movement pedagogy make change happen in drama schools, or how we could *respond* to change by updating our pedagogies?

Three movement practitioners were invited to deliver keynote speeches. The topics covered how to reform systemic problems in a drama school, how to enhance Pure Movement training, and how to embody anti-racism in our teaching practice.

1. Niamh Dowling proposed treating an institution as a 'body' in somatic practice. This would implement holistic change in educational management settings. Niamh Dowling was the new Principal of RADA when she gave this talk.
2. Claudia Mannini delivered a talk on how she was expanding the principles of Pure Movement in drama schools and theatres in Barcelona, to include the more dynamic and acrobatic Grotowski-based training of the actors she worked with. Claudia Mannini is a movement teacher in Barcelona.
3. Ingrid Mackinnon delivered 'Empathy as a movement practice' to enhance anti-racism in movement classes. Mackinnon is a movement teacher, director and intimacy co-ordinator. I wish to focus on Mackinnon's talk, because it directly addressed how to improve inclusive teaching and considers some of my observations above.

---

[43]Senior Lecturer at Central School of Speech and Drama.

Mackinnon recognized that movement teachers have a special skill in 'holding space', but this skill needs to grow into an active form of empathy if we are to implement anti-racism fully in our teaching. Empathy is an 'important tool to decolonize our curriculums'.[44] It allows us to notice our difference in relation to the students we are teaching.

> Holding space must now involve understanding your 'positionality' in relation to the students we teach.[45]

She proposed that we might be very different to the students we teach, who might be different to each other. There is no simple way to view a body, and we ourselves (as teachers) bring our own history and context into a teaching space, which students notice. Education systems and teaching spaces encourage us to view the students as 'bodies with outcomes'. But does this help us see them as people? Are we being empathetic?

Mackinnon suggested that a conscious use of empathy can help us change 'what is happening in our spaces'. It helps us slow down, take stock, see the people in front of us as individuals. Students will experience our teaching from their unique perspective[46] so now we should notice how students take up the work as individuals, and as teachers facilitate them to go further with this. A student taking part in the class is not enough: how do we as educators create a space where they can fully participate with their whole self? 'Silence is an indicator that something is disconnected' and that the student could be feeling 'not seen'.

Mackinnon reminded us how the impact of micro-aggressions can manifest as students being withdrawn and compliant in class. Perhaps revealed when the same student is more expressive and alive in the corridor. We should question why this student isn't comfortable with risk taking in our classes? Is it because they don't feel 'seen', and they don't feel safe? Her focus was on communicating the importance of fully embracing ways to decolonize our teaching practices, which will allow us to be genuinely inclusive and informed in how we teach movement to students from the Black and Global Majority. She was proposing empathy, over theory, to enable this – which leans into the skills movement teachers have developed.

Mackinnon's view is that students are much more political today[47] and come with their own points of view that they want addressed. Her reflections, however, propose a pedagogy that is relational, and relative. My sense is that movement teachers experience a sense of change, in much the same way as sitting in a stationary train, feeling as if we are moving, as the train next to us moves. But we also need to move. To change.

> There are young activists in my room, who are asking questions in their own right .... young people know their stuff, they have questions about the systems we are offering. What system we come from. (Mackinnon, July 2023)

---

[44] I.Mackinnon (2023), *Empathy and Difference*. London.
[45] Ibid.
[46] As mentioned previously I start with the body in front of me when I teach. How to teach students who will see you from their perspective needs research and development. Pure Movement works with stillness, and starts in silence and the work evolves at the pace of the student.
[47] My experience was that students were more focused on learning how to be 'good actors', but the two aren't mutually exclusive.

My analysis is that drama schools have historically asked students to leave their politics, mood and struggles outside the door, with everyone working together in an 'open' space. This was to facilitate saying 'yes' to the offers in the room, not to avoid the struggle this might entail. Struggles shape us, as they also shape each student. Movement classes could be adjusted to reveal how this shaping takes place. More empathetic understanding could facilitate transformation that is culturally sensitive, taking students to a deeper sense of transformation and expression. The students have questions about the systems we teach them, but until we as teachers fully question the legacy of our systems, the sensation of moving on will be illusory.

Mackinnon proposed that students are more political than before. But looking at the examples I refer to from the 1960s and 1970s I question this. Mackinnon's suggestion that drama schools should include an activist understanding of education is radical and could have exciting consequences if we found a methodology and a pedagogy to work with and the teachers to teach it. Do students want this? Many acting students also want value for money in their training.

> An actors' education is a constant dialogue with socio-political forces. (Mackinnon, 2023)

Perhaps the answer lies here. Socio-political forces aren't constant, they change. 'Othering' has a long and dangerous reach as Ginther in *Stages of Reckoning* reminds us.

> When students who have been racially othered enter an educated space where the teacher wishes them to find breath, release physical tension, find vulnerability and explore connection with others, they bring what has happened to their communities to that space. (Ginther, 2023)

Ginther's view that opening the breath and the body, and the need to find a vulnerability, does not chime with how I deliver a movement training for actors. Vulnerability and connection are neither the sole basis of acting, nor the sole focus of a movement class. The opposite is also true for movement – expression, action, dynamic, situation and artistic interpretation. But it is true that we bring what has happened in our communities into the creative spaces we work in. And I am grateful to Ginther for pointing this out. It will form the basis for the next part of the chapter.

The perils of saying yes

If Alexander Technique is based on saying 'no', being ready and open is based on saying 'yes'.

There was an actor at the Stratford Festival Theatre who was uncomfortable with the exercise of rounding and hollowing the spine. He was 'blocking' (his words) and questioned how working on all fours could benefit a classically trained, psychological actor. Then he said, 'no paralysis by analysis' and did it. I thought he was right; we can overthink the point of a physical exercise to oblivion, but I was interested in his struggle to accept doing an exercise, simply because I had asked him to.

There is an apocryphal joke in theatre circles: 'what is the difference between an actor and a dancer?', 'when you ask a dancer to jump, they will ask "how high?"', when you ask an actor to jump, they will ask "why?"' One will do it, one will discuss, perhaps, for hours, the reasons to do it.

Saying 'yes' is another way to stay open to new experiences. But it is also a leap of faith, a commitment to risk taking, and requires mutual trust between teacher and student. Lecoq reminded us that exploring new sensations was the basis of play and was pleasurable. Play is how children learn. Physical play and exploration bypasses inhibitions. But play is a serious matter: a child can act out through play some strong and troubling experiences.

Sometimes students resist an exercise because it will change them too much. They don't want to transform. Or they want to be seen first for who they are, before they transform. This was discussed in the RADA Student Action Plan:

> Students have heard multiple times that they should say yes to everything. (RADA, June 2020)

Which also meant we didn't take account of who they were, because they were 'asked to ignore their race and differences in the service of the text' (RADA, June 2020).

An artist might resist something that doesn't sit well with them, and this is also part of their creative process. The question is: what are we saying yes to? And what are the perils to saying yes?

Sometimes the resonance of the work and its history is very powerful and can be overwhelming.

The Arrow Swing and the Olympic Games Germany 1936

I will explore my own resistance to saying yes, and what discoveries it led to.

The Arrow Swing is part of a repertoire of swings. The sequence I teach (which Arnold showed me) builds from a simple swing of the arm from back, to front, to back, with the torso supporting the swing upright. It then develops into dropping down, as you swing the arm, forwards and backwards, involving a powerful sensation of a change of weight as you swing, and leads you to dynamically galloping down a diagonal line of the room. It can be taught referencing its relationship to the 'diagonals' (taken from Laban's Kinesphere),[48] or as a simple swing from shoulder to finger, reaching towards something or someone just out of reach.

Trish Arnold taught me this sequence of movements in relation to an imaginary box[49] I was inside. I started by touching all eight corners of this imaginary box – four in front of us, and four behind. Up, down, behind, in front – and the diagonals – high back left to high front right.

Reaching forward along the diagonal, to focus my gaze on a point in the distance, felt aspirational and idealistic. I felt someone else's aspiration. It unsettled me. Maybe it was because I was expanding my back along this diagonal line, and filling a bigger space? But where did the energy beyond my fingertips reach to? I asked her. 'Beyond', she said. Beyond?

---

[48] The Arrow Swing is one of the exercises I learned from Trish Arnold, which I will describe in more detail in Chapter 5.
[49] The Kinesphere – as developed by Laban.

Beyond was, I discovered, a concept. My research has led me to understand that this was the movement the young Aryan women used in the opening to the Olympic Games in Germany – that I had good reason to question the idea of 'beyond'.

German Dance

By 1936 Free Dance and the avant-garde practitioners and dance forms that had taken over Central European dance, re-defining dance as radically different to other forms of dance,[50] were gathered under the command and control of Goebbels at the Ministry of Propaganda.

All dancers were instructed to register with the Reich Chamber of Culture. It was no longer known as Free Dance but German Dance. This corresponded with 'The Law of the re-establishment of the Professional Civil Service', which was the first of a series of laws to officially exclude Jews from the 'Aryan Community'. According to Lilian Karina, who was in Germany before 1933 and during the Third Reich, the proclamations of hatred against the Jews were clear, and once the Nazis were in power their intentions were realized.

In September 1933, the Reich Culture Chamber of the Reich Ministry for Popular Entertainment and Propaganda had been set up. The Reich Theatre Chamber was one of its sections, under which dance was managed. The Dance community was divided into two: one, the professional dancers working on stage – the other, Free Dance practitioners, dance pedagogues and directors of movement choirs. All dancers were required to register with the Reich Chamber of Culture. The Ministry's intention was to control and frame all cultural expression to fit the ideology of the Third Reich: and artists who adapted their ideas to the Nazis were protected and favoured.

Every aspect of artistic expression was moulded to fit the regime. Goebbels controlled the press and every form of literary censorship.[51] He exploited film as propaganda, which Leni Riefenstahl acknowledged when she made her films for Germany.[52] Radio was used to broadcast Hitler's speeches, and could be considered as an instrument of rule. The Degenerative Art Exhibition in 1937, coupled with the art exhibition in Munich, showed what was desirable and undesirable in painting, and art. Theatre, according to Karina and Kant, classified what modern plays were acceptable and, tellingly, the authorities 'tried to eliminate silences' in productions – a fascinating insight. The power of silence that speaks louder than words – to tell stories that are forbidden or in the margins. This is the theme of this book, and was to influence the renewal of Mime after the Second World War.

In music, concerts and opera all Jewish and non-Aryan composers were censored. Wagner, one of Hitler's favourite composers, already placed art within politics. The Aryan race was promoted through art and aesthetic, which he described in his essay 'Das Judenthum

---

[50] German Folk Dances and Classical Ballet.
[51] Book burning started and journalists and writers were sent to Concentration Camps.
[52] In 1940 Goebbals requested the production of the infamous antisemitic Nazi German historical propaganda film *Judd Suss*, directed by Velt Harlan.

in der Musik' (concerning Jewishness in music) published in the nineteenth century – with calls to silence Jewish artists. Stephen Moss described it in the *Guardian* as 'a racist tract that no amount of contextualising can redeem' (Moss, 2013), and it was adopted by Hitler as an expression of his ideas on how Jews could never be original composers. Jews live 'outside society' and can never produce authentic work, incapable of real creativity. Jewish artists would bring about cultural degeneration, so they should be excluded from all cultural enterprises, and this included music and composition. And as it turned out, the dance experimenters who didn't conform still danced with the spirit of the Weimar Republic, or were Jews or communists.

With dance, there was no clear political direction of what was acceptable during the Nazi years. But according to Karina, many of the proponents of German Dance were happy to adapt to the ruling Nazi ideology, because they believed that the modern dance they had developed was, by its nature, an expression of Nazi ideas and racial purity.

In 1933 Laban went to work for the Ministry of Propaganda. (This was when both Sigurd Leeder and Kurt Jooss left Germany and came to Dartington, where they developed their dance theatre into a pedagogy.) For three years German Dance was used by Nazi organizers, particularly Goebbels and the Ministry of Propaganda, to promote German culture. These dance forms had originated from Laban's research into movement.[53]

Nazis added German Dance for the advent of the Olympic Games. In 1936 Laban was commissioned to direct a celebration of German Dance at the Outdoor Theatre, using his Movement Choirs (referred to later). His choreography – called Spring, Wind and Joy – was only seen for the first time at the dress rehearsal and was banned by Goebbels. According to Elizabeth A. Hanley (2017), the choreography was considered too intellectual for Germans to relate to. Goebbels hadn't appreciated how experimental Laban's work was, and Hanley points out that the Nazis viewed as decadent any form of art they saw as intellectual. However, Mary Wigman danced in the ceremony and was filmed, so it wasn't the movements themselves they saw as decadent, but the composition. These movements derived from Laban's techniques were not censored and were also seen in the German propaganda films that Leni Riefenstahl filmed in her documentaries, *The Olympic Games* (released in 1938) and *The Triumph of the Will*, celebrating the resurgence of Germany as a militaristic state.

When I analyse the movement of the Arrow Swing in its components and link it to my historical research, I understand the meaning that I had unknowingly tapped into. You extend your front arm out forwards towards the 'beyond', with the feet in an open stance, like an open fourth position in ballet; you have a body that not only reaches for hope but also to a universal being and the Wagnerian implications of this.

The body tells a story, a story that wasn't your intention, *because* the movement was once used to tell another story – in this case the story of white supremacy. Gesture is powerful, as Lecoq's training taught me.

*

---

[53]More on this later in this chapter.

Lecoq describes how in 1947 in Koblenz teaching the Noble Mask (to become the Neutral Mask) in a teacher training college, he de-nazified the students by getting them to do a movement differently to how they automatically did it.

> I like to think I helped a little in the 'denazification' of Germany: I tried out a relaxation exercise which consisted of lifting the arm and letting it drop. I found that their way of doing the gesture was stiffer and different from ours, so I taught them to loosen up.
> (Lecoq, 2002 [1997])

The habit of the Nazi salutes had congealed their bodies. Lecoq's relaxation of this movement de-programmed them. Lecoq was able to do this because he knew how to teach a gesture with a different intention. Breath can lead to relaxation and isn't always courting vulnerability. Openness is not always triggering, but is also full of possibility, regenerative.

A baby lies asleep – their body open, their arms, open and their breath gently inflating and softening their lungs and their bellies.

Never move without awareness of the meaning you are making, or the source of the gesture. It is important to understand the wider social and political context of a gesture and the story it can tell.

*

How do we navigate this troubling heritage? The practice of Laban is embedded in most drama school training.

Much of the teaching of Laban in drama schools follows a schematic understanding of how the body moves, but of course the teachers and schools aren't aware of its connections to this idea of the universal. This is different to the principles of Free Dance, as interpreted by dancers who were experimenters and dance artists, and part of the cultural landscape of the Weimar Republic, before the Nazis came to power. Many of these dancers were forced to leave. Many Jewish dancers were forced to leave. Racism leaves traces, even in its absences.

How to teach physically and avoid the perils of provenance

There is a technique and a specificity to teaching Pure Movement which Trish Arnold taught me. And all the exercises are designed to open an actor up to their own impulses and expression. In fact, the more detail and technique, the less spiritual the work is. The intention behind the work can also change how it is received and how it is expressed.

Litz Pisk's exercises, as noted in her book, were taught with detail – often using a figure of eight to release a swing of shoulder, arm, or wrist.

> A shoulder might go
> Down, up, Down
> Up, down, Up
> Combining
> Back forward Back
> Forward back Forward

With a sense of swing in the rhythm – And 1 and a 2/And 1 and a 2.

To work with technique ensures that actors and dancers and theatre makers are empowered to make the meaning they want, with their understanding of their craft.

Mount Verita

For Laban the principles of human movement were for everyone, because everyone is a dancer, or can be a dancer. Dance was seen to be spiritually and socially beneficial, but didn't need to be technically accurate.

From 1913 to 1918 Rudolph Laban ran a 'School of Art' on Monte Verita with Mary Wigman. They developed practical and theoretical research into the principles of human movement that developed a holistic connection between mind, body and spirit. Movement and meaning could be understood as inner impulse and outer expression and were reciprocal: in harmony with each other and with the universe. The mover's motivation and expression were bound together, a unity of action and inner truth that is not exactly dance.

It was later that Laban's principles were refined into a technique by the teachers who taught his work – like Sigurd Leeder for example.

Their modern dance innovations mirrored Third Reich ideologies, such as the rhythmic use of space and the idea of movement to cleanse and purify the people. Race and racial hygiene were adopted by many of the dance teachers who subscribed to the Nazis' ideology of racial superiority (Karina and Kant, 2004).

Sigurd Leeder and Kurt Jooss then went on to develop the principles they had learned with Laban into a pedagogy and teaching practice for dancers. Their focus was on dance theatre and the training systems of ballet – applied to the more freeing aspects of this new form of dance and the stories that could be communicated on stage.

However, the one fundamental contribution that Laban made to dance was to make it three-dimensional. The work on three dimensions was notated and also influences movement teaching for actors.

*

Three dimensions: Space and expression

The experiments on Mount Verita led to two fundamental theories on movement, spatial form and dynamics:

- Choreutics – spatial forms
- Eukinetics – the expressive dynamics of movement

Choreutics: How you move through space, shaping your spatial environment
Expanding and contracting
Rising and Lowering
Eukinetics: The experience of force, later called weight, and in relation to gravity
Heavy/Light or Strong/Weak
PLUS
Time Tempo/Speed
Space as above

Flux later called Flow and moving between Bound Flow and Free Flow.

The combination of all the above forces and tempi create the effort actions which most Laban-based techniques use in drama schools.

The theory is that the combination of these factors is what gives movement its expression, with each one being on a continuum between the extremes, of, for instance

V E R Y F A S T--------------------to V E R Y S L O W

*

The dancers used the techniques in choreutics and eukinetics to create abstract meaning – stories of myth, or personal expression, often imagistic, associative, sometimes dreamlike. This is different to the set vocabulary of movements for ballet where the dancers tell their stories with the help of the music, often specially composed.[54] But how did these techniques align with The Third Reich?

Marion Kant

I met Marion Kant, one of the authors of *Hitler's Dancers*, because I had seen a talk she gave online about Laban's collaboration with Goebbels and the Nazi regime. It was the first time I had understood this historical connection, though I had always found the Kinesphere and the effort actions difficult to understand as ideas that helped me to move. I was curious to understand further Laban's connection to the Third Reich when he worked for the Ministry of Propaganda and Goebbels, and how he used his movement philosophy and techniques to create the mass Movement Choirs (Karina and Kant, 2004).

Kant outlined for me the direct links that Laban had with the regime. His work at the Ministry of Propaganda directly contributed to the implementation of Goebbels' cultural policy, as described above. Despite claims that Laban either didn't know the political significance of working for Goebbels, or felt he didn't have a choice, my conversation with Kant suggested there had been different paths to take for those professional dancers working with Free Dance; that there were clear political differences between the artists who were part of the 'Free Dance' movements, and even between those that had been pupils of Laban (like Leeder and Jooss).

Marion Kant has direct experience of how developments in modern dance in Germany could be interpreted differently. She was trained at the Comic Opera in East Berlin and was part of Jean Weidt's dance company. Jean Wiedt had been trained by Sigurd Leeder (who was Trish Arnold's teacher and had studied with Laban) and was known as 'the red dancer'. His work created an antidote to Laban's mass Movement Choirs, through his 'red groups' of the workers movement.

In *Hitler's Dancers* Lilian Karina notes this emergence in the 1930s of creative artists as part of the 'new realism' or *Die neue Sachlich keit* (translated as 'the new matter-of-factness'), which became the 'realistic dance theatre' (Karina and Kant, 2004). This was

---

[54]*The Rite of Spring* by Stravinsky, which Nijinsky danced in, also expanded the dance vocabulary for ballet, as the feet turned inwards, and the dancers turned their backs to the audience.

committed to making work that was political and was a departure from Expressionism. But Expressionism (as I have shown earlier) could also be political.[55]

Kurt Jooss, whose anti-war ballet *The Green Table*, was to win first prize at the Concours Internationale de Chorégraphie in 1932, argued for dance as an artistic and creative discipline. He had created a structure to train dancers for theatre dance, combining Laban's innovations with the methodology of dance teaching. He didn't seek to dismantle the artistic activities of theatre (which Laban sought to do), but saw theatre, opera and dance as a 'historical reality'. Ironically, Jooss used Labanotation to record his choreography, but the ballet was a response to the growing advance of Nazism, with variations on the theme of war and death.

The difference between Laban and Jooss (and Leeder) is that Jooss, and later Leeder, saw the expression of the new dance not as 'dance for dance's sake', but to make meaning that was expressed clearly in the choreography and delivered through a precision in the dancers' bodies.

How much is known about the connection between Laban and Goebbels?

Kant suggests that as there has been a discussion about Wagner, which hasn't resulted in his music being censored; we should at least look at the time Laban was working for Goebbels to discuss what aspects of his theory and practice underpinned Nazi ideology.

This chimes with my own questions as to why so many movement systems and classes in drama schools still focus on teaching Laban for actors, without questioning the nature of its abstraction – for it was the abstraction that always bothered me.

The 'Kinesphere' or the 'Box' exercise trains an actor in spatial awareness to move in three dimensions. The 'Box' is an embodied insight into how Laban's movement works, precisely because there is no story or literal meaning. Previously, my understanding of a body in space came from my work at Lecoq, and my training in ballet. Lecoq taught 'Movement Analysis' classes applied to the body in action and to nature: we worked on pulling, pushing, climbing, running, etc. In his book *The Moving Body* (Lecoq, 2002 [1997]), he describes this as:

> actions which lay down circuits in the body, through which emotions flow. Feelings, states and passions are expressed through gestures, attitudes and movements similar to those of physical actions.

This provided reference points from where characters might lead: push, pull, move backwards, forwards, etc. Every movement sequence or set of actions we learned was then immediately applied through our imaginations to what the dramatic story or the attitude might be, or who we might be.

By contrast, the work in the 'Box' didn't seem to be based on an observation of real action but a re-enactment of an abstract idea.[56] However, as a technical exercise to explore

---

[55]See below, references to Kurt Jooss, Sigurd Leeder, Anna Sokolow and Hannah Berger.
[56]Interesting to note, when students were taught this and you left them alone to find the imaginative story in this, you could see some powerful images: children playing with sandcastles in 'low forward': or using these journeys in space as 'shape-shifting' for 'supernatural' characters, like the Three Witches in *Macbeth*.

practical orientations in space it is very useful. But the ultimate direction of this travel of movement from inner to outer was 'beyond' – into a universal spiritual truth,[57] which doesn't seem applicable to acting, or dancing or education.

I stress for those who are Laban trained in depth that I don't teach Laban and am considering some of the ideas underpinning his premises, to interrogate how the idealogy of the Third Reich flowed in and out of Laban's principles. I also recognize, as with Alexander, the cultural importance of Laban's work to the art of movement, and of theatre. But his relationship with the Third Reich can't be overlooked.

The problem of Laban and politics and influence on German culture in the Third Reich

One key area of discussion that Marion Kant shared with me is how Laban's legacy is viewed. Germany and many of the key artists contributing to the culture of the Nazis were forced to de-Nazify. Laban never had to explain his time at the Ministry of Propaganda working for Goebbels or choreographing his Movement Choirs for the Olympic Games. Many believe that Laban ought not to be held accountable for working for Goebbels and contributing to the creation of German Dance and how it was used as part of the Nazi propaganda machine.[58] As such, according to Kant, the history of Laban's politics underpinning his work has been 'eroded'. This could be excused as his lack of political awareness, while the approaches to movement and dance he and Mary Wigman developed are too culturally important to question their context. However, he collaborated with the Nazis' views of racial purity, and while many other artist collaborators were tried or imprisoned, or at least forced to de-Nazify, Laban has been left unscathed – certainly in this country.

His movement approaches weren't based on the observation of the world around us, but were spiritually orientated, seeking purification and harmony that chimed with the Aryan promotion of racial purity. Some of this can be understood through Laban's Movement Choirs.

Laban's Movement Choirs

Part of Laban's research into movement was his development of the Movement Choirs, which he had been exploring since Mount Verita. At a Dance Congress in 1928, different dance practitioners shared their visions of the future of dance. Laban argued for community dance over theatrical dance, through his 'Choric Art Work'. The Movement Choirs transformed the individual into spiritually collective, heightened physical activity. He argued this was the 'true spirit' of community, creating a harmonious order. Laban's success with Movement Choirs was used to choreograph events to celebrate the Olympic Games.[59]

---

[57]My analysis is based on several key texts: *Hitler's Dancers* by Lilian Karina and Marion Kant, *Alien Bodies* by Ramsey Burt, *Ecstasy and the Demon* by Susan Manning.

[58]This distinction is important. Kurt Jooss returned to Germany after the war and developed German Dance – Pina Bausch was one of his pupils.

[59]See above.

Laban's Movement Choirs created choreography with a group of 'lay dancers' moving as one organic being. There is evidence of this in the films of Nazi Germany, where this uniform power is shown as a group of idealized Aryan young men or women, as they move together with similar aspirations. The young movers were chosen for their Aryan features. This linked in part to the right-wing folkish colonies – whose task was to 'preserve the white race' with a connection to eugenics[60] where only the right people should reproduce and keep the race 'clean' to survive. Laban's overall frame of reference was purification of society through 'the people' to create a 'dancing society', where dancing had converted them to the right way of thinking. In this context it is hard to simply focus on the art form that Laban was developing, without looking at the context in which he was working and the philosophy that was driving it. We could focus on Laban's discoveries of how movement and dance are beneficial holistically: or we could interrogate further what he was contributing to, and how it served the Nazi regime. It is remarkable, given the current conversation about racism, that this hasn't happened.

Drama schools and the eight effort actions

Most drama schools I have taught at, and directors I have worked with, have asked if I do 'Laban'. They usually mean 'the effort actions' which produce transformative results in trained actors. A physical action can be embodied through a combination of speed, weight and energy and the use of space to channel an acting intention or a physical characterization. My exposure to these ideas came from training with Trish Arnold, who had taken them from Sigurd Leeder: which I then re-connected with my training at Lecoq. I prefer to describe the 'effort actions' less theoretically as 'movement qualities'.[61]

The eight effort actions which come from the principles of space and the dynamic expression of movement through force, flow and tempo (see above) are taught in most of the schools even now.

They are:

DIRECTION and FLOW	LIGHT	STRONG
DIRECT and BOUND	GLIDING – slow	PRESSING – Slow
INDIRECT and FREE	FLICKING – fast	SLASHING – Fast
INDIRECT and BOUND	FLOATING – slow	WRINGING – Slow
DIRECT and FREE	DABBING – fast	PUNCHING – Fast

---

[60]This is referred to as 'killing life' in Laban's book *Die Welt des Tänzers* (1920). On page 112 he refers to breeding, illness and death as a necessity for 'renewal'. 'Every illness is an attempt by nature to create space for re-building of fresh cells, sensations and ideas ... [it] often demands unnatural ... interventions.' He also refers to this, as a 'dance-like understanding' that is 'needed everywhere'. In 1922 the volkish right-wing movement invited his dance group to Gleschendorf near Lübeck, to choreograph Solstice celebrations in the shape of the swastiska. (From conversations with Dr Marion Kant)
[61]See below for more detail.

They are used for character transformation, text work and action playing, and are often considered fundamental to a Stanislavski-based training. The words are clear in how the movement is designed to be 'played', and give some instant results, but the theory behind these descriptions is much more complex.[62]

Movement is making meaning and creating action and drama. But if the ideas that gave rise to a practice are for spiritual enlightenment, and racial purity, surely, we should at least consider this? Surely we should consider who employed Laban from 1933 to 1935.

Interestingly, Marion Kant wasn't aware of Laban's influence on actor training, nor our lack of awareness of its provenance, but she thinks we should question Laban's collaboration and connection to the Third Reich and by association, his endorsement of racism.

*

The RADA Student Action Plan invited us to consider training in relation to racism. It criticized what it saw as an outmoded delivery, proposing that too often RADA upholds:

> the classical training without a clear understanding of why it is doing so [whilst] the current model is perpetuating a racist and wholly outdated standard. (RADA, June 2020)

I had come to 'Free Dance', 'Expressionism' (as described above) through my training with Trish Arnold as a practical technique. I had also trained in modern dance, which as I will show, shares many techniques with Expressionistic dance. How to untangle these associations? I discovered a shadow that underpinned its provenance. The shadow was Laban and his links to the Third Reich and racial purity.

The question remains: if the origin of a practice is questionable in terms of racism, should we continue to teach it; with the caveat that Litz Pisk left Austria in 1933, and Kurt Jooss and Sigurd Leeder diverted their training with Laban to a professional pedagogy and theatre dance, and left Germany in 1933. But does that excuse the practice I teach?

The history of the Free Dance experimenters, and their relationship with the Third Reich is complex. Many dancers, for instance, worked for the Nazis, because they were compelled to, while also working for the Resistance. Some lost their lives, by working for the Resistance, while also trying to keep working within the constraints of the regime. This is a common story for many artists.

The Free Dance experimenter, who was also a sculptor, Oda Schottmüller (1905–43) initially refused to register with the Reich Chamber of Culture. The expressive and experimental dance she had performed in the Weimer Republic, before the rise of the Nazis, was prohibited. The titles of the dances she performed reflected what she felt about the regime. Titles like 'Outrage' and 'Tragedy'. She worked for the resistance, but eventually she also registered for the Reich Chamber of Culture, so she could dance in the Olympic Games in 1936. But in 1943 she was captured by the Nazis and sentenced to death. She was executed in Plötzensee Prison in July 1943.

---

[62] Try playing these different actions, and speaking as you do it. Very different sensations emerge, reflecting different intention.

Figure 3 Oda Schottmüller performing in her solo *Tragoedie* with the mask she had designed, Getty

Is Pure Movement exempt?

The practice of 'Pure Movement' focuses on the body in front of you, which Lisa Peck refers to as a '*via positiva*' particular to 'women's movement practices' (Peck, 2021), quoting me as saying that you start with a group of bodies:

> and they are all different ... [with] ... completely different experiences and you work with the bodies that are there .... everybody is learning together but everybody processes it slightly differently. I think there is a lot of freedom in that. You just need to go on the journey and see what happens and I think that is quite female.

And earlier Peck had said that my 'female space points to the relational and mutually receptive exchange of joint experimentation'. I am encouraged my practice can be viewed like this, but we have been asked to de-colonize our practices. And as teachers, many of us were asked to consider our own contribution to racism through our practices.

As Vanessa Ewan and I proposed in the *Conservatoire Conversations on Movement* symposium in our mission statement, we need to discuss 'the implications, discoveries and challenges of teaching movement today, post-pandemic, through a cost-of-living crisis ... [to include] ... the challenges facing our students in an uncertain world for an industry that is also changing rapidly thanks to the energy of #MeToo and the urgencies of anti-racism. We are all navigating waves of change' (Ewan and Morris, 2023).

But to do that, we need to know what we have left behind.

Notes from the past

For many years I would visit Vienna annually to teach movement at the Vienna Kinder Theatre. I walked the melancholy, beautiful streets, visiting Freud's Museum, and the Belvedere. I ate in the Gästehäuser with my friends, and visited the Holocaust Museum in Judenplatz, known as the Nameless Library, designed by the British artist Rachel Whiteread. I was drawn to the baroque churches, spilling out the music of Mozart, which felt more uplifting, and spoke of the Enlightenment, and the ornamental beauty of the courts. In many ways it was delightful, but I was never at ease. One day I took a tram to the Volkesparker, famous for the Ferris Wheel where Holly Martins met Harry Lime in *The Third Man*. An old woman with white hair in a bun and sparkling blue eyes – maybe 80 years old (this was in 2005) – sat opposite me. She repeatedly looked at me piercingly, and then pointedly moved away. Was I imagining why?

One April In Vienna, I was invited back to teach movement on a weekend workshop for teachers working for the Kinder Theatre. Afterwards we sat in a circle to debrief. Many of the teachers were music teachers, working with Eurythmy, so were familiar with rhythm and movement – but they hadn't encountered movement that was about expression or communication, or could be used for character. They hadn't encountered movement that asked them to discover their own way of moving – expressive, dynamic, spontaneous, surprising.

'Where does this movement come from?' I was asked. I said it was based on Sigurd Leeder and some of Litz Pisk's work.

'Where were they from?'

I told them.

'Why did they leave?'

I paused. They paused.

'They left in the 1930s', I said, feeling very uncomfortable.

One older woman looked down and started to cry.

'We have lost so much'.

I propose that drama schools, to acknowledge all aspects of racism, need to understand what else has yet not been spoken about. Laban and his connection to Goebbels.

It is why Litz Pisk taught at RADA in the 1930s. It is why Sigurd Leeder came to the UK, and taught Trish Arnold.

Part II The body as a play text

5 Trish Arnold and her legacy

Teachers and teaching

Pure Movement and Expressive Movement: my personal experience of working with Trish Arnold

> Pure Movement is doing something in depth – it is totally about acting – learning something in depth over the years. Training is not a smorgasbord but something that is embedded for the rest of their lives. (Latham, 2023)[1]

This quote from David Latham endorses the long slow journey of transformation that occurs through the teaching of Pure Movement, as developed by Trish Arnold. In 2003 I was invited to the Stratford Festival Theatre in Canada, to teach for the Birmingham Conservatoire. This was a training programme for emerging actors that David Latham ran, with actors progressing to work as apprentices at the theatre. I was nervous as I walked into class with my drum. Would a group of young actors drawn from all over Canada, who I had never met before, want to move with me? I was only to teach Pure Movement, and I wasn't even sure if they knew what to expect. Before arriving, we had talked on the phone about my practice, my teachers and what I would teach. As I ran my first class, veering from caution to confidence, David Latham watched me, inscrutably calm and still. Had what I taught measured up?

'Was that alright?' I asked afterwards.

'Oh yes.'

He was delighted that I had brought Pure Movement and Trish Arnold's practice back to the Festival Theatre.[2]

*

When I first started to work with Trish Arnold in 1996, my understanding of movement was as an actor, a dancer and a mime. I was yet to experience how a movement practice could both ground my body and focus my imagination, to help me be physically present and truthful on stage. Arnold introduced me to the 'body' as an expressive instrument that could be trained technically, specifically for the craft of acting. This was an entirely new experience, despite my dance training, and my time at Lecoq.

She taught me how to teach a physical discipline and to work with the breath and her practice emphasized teaching as much as movement. I learned how to build exercises progressively, embracing a physical technique designed specifically for actors, with the

---

[1] Notes from an interview with David Latham (2023).
[2] Trish Arnold had worked at the Stratford Festival Theatre in Ontario, Canada.

same rigour as my dance training. I learned to think about how a body communicates meaning and emotional life, through specificity and a vocabulary – both of which I had appreciated at Lecoq, but for a different outcome. She taught me how to select exercises that unlocked the actor and what order to teach them in. In helping me work with students she introduced me to the importance of physical development and how to build up teaching brick by brick. She taught me both a practice and a pedagogy. She was a wonderful teacher and even at the age of 80 a beautiful mover.

Pure Movement: The focus for the transformation of the actors, not the teacher

One of the key aspects of Pure Movement was Trish Arnold's understanding of the craft of teaching itself and how to apply that to the training of an actor. As a teacher you focus on the work trying not to be the important energy in the room. She described herself as an instinctive teacher, inventing ways in class to break an exercise down to help the actors she was teaching, do her exercises better. 'Better' was about improving the technique of the body to allow the actor to make clear movement decisions that could inform their acting choices, not as an end but as a way to give actors options for transformation.

Pure and Expressive Movement

When I first started to train with Trish Arnold, she told me the name of her practice was 'Pure Movement'. I discovered the name was important as it described both the approach and the ethos of the classes and was taught in several drama schools at that time, which distinguished it from other systems. Her classes seemed simple but weren't easy to do. I was encouraged not to 'act' or 'show' – just to respond. We focused on how I moved, not what my physical issues might be. I needed to dig into the source of the movement, not dance or embellish. To really 'do' it, but with technical accuracy. The movement was a physical text, to bring to life.

The techniques and exercises were taken from her training with Sigurd Leeder but adapted for acting. After a few months the connection between the 'Pure Movement' I was learning with Arnold and Leeder's Expressionism began to make sense. It was the movement of the human body in space, informed by gravity and momentum, emanating from inside. This is different to the utopian or idealized abstractions of 'inner' to 'outer', of the Laban-based techniques in the 1930s, as the outcome was for an actor, working on text, or on character, not for self-improvement or national identity. I believe this is one of the reasons why Arnold was always very clear to distance her practice from claims that it could improve well-being or was therapeutic.

There is currently a critical debate around the term 'Pure Movement'. A concern that it doesn't include students and teachers from the Global Majority and the Global South.[3] But as a technique that requires detail, which the specific exercises in the book will show, it

---

[3] Mark Evans, Vanessa Ewan and Lisa Peck have raised concerns about this – also in its conflation with 'Neutral' as a term. Concerns were also raised at RADA in the public meetings by members of staff, that it had Aryan connotations.

moves us away from the small space of 'who' we are – to the bigger space of 'why' we are moving and offers the actor/student developmental teaching. And by extension, helps the actor discover how the character they might play, moves. The word 'Pure' means to not lay anything on top of the movement and 'let the movement (embodied within the exercises) change you'. It could and has been described as 'functional movement for actors'. This is not aesthetic or, I hope, cultural, and I believe it addresses the question of cultural difference if it is taught inclusively.

'Pure Movement' and 'Expressive Movement' is a system that only works if it is taught incrementally. As I demonstrate later in the chapter, exercises are taught inclusively by inviting students to work within their own parameters. An example (for instance) might be to do with a students' flexibility. Instead of asking them to drop their torso fully to the ground, you might invite them to hang down as low as is 'available' to them – focusing on feeling the drop of their torso, and the placement of the pelvis, rather than stretching the backs of their legs. Balance is another example where the ability to stand on one leg, or change weight suddenly, can differ from day to day; it is not a finite skill to be achieved, but an appreciation of how the distribution of weight through your feet is constantly shifting. When I advocate for a gentler approach to movement teaching, sometimes there is concern that students might not acquire the skills they need. But anyone who takes physical classes will know, being invited to try something is how incremental learning works, and acquiring a skill is a process. Movement and dance teaching focuses on 'how' we move; and 'Pure Movement', as I have come to understand it, allows the student/actor to decide for themselves how far to go with an exercise. A subjective response, based on how you might experience the movement – phenomenological, rather than theoretical.

Classes with Trish Arnold didn't focus on fixing my physical problems, although she corrected my shoulders and the placement of my pelvis frequently.[4] I learned through watching, or from the sensation of doing, or from a series of experiential explorations – one of which I show below. I never looked in a mirror. Instead, a drumbeat or guided prompts, often rhythmic, would suggest the impulse to move – which made it closer to an improvisation for an acting class. Often these techniques were extremely dynamic, threaded into sequences, challenging in their use of space and direction. To 'let the movement change you' revealed its meaning as you did it,[5] and suggested inner impulses – leading you towards freer movement.

The Gravity Swing, an overview

Much of Pure Movement is taught through a repertoire of swings. They are called 'Gravity Swings' as they work in concert with gravity. 'The swing' contains within it many things you might experience physically as an actor. You let the weight fall, and momentum is released in relation to gravity – the swing – until it suspends in an active stillness, hovering in the opposite direction to where you started. Then you let it fall and swing back again, returning

---

[4]Fixing a student's faults was something I resisted throughout my whole movement career, because it suggested there was something wrong with the student. You work with the body that is in front of you. Drama schools, however, are committed to delivering development through 'learning outcomes'.
[5]An exercise I will explain later is called 'justify the movement'.

to its starting point. The impulse moves you through time and space. The body feels different afterwards: rebalanced, elastic. The swing helps you find your alignment and grounds you. You have let go into the movement, which is called 'release'. An actor is also propelled through the time and space of a play or performance. They are moved by different stimuli, moving through huge and varied arcs of feeling and action, but they come back to themselves.

How I discovered Expressive Movement as a pedagogy

It took me a while to understand the connection between Arnold's movement and acting and I asked her about Pure Movement's connection to an actor's work of interpretation and physical acting. This is still an important question for all forms of Actors' Movement. To help me think how to do this, Arnold introduced me to some expressive improvisations which were very playful, but started from the body, rather than from an idea. This interested me, as it connected to my experiences with Veronika Sherbourn, and later at Lecoq. The only time, as a professional actor, I had experienced a real sense of exploration and embodiment through physical improvisation was with Nancy Meckler, whose approach to exploring movement that lay underneath the text was revelatory.[6]

One of the classes Arnold introduced me to was 'Insides and Outsides', the other 'Symmetrical and Asymmetrical' and another 'Flirtatious Feet'. I trialled these classes at Rose Bruford, and they were great fun and liberated students' physical imaginations. For this the students would split into pairs. For 'Insides and Outsides', one actor physicalized the inside of an object, the other the outside. I remember two students acted a book: the outside of the book was an actor reading it, the inside, an actor embodying the content. Another two students chose a boot. One was the shape of a battered boot, the other a gnarled and ancient foot inside it. 'Symmetrical and Asymmetrical' was a conversation – one person would make a symmetrical shape, the other answer with a different shape: and then the same with asymmetrical shapes. A symmetrical conversation is direct, uncompromising, clear – an asymmetrical conversation complicated, indirect, contorted. 'Flirtatious Feet' speaks for itself but involved a delightful variety of physical conversations: sitting at dinner tables, or running away from someone, putting on new shoes, walking barefoot outside.

Although, when I finalized the syllabus, I didn't use these exercises, they showed me how you can create a narrative out of relationships based on physical action and physical shapes: how to create magical and fantastical transformations that had a logic for the performer.

*

As a rule, it is drama schools, and not movement teachers, that determine the length, and the frequency of movement classes – usually scheduled for one-and-a-half hours and running for a set number of weeks each term. At Rose Bruford in 1997, each year group would be given four movement classes a week, with seventy-five students in each year. Each year divided into five groups of fifteen students. This was a three-year course, so there were 225 students, divided into fifteen groups. A lot of bodies to take care of and classes

---

[6]Nancy Meckler was the Artistic Director of 'Shared Experience'.

to keep track of! That, alongside the number of subjects acting students are expected to do in any one day, meant that students frequently switched modalities. My preferred, more organic method would be to lay down in depth a movement-intensive training in the first term – focusing on technique, stamina, body-awareness and physical improvisation – introducing students to the basic techniques, swings and the use of breath, and simple scenarios. This would go on to form the basis for a daily class of one and a quarter hours and team teaching[7] on projects to help students apply the work. Sadly, I only encountered this when I went to teach a project at the Institut del Teatre in Barcelona in 2001, and it is not common practice to work intensively with physicality like this in the first months of training on a BA Acting course. MA courses may include this but often stop teaching movement regularly after the first term, which is different.

At Rose Bruford I was scheduled to teach each first and second year student two classes a week and provide movement input and movement directing for all Third Year Shows; I was teaching twenty classes a week, as well as providing movement for up to four projects and rehearsals a term, in the third year. To clarify my pedagogy with a clear developmental arc, I divided my classes into two strands, that 'spoke to each other': one focusing on the body, the other focusing on movement into acting. One class was called Pure Movement, which would be a technical class. The other, Expressive Movement, was to study more creative techniques, as a bridge into acting.

Teaching Pure Movement and Expressive Movement in tandem has now become my pedagogy – and as I mention earlier made sense to me, from the training I received at Lecoq. The other two strands of movement training I oversaw, were Fight, or Stage Combat, and Social Dance. Which this book doesn't address.

Pure and Expressive Movement and the influence of 'autocours'

The content of the two classes and their aims needed to be decided, along with the arc of training, so that the work could go on a journey.[8]

Some of the syllabus in both Pure and Expressive Movement would look at period, genre or text – such as Greek Tragedy or Shakespeare. Some classes in Expressive Movement, would work with analogy – moving 'like something' to embody a movement quality or an idea, 'transposed' into character or situation.

My classes in Expressive Movement were an amalgam of work I had encountered at Lecoq, alongside exercises Arnold had passed on to me with many inventions of my own. The BA Acting courses were informed by Stanislavski or psychological realism, so my focus became exercises that linked movement with motivation, and text. For Expressive Movement, the autocours from Lecoq provided inspiration and structure.[9]

---

[7] Team teaching is when movement, voice and acting teachers work as a team with students to create their projects and direct their plays. This was an approach I encountered at the Institut del Teatre in Barcelona, helping students to experience how voice, body and acting are all connected, and happen at once.
[8] A learning journey was something we had to reflect on at Rose Bruford. But the idea of a journey was also part of Lecoq's pedagogy.
[9] See more detailed reference to autocours in *The Moving Body* (Lecoq, 2002 [1997]).

'Autocours' was Lecoq's revolutionary pedagogy[10] that integrated his unorthodox training systems into opportunities to make theatre – developed from his 'lores of movement'. Each Friday, Lecoq would give us a 'title' to create a piece of theatre to present the following Friday for him to critique in front of the whole school. We found our troupe for the week and rehearsed daily. A mini weekly festival. Simon McBurney mentions in his introduction to *The Moving Body* that Lecoq could 'see well' and his school also taught his students to see well, and critique with accuracy. The autocours helped us craft what we wanted to say into physical action. But it was a collective experience, where 'personalized' Stanislavski responses were less pressing, than trying to work out what you wanted the piece to 'say'.[11] There is an inherent tension in the two traditions of an actor being inside their role, and at the same time crafting what they want an audience to understand. The connection between structure and form, to create meaning, was a shared enterprise – rather than an 'auteur's' voice shaping their personal meaning through the actors, or the actor being reliant on the director to decide how their role relates to the whole production. We had to do both at the same time – work with personal integrity, and work as a group. Lecoq introduced 'autocours' (which translates as 'teach yourself') as a response to May '68.[12] It was part of a broader social revolution[13] and one of the most important innovations of the school.

The autocours were noisy and combative experiences. We created what we wanted to say, every week, grappling with content and execution. We often fell out and fiercely disagreed, but the weekly deadline forced a compromise. No one wanted the ignominy of not having got a piece of work together. Some of the work was dreadful – 'la tasse' – but we mostly owned the process. Democracy in action. We also found our 'troupes' – those we wanted to work with, whose chemistry and ideas challenged or stimulated.

The second year at Lecoq introduced us to different styles or genres of theatre, each taught over several weeks[14] – Pantomime Blanche, Commedia dell'Arte or Tragedy, for example. 'Autocours' made us expand these techniques and reinvent them to express our worldview, or our imaginations.

Movement was the starting point from which to incorporate text, character, relationships, use of space. With the theme of melodrama, for instance, the group I was in made a piece called 'The landlord throws her into the snow'. Highlighting poverty in the Victorian age, we drew on the melodramas of Boucicault to lambast Victorian social attitudes towards poverty. The physical techniques we used – the strong gestures for emotional emphasis – or still points creating tableaux – embodied these ideas.[15]

'Expressive Movement' became a new addition to the movement classes, as part of the curriculum at Rose Bruford,[16] and then at RADA.[17] It would follow the journey of the

---

[10]There is a similarity to devising, but the emphasis was different – how to make meaning **through** movement as a starting point.

[11]How you or your character responds to a situation, because of who they are and what they need, in any given moment.

[12]See Chapter 4 'The Need for a System' for details of May '68.

[13]Please see Chapter 4 for some more detailed accounts of how the French students in May 1968 challenged the theatrical status quo.

[14]See *The Moving Body* (Lecoq 2002 [1997]) for details.

[15]See Figure 5 for reference.

[16]1997–2005.

[17]2015–22.

Figure 4 Commedia dell'Arte autocours mask work. Lecoq 1977 shows how the work was updated to cover contemporary themes.

BA Acting classes and rehearsal exercises, so changed from school to school. The content included 'Animal Study', 'Animal into Character', 'Chorus Work', 'Character Work', 'Neutral Mask', 'Paintings', 'Music' and 'Physical Characterization'. The classes often led to scenarios, following the 'autocours' model, and followed the techniques of 'Pure Movement'.

My conversations with Trish Arnold helped me clarify the fundamental principles actors need to learn when training their body for the stage. The separate distinctions of Pure Movement and Expressive Movement helped to plan classes and student development.

Pure Movement

- Exercises and classes to develop technical ability: main focus – the spine, the Gravity Swing, spatial awareness and body awareness

Figure 5 'The landlord throws her into the snow' – autocours. Lecoq 1978 shows the use of space and emotion in gesture and physical attitude.

- Derives from the Sigurd Leeder Expressionistic technique for dancers, adapted for actors by Trish Arnold and a community of practice
- The classes delivered incrementally, following the educational needs of the group
- Pure Movement connects to the breath and breath is a constant presence in all the work
- Pure Movement improves the actor's technical ability – co-ordination, flexibility, stamina, strength, relaxation, balance and alignment.

Expressive Movement

- Helps actors physicalize their interpretations of a role: intention, characterization and different acting styles
- Development of physical characterization, in a context (personal or a particular period)
- Understanding of how to plot the physical life of your character in the story/play/text
- It explores a variety of techniques
  - Abstract – dynamic, tempo, rhythm, weight and flow
  - Spatial dimensions and levels
  - Changes of weight
  - Identification with the natural world through analogy: moving 'like' something to find movement qualities
  - Steps and dance (see the description of how dance can be adapted for movement)

- How the world of the play determines character, status and relationships
- Time and place.

The subjects of Expressive Movement

- Mask work, chorus work, animal study, paintings, music, physical characterization, the elements, observation of real life
- The techniques derive from Lecoq and Sigurd Leeder and Stanislavski-based techniques
- The expression and transformation actors learn is on a continuum, from naturalism to heightened expression – always connected to a sense of truth, but helping actors develop a playful and informed understanding of the 'world of the play'.

*

The community of practice and lineage of movement teachers for Pure Movement

The techniques of Pure Movement were enhanced through the community of practice to which I am affiliated. The exercises that derived from the connection of expressionism to the breath applied to an actor's body, are the techniques particular to Pure Movement. The Pure Movement work I taught developed collegiately, without a hierarchy, continuing the radicalism and modernism that is part of its provenance. Though there isn't (and wasn't) a hierarchy, there is an awareness of seniority. This is a body of work that a group of practitioners developed together and passed on, albeit informally.

The teachers instrumental in creating this pedagogy, alongside Trish Arnold, are Sue Lefton and Jane Gibson. Wendy Allnutt developed it further and later Jackie Snow helped develop the inclusion of parts of Grotowski's 'The Cat'. I became part of this collaborative, supportive network, when I started to train with Trish Arnold. Lefton, Gibson, Allnutt and Snow also taught Period Dance. Lefton and Gibson developed it as a pedagogy specific to actors and taught Period Dance classes and developed projects together. Their research into the curating of dances for specific periods of plays and literature is long and deep.

The lineage also goes beyond Trish Arnold. Pure Movement includes the work of Litz Pisk who came from the same tradition of Free Dance, and whose work already had a strong presence at RADA, the Old Vic Theatre School and Central School of Speech and Drama, when Trish Arnold started to teach and develop her practice.[18] Sue Lefton, Jane Gibson and Wendy Allnut had all been taught by Litz Pisk at Central School of Speech and Drama. And when Arnold started to research how to adapt her work for actors, she worked with Litz Pisk.

This focus on this community of practice was to consider teaching problems, sharing how to break movements down, or how to combine sequences, or identify common problems that students might present with – or even develop new ideas. The quality of the

---

[18]As mentioned below, Litz Pisk taught my father, who passed on some of her exercises to me.

research was highly professional and properly interrogated, though none of it was funded, or officially recorded.

Leaving this research undocumented can lead to misinterpretation[19] – though Merry Conway's film *Tea With Trish* was a record of some of the exercises,[20] and Lizzie Ballinger's book *Trish Arnold* also lays out her work and exercises with clarity.[21]

We supported each other by watching our classes, sharing new exercises, or attending each other's productions. It is common to think that 'Pure Movement' is just about 'the swings'. But it has developed into a complex body of work with its connection to Expressionism, and Lecoq: and has been developed to facilitate the voice (which I refer to below). Many of us have also developed how to connect the swings to characterization, and different playing styles in theatre.

But it is often seen as the strange woman with a drum.[22] Foreign, alien and clever.

The connection between Jacques Lecoq and Pure Movement

While Arnold was developing her pedagogy at LAMDA, she also went to train with Lecoq at his workshops and Summer Schools in Paris. There she became particularly interested in mask work. Much of Lecoq's work has influenced Pure Movement practice. The development of Pure Movement remained open to new influences, its teachers often introducing other movement techniques, which they encountered through personal training or working with international practitioners.[23] Pure Movement uses the Gravity Swing as the foundation of the practice and its teachers have adapted it to accommodate various cultural expectations and forms of expression.

I was also trained by Monika Pagneux in Paris (when she was teaching at Lecoq), and her work has informed some of the exercises I teach.[24] Specifically, the spiral. Moving with the dynamic of a spiral unlocks different parts of the body, winding or unwinding, curving often in countermotion, and creating its own momentum in the process. It is also spatially dynamic. If you turn the arm and shoulder inwards, the journey follows round in an inward turning spiral, as you walk – if outwards, the arm travels on an outward turn, seeing into the world. These spirals open and close the body as you move, following pathways of turning in on yourself, or expanding.

Pagneux's approach was more contained, influenced by Feldenkrais, focusing on the spine. The spiral starts with the head leading a sequence, turning the shoulder, hip, knee and feet spiralling around you as you turn. Pagneux's spiral is nuanced, as if turning in

---

[19]Particularly because of the term 'pure': but also a lack of awareness that it is technical and precise, and works alongside voice training.
[20]*Tea With Trish*, directed by Merry Conway: http://conwayandprattprojects.org
[21]*Trish Arnold* by Lizzie Ballinger (Ballinger, 2023).
[22]See Chapter 4.
[23]For example, Claudia Mannini is an Italian movement teacher working in Barcelona, who trained as a movement teacher at Guildhall with Wendy Allnutt. She has developed Pure Movement to include the more dynamic and acrobatic-based training of the actors she works with in Barcelona.
[24]Pagneux's training with Feldenkrais then influenced some Pure Movement teachers to study this technique in more depth: and some of the exercises have found their way into Pure Movement training.

response to something you have heard or seen. The dance version, described above, coming from the torso, is more dynamically expressive.[25]

Pure Movement is a complete curated pedagogy developed over a critical period of experiment and research, from the 1970s to the 2020s, and is open to change and development. The practice was developed at LAMDA, Guildhall, RADA, Rose Bruford, but these institutions may not be aware of this today.[26] There are no exams or objective measures to provide official validation. Instead, the work is transmitted informally, allowing it to evolve through those who teach it and adapt to current needs. It is a 'river of work' and, as it is hard to quantify, it sometimes raises questions of its authorship and how to advocate for its relevance. Transmission – can it be measured?

Pure Movement: Why it is unique

- Pure Movement is a calibrated series of exercises that have been scrupulously *adapted* for acting and text-based and psychological performance, and stage movement.[27]
- It trains the whole body to move in an integrated way and helps actors take up space and learn how to move *through* space, to apply to the craft of acting.
- It connects an actor to an impulse, and helps them eradicate tension that doesn't belong to the character or the situation.
- It also provides the actor with the means to work safely with tension, when the situation or character demands it.
- It works technically with Gravity Swings, the spine, placement of breath and weight.
- It can be adapted to fit different performance styles.
- It teaches the actor how to work with the breath when moving.

The lineage of Pure Movement is:

Sigurd Leeder – Jacques Lecoq – Litz Pisk
|
Trish Arnold
|
The community of practice (as described above)

Movement teaching as a craft and a technique – Transmission

There are some fundamental principles that movement and dance teachers share – embodying the work being the most obvious. Much needs to be embodied by the teacher,

---

[25] See below for specific exercises.
[26] LAMDA, Guildhall, RADA, Rose Bruford for example.
[27] The state of readiness and relaxation is an excellent starting point from which to develop a psychological understanding of character. The release and understanding of how to use the breath helps the actor to play and explore text. The understanding of how to move effectively in the space equips them to work on a stage in three dimensions.

for them to teach effectively. This is often very clear when you watch a dance teacher, as they will have been trained as a dancer as well.

Many dance teachers and companies have found methods to teach diverse groups of individuals, helping them find their own capacity to move. I discovered that drama schools could benefit greatly from following the example of this flexible knowledge held by dance instructors which makes their movement training inclusive, when researching inclusive movement practices with RADA's Access Advocate, Angela Gasparetto. In 2017 Angela Gasparetto and myself consulted with Candoco Dance Company – the first professional dance company for disabled and non-disabled dancers working together. We were specifically interested in methodologies to enable full participation in movement and dance classes at RADA for wheelchair users and physically disabled students. Candoco Dance Company was founded by Celeste Dandeker-Arnold who trained at The Place in London. Candoco clarified for us the principles of adaptation for movement. It is a practical change you make, based on the aim of the exercise and the mover themselves. Exercises aren't fixed but instead relate to who is doing them – and (crucially) ensure that they are equally expressive for everyone. You are teaching the individual, with techniques that extend and transform to fit *them*.

I interviewed Sarah Miller, who teaches classes for over-sixties at The Place,[28] to ask how she adapted her teaching to accommodate dancers with different ranges of movement. Reviewing Miller's weekly teaching schedule revealed a diverse group of students. Besides classes for the over-sixties, she also teaches children at the Young Place, and 'has diversified to teaching in schools' (Miller, 2024). At the other end of the scale, she also works for the Centre for Advanced Training at Trinity Laban, teaching creativity to very talented dance students. She needs to adapt her pedagogy to different circumstances – adapting her technique to the level of the students she teaches. Miller viewed the lineage of her practice as an important part to this, as it helps ground her in specific principles when she works with her different groups of students. She has been training at The Place since she was four but also trained as a teacher at the Young Place, working as the demonstrator for her teacher and mentor, Iris Tomlinson.

The lineage she is part of goes as follows:

- Her seminal teacher was Iris Tomlinson, who mentored her as a dance teacher.
- Iris Tomlinson was trained by Jane Dudley.
- Jane Dudley was an American Dancer, whose influences from Expressionism and Free Dance (and Martha Graham) led her to create dances that were socially relevant and linked them to themes from (for instance) the Great Depression.
- Jane Dudley was trained by Martha Graham, whose rigorous dance technique is a vital part of the modern dance lineage.

This foundation in a strong technique and lineage gave Miller the basis to explore other techniques offered at The Place.

---

[28] I'm not suggesting there is a correlation between the two. I am looking at the creative possibilities of adaptation and accessibility.

> I did Cunningham, Bartinieff fundamentals – release technique. Lots of practitioners came in and did projects with us, Russell Malliphant worked with us just after his baby was born and looked at small ways of moving, from Bartinieff. (Miller, 2024)

The practitioners she mentioned illustrated how teaching can connect to 'life', something which Lecoq's pedagogy and creative approaches also shared.

How to plan a class, so that everyone can participate

I also asked Miller how she structured her classes, to consider the similarities between movement and dance classes. Part of this book explores how to structure classes, whose methodology is to learn through doing. Teachers transmit the material they teach, from their own body knowledge to other bodies. But the class needs to respond to the students and is a living breathing entity. What specific physical adjustments does a dance teacher like Miller make to create an inclusive classroom?

Teaching dancers over 60 is to create a space that can positively include their limitations, as well as developing their technique. The teacher offers three or four different options with full creative expression. The message from this approach is that there is no one version better than another. This is also how movement teachers work with actors.

I asked Miller to provide insight to planning her movement classes in this way.

Interview with Sarah Miller: How she plans her classes and works with older artists/dancers

> I plan my classes by starting with the end, and the phrase I want to teach. Then I decide what skills they will need to create these exercises and sequences. Teaching safely – so it is important to give a good warm-up, working with the kind of movements that the students will need later. You can teach a class, or you can give class.

Teaching older people: The experience of life

Miller's thoughts on teaching modern dance to over sixties chimed with how Actors' Movement has adapted certain techniques from modern dance and applied them to an actor's movement and physicality. The emphasis is on human expression, rather than virtuosity in movement. In many ways, Actors' Movement and Miller's application of dance to everyday life and human experience are linked.

> I now understand how bringing your life experience to dance can be very enriching. An older dancer has lived their life as a human.

An older performer brings their lived experience to a movement, much like an actor does. An actor brings the history of self or the character they are playing to the movement they are making. The audience connects to the 'why' the actor moves, which is expressed in 'how' they move.

However, there is a distinction between dance and Actors' Movement, which Arnold discovered for herself, and then developed a unique practice which she transmitted into the

Drama Schools. She worked on this, through trial and error, empirically, and pioneered a pedagogy. Much of this, I describe below, and comes from discussions we had, and notes Arnold gave me.

Progressive and expressive pedagogy of Trish Arnold

Trish Arnold trained with Sigurd Leeder, in search of a more liberating form of dance than Ballet (Arnold, 1997). She took the dance pedagogy she learnt from Leeder into something much more interesting for her: movement teaching for professional actors.

I will now consider how the Pure Movement that Trish Arnold taught, and inherited, was about the expression of the individual artist.

Sigurd Leeder and Kurt Jooss were both trained by Laban but left Germany in 1933 (largely because of the Nazi's Aryan policies against Jews).[29] They had used Laban's discoveries to create a professional pedagogy with a calibrated technique of their own.[30] Their training was for dance artists to learn how to perform the techniques of modern dance for the stage.

The Green Table, choreographed by Kurt Jooss in 1932, is a ballet that depicts the futility of war and the dangers of militarism, through a series of dramatic danced motifs, referencing medieval woodcuts from the Dance of Death. The dance opens with diplomats and politicians, debating terms of war and peace.[31] There is also a rigorous technique in this 'dance drama' with individual performances communicating a modern fable. Soldiers, refugees and profiteers are overshadowed by the figure of death in a Roman helmet – his body and costume made up like a skeleton. This ballet is frequently revived – with both the rigorous technique and the Labanotation which recorded it making it possible to transmit both the dance, and the ideas and viewpoints about war it embodied.

When I first trained with Arnold I hadn't understood Leeder's connection to Laban, nor the political engagement that came through the dances that he worked on with Jooss. Only after Arnold taught me 'the Box' did I appreciate the teleology, threading back to Laban, and the variety of possibilities of how meaning could be crafted through dynamic and abstract movement, in ways that were artistic and benefitted the individual artist. Pure Movement had a context, just like Lecoq's work, and Arnold had developed it, so that actors learned to express themselves, through their whole body, using the whole space.

*

When I first taught Pure Movement at Rose Bruford, one of the students later told me how he discovered the movement was about him, about the self.

The range of the Pure Movement practice, and how it enables us to express deep impulses makes it eminently suitable for a Stanislavski-based approach to acting. The means to explore the release of the body and intention was through the Gravity Swing. The Gravity Swing, as developed by Arnold in connection with the breath, created a combination of

---

[29] I discussed this in greater detail in the last chapter: Kurt Jooss's wife was Jewish as were many of the dancers in his dance troupe.
[30] See below for more details.
[31] To see the ballet online refer to the Joffe Ballet: the ballet is frequently revived.

Figure 6 *The Green Table*, choreographed by Kurt Jooss. Getty.

release of the musculature self-awareness of how an actor moved, and a sharpness of observation, which she understood and frequently talked about.

> It is the release of muscles and the sharpness of the actor's observation and awareness which – freed of his own habitual tensions and personal quirks – will be a major factor to inhabit the character he is playing. (Arnold, 1997)

Arnold was a dancer who adapted her technique for acting. She took years to research the different emphasis she needed to develop: the connection of the breath and impulse into movement. A specialist mover, teaching actors to extend their physicality for acting, Arnold focused on the meaning of the movement, not its somatic or therapeutic outcomes, or mysterious utopian possibilities, as expressed in German dance.

> Although it is true there can be a feeling of well-being after a 'work-out' the state which we aim for is much subtler. (Arnold, 1997)

When I watched and took part in Trish Arnold's classes, her expertise transmitted both meaning and craft across the space. But her pedagogy emphasized expression and placement more than expertise. Once the actors acquired these skills they might 'look' very different to the 'movement experts' delivering the work. The change in the body comes from the exercises in relation to how each body moves as an individual, not from copying the exercises correctly. Arnold's release of musculature (as she put it) was a training for actors to make the choice they needed for character or situation. Actors' movement, Pure Movement, is a craft specifically developed for acting.

> This is not merely letting go of muscular tension but an intimate knowledge of what the body is doing in any given action …. It is the ability to 'read' what the body is saying and therefore the ability for the body to 'say' what we choose. I.e.: knock-knees do not look confident. Wrinkled forehead does not look happy or calm. (Arnold, 1997)

Arnold expressed herself and explained her work in simple and direct ways.

Her focus was on teaching and finding the right way to pass on and explain the exercises. Here is an example from the notes she gave me.

> **Swings 'The Liberators':**
> The use of gravity. The exercises which swing the arms, legs and torso are the most important in giving the experience of weight and lightness and discovering the full range of movement from high to low, heavy to light.
> Time, space and energy are the dynamics in swings, and they are crucial in the discovery of release and the sense of being grounded (anchored). (Arnold, 1997)

*

I worked with Trish until she was nearly 90 and watched her teach on many occasions. Her classes, though always technically demanding, were never pushed and showed me the value of giving actors space to breathe and be present. There is space between them and space for them. The pattern of the class moves with ease and flow, starting with simple stretches and release exercises, and often finishing with dynamic travelling sequences, or physical improvisations, using the work covered.[32]

Pure Movement in the post-war drama school project was specifically developed in response to the schools Arnold was working in. Their acting techniques referenced Stanislavski, in particular the emphasis on relaxation to open out the imagination and the inner life. However, Pure Movement is also designed to allow the actor to adapt to many forms of theatre, not one approach, not even just for Stanislavski. Movement training also creates possibilities for experiment, and improvisation. I have been as interested in its experimental aspects as I have in serving a naturalistic approach to theatre and acting.

*

The Jooss-Leeder method is much nearer to human feelings and emotions

Jane Winearls' book *Modern Dance, the Jooss-Leeder Method* (Winearls, 1958) charts the pedagogy of both these practitioners. She describes the development of twentieth-century

---

[32] I will go into the structure and classes in more depth.

modern dance as an 'expressive style quite different from that of other forms' of dance. The book is an illustrated manual of many of Kurt Jooss and Sigurd Leeder's developmental and calibrated exercises that made up their method.

As one of the many refugee artists fleeing Nazi Germany, Leeder went on to establish a London school in 1947. There (according to Winearls), actors, dancers, film stars and many people from diverse backgrounds learned how to dance. The training combined the form of rigorous ballet training with the vocabulary and expression of more modern forms of movement and Free Dance.[33] As Trish Arnold trained with Sigurd Leeder in London, she was directly influenced by this new European physical expression and pedagogy and experiment. As Winearls' book shows, the Jooss-Leeder method was rigorous and very creative, often exploring movement from everyday actions or extrapolating from the physicality that emerges from a relationship to gravity.[34] But Arnold changed and developed the exercises specifically for drama schools. This is significant, and further removes her from any connection with Laban, and his troubling connection to the Nazis.

*

Referring to notes that Trish Arnold gave me personally, I quote from an article she wrote for *Reverberations*, a voice teachers' house magazine, where she describes how she came to teach movement to actors and arrived at the 'particular series of exercises' she used. Only a few of the exercises she taught me are included in Winearls' book, proving that Arnold was focusing specifically on serving the needs of the actors in developing their physicality for acting, rather than shoehorning her dance training into the Actors' Movement syllabus. She also firmly places Jooss and Leeder in the German cultural renaissance, which pre-dates the Nazis, and reminds us that the movement that came out of the Weimar Republic, and the influence of Leeder and Jooss in Germany, was quashed by the Nazis.[35]

In *Reverberations*, Arnold explains that she was initially a classical ballet dancer for the Royal Ballet at Sadlers Wells and describes her change of direction.

> My interest was aroused by a teacher called Sigurd Leeder, an Austrian who had been a member of the Kurt Jooss company before the Second World War. The Jooss Ballet came out of the German Cultural Renaissance in the 1920s based in the Bauhaus, a multi-art centre which covered dance, music, drama and architecture. This movement was highly influential (in many diverse arts). It ended when Hitler came to power, and the various artists took their skills to other parts of the world – including the States.
>
> After the war Sigurd Leeder opened a studio for 'Modern Ballet' in London and in 1950 or 51 I heard of him: on visiting him I saw that this was work which interested me much more than the classical ballet form. It seemed much nearer to human feelings and emotions.
>
> I took a two-year course with him during which I learned about 'swing', dynamics, and space in relation to the body and their use in freeing the body to enable it to become an expressive instrument. It was a new world. I should add that the emphasis was on dance. (Arnold, n.d.)

---

[33] As Winearls outlined in *Modern Dance: The Jooss-Leeder Method*.
[34] See below.
[35] Many dancers in Jooss's troupe were Jewish, as was his wife, and the composer for *The Green Table*. No doubt these were also compelling reasons for why he left Germany in 1933.

She then introduced this movement to LAMDA, after a successful interview for the post of movement teacher, where Michael McCowan was looking for a dance teacher in the 'Michel Saint-Denis tradition'. Here her comments show the moment she understood the importance of the breath as a new 'concept' to add to the Expressive Movement she was to teach the students:

> I had an interview with McCowan and Warren and a sort of audition where I demonstrated some of Leeder's swings and spinal exercises. Miss Warren said: 'I hope you are not going to do anything which stops them breathing'. It was the first time I had even heard of breathing in connection with movement. Of course I said: 'No' and got the job. So, I began teaching with a new concept added to Leeder's movement. (Arnold, n.d.)

The movement in the Michel Saint-Denis tradition that McCowan referenced when asking for a tutor was the Saint-Denis' school at the Old Vic.[36]

> Since the Second World War, a growing interest in body-based acting teaching[37] ... had begun to challenge the domination of the spoken word. Two approaches imported from the Continent offered themselves as key alternatives: expressionist dance ... and the playful tradition regenerated in France by Jacques Copeau and brought to London by his nephew ... Michel St Denis (V. Mirodan, *Lecoq's Influence on Drama Schools*: p. 208). (Mark Evans and Rick Kemp, 2016)

How Arnold's technique evolved through working with Kristin Linklater

Once employed at LAMDA, Trish Arnold adapted her movement classes away from dance, as few actors 'were built for the more extreme extensions required for dancers'. The practice was developed for the dramatic needs of the actor, and to support voice training.

Arnold was always pragmatic. She told me that over the years she discovered and introduced many exercises from different sources. Her relationship with Kristin Linklater was seminal in developing a more forensic approach to her work. This was particularly important in the use of the breath, and how to look at the impact of a movement, on a body, in detail.

> The big development came for me when Kristin invited me on her course at the Working Theatre in New York. For the first time I had to really analyse what I was doing and answer penetrating questions. I often had to say, 'I'll think about that one' and hope to come back with an answer. (Arnold, n.d.)

The demands of the students asking for analysis of how to solve movement, voice or breath issues was a big leap for her, making her work clearer and more powerful. Working with voice teachers helped her develop an emphasis on relaxation, over strength, combined with extension and expressive use of the body. She began to focus on the relation of spine, head, pelvis and freeing the joints to facilitate vocal techniques, and of course, the breath.

---

[36]See later references to Lee Montague's experience at the Old Vic.
[37]Body-based as opposed to text-based acting.

All these discoveries have been incorporated into the practice of what I refer to as Pure Movement. Arnold's techniques connect both to dynamic movement, and to suspension – an active stillness, where the breath still flows.

There are two important factors for an actor's training today. One, that built within the practice, is an approach that is relational and ready to respond to what is needed. Two, that the connection to the innovations that Laban developed came through the dance artists who rejected his collaboration with the Third Reich, and who left Germany because of that. There is an open-ended spirit of enquiry that is not dogmatic and not influenced by politics or ideology. This is not a theory but a practice.

Arnold's enjoyment of movement never left her. She used to volunteer in the local primary school, helping 5-year-olds with their reading. One day she physically embodied a little girl more interested in looking around her than in reading. She described her as so free and full of life.

With this idea of experiment, let us play with gravity, without politics and without ideology.

What is the Gravity Swing for an actor?

1. What is a 'Gravity Swing'? Let us experience gravity itself
   - Lift your arm up, hold it for a moment and then 'let' it fall.
   - Hold a tennis ball in your hand and release your grip.

   The movement, or momentum is in relation to gravity. Once the ball drops or the arm falls, its journey has started and will only stop if your arm freezes or you grab the ball to stop it falling.

2. Let us consider 'the swing'

   Like a swing in a children's playground, this movement starts from a point of stillness or inertia into a gathering momentum, energy and dynamic along a specific pathway in space, until it reaches the end of its trajectory, hovers in suspension, to swing-return to its starting point.
   - Drop, swing, suspension – three elements of action.

3. The Gravity Swing and momentum

   Gravity is a force and when your body harnesses its momentum through 'swings' it helps you to move freely. By letting the movement happen to you, you are letting yourself be changed or affected by something outside of yourself.

The 'Gravity Swing' and how it develops our imaginative understanding of movement

- The Gravity Swing taps into how your body moves and can help us create movement on stage that is alive and authentic and develops your ability to make physical choices.
- Swings can also be used as liberators, freeing joints, and opening your range of movement.
- The swing develops an actor's powers of expression.

Gravity and the universe: No longer of interest

Gravity is the force which pulls everything towards the centre of the earth. In order to move, this force must be overcome by energy, and so in all orders of life we see a rhythmic waxing and waning of energies. In all forms of life deviations and disturbances may occur, but the underlying rhythmic harmony continues from day to day and from season to season. (Winearls, 1958)

This is again from Winearls' book, and we can see the quasi-religious or spiritual connotations in the language she uses. The idea of rhythmic harmony refers to the Universal as an abstract that we should seek. Deviations and disturbances are part of 'life' but there is a harmony underneath, that the force of gravity returns us to. As the previous chapter explores, these were ideas prevalent at the time – how movement can encompass a more universal state of being. But this analysis is no longer relevant in a world where the harmony of the seasons no longer exists.

> Rheumatic diseases do abound.
> And through this distemperature we see
> The seasons alter: hoary headed frosts
> Fall into the fresh lap of the crimson rose,
> And old Hiems' thin and icy crown
> Is, as in mockery, set.
> (Shakespeare, *A Midsummer Night's Dream*, 1984)

Diversity and unpredictability. The world is shifting; the times are changing.

The drama of a swing is not in the 'universal' but in the element of risk, surprise, transformation and change it allows, shifting weight and balance and exploring variations in tempo and breath. It harnesses gravity and plays with it.

Innovation, surprise, invention: Lecoq and Arnold

The swing as dramatic action

The swing's journey through high to low, wide to closed, forward to back, is all you need to know about the body's possibility for dramatic response. Lecoq also talks of the dramatic potential of a swing, the risk before 'la chute' at the top of the Pendulum Swing.

He describes its different stages. First you learn the movement breaking it down into its mechanics. Then you 'expand' the movement – seeing how far you can take it in space almost until you overbalance. Then you learn its components, breaking it down to feel the 'dramatic dynamics'. The moment of the fall and the moment of recovery is where the drama lies, with possibilities for smaller actions in between.

'The state of suspension just before the beginning is part of the dynamics of risk (risk of falling) and includes a sense of anguish. Conversely the concluding suspension is one of landing, returning to a state of calm, coming closer to … serenity.'[38]

---

[38] *The Moving Body* (Lecoq, 2002 [1997]).

Working separately with these dramatic dynamics, you can make a story: the moment of risk, when you are about to fall, or relief after diving into a river. Lecoq's description of this swing has more definition, with more emphasis on the pendulum in the swing, than release. But Arnold would also remind me to tell my students that 'there is no movement without thought'.[39]

Both Lecoq and Arnold developed pedagogies using the swing, but both felt technique was only useful if it contributed to the 'dramatic moment' and an actor's awareness of what it could mean or what the story was.[40]

I have done this swing – the Pendulum Swing – in many ways, searching for a different experience to share with actors and students. Trish Arnold called it 'Tree Topple'. Sue Lefton described to me how Litz Pisk would do a similar swing from high, but with a fluid spine 'like a wave'.

Meaning is not fixed. The importance is being able to a teach a technique with specificity, and that allows the actor to find the connection.

The swing, the breath and emotional release, and human emotions and power

The swing frees the breath and the actor's impulse at the same time. The sensation of freeing the breath through movement can be the first time an actor experiences a deep and full sensation of physical life and is sometimes very emotional. This can be surprising because it comes through sensation, rather than through an acting exercise. When the body moves dynamically in response to the pull of gravity, the breath is engaged and drops into the movement. 'Letting go' and 'giving in' are terms to describe this.

The swings have placements for their starting point. As the body is freed in response to gravity, it is brought into an easier and more balanced alignment. The suspension, at the end of the swing, is a form of recovery, where the action leaves the actor for a moment, and they can wait for the next thing to happen.

Transformation through Gravity Swings and Pure Movement: Different to a psychological approach

There are different ways to approach the idea of transformation; for many Stanislavski-trained actors it could be described as a subtle shift internally, a repositioning through the imagination, which alters physical behaviour in an unforced way. Choices are made naturally and 'in the moment', with the actor working from the logic and physical life of the character, and the situation they are in. Stanislavski-based techniques, arguably, see the actor as a transforming artist.

To be able to play the scales of movement that your body offers you – your body with all its nuances, rather than an ideal body – gives the actor physical options from which to

---

[39] Morris, notes taken from a class with Arnold.
[40] Ibid.

transform. Some of those choices might be for psychologically truthful acting alone, some for experimental forms of expression, and some for a form of theatre yet to be discovered.

The legacy of Trish Arnold remains in the body of work she passed on to those that teach Pure Movement. I have considered how the elements of Expressionism that she was trained in diverge from Laban. The practice is re-examined and reappraised to meet the requirements of today, every time a new teacher learns the exercises, and to find their unique ways to explore them with young actors and students. Lecoq's pedagogy, which also forms part of the practice of Pure Movement, has built within it scope for renewal. The next chapters discuss future directions for teaching Pure Movement exercises. To end the chapter I provide, as a historic document, two of Trish Arnold's classes that I have transcribed from her notes.

Trish Arnold's class

Warm up 4 June 1991

Walk 4 or 5 steps – handshake – Hullo – to drumbeat

1. Run on spot, trot on spot, arms over head, floppy wrists, circle – feel feet
2. Rib stretches in all directions. Then arm over in big lunging side bend – clasping hands together
3. Flop down, shake shoulders, build up spine
4. Bounce knees, drop spine down in 4 counts + UP SLOW
5. Then in 8 counts faster rhythm 8 down, 8 up arms thrown up on the 8th beat up
6. On hands and knees

    Simple arch

    Ripple arch

    Animal arch (sinuous and circle)

    Animal drinking

    Folded leaf rest
7. Swings

    R. arm up vertical, until tired, allow to drop in wide arc outwards

    Let alone till stops swinging

    Diagonal swing arm only,

    Then involve some body movement

No movement w/out thought: Warm up 5 June 1991

Spine is centre. Stiff spine – stiff expression. Joints and skeleton

1. Explore movement of spine
2. Rib stretches (use elbow to get ribs activated)

3. Bounces, drop sections of spine on each of 4 bounces (7th, 8th, 9th vertebrae first and so on till hanging head down)
4. Hands on knees (this is with knees bent, so body is supported by the hands resting on thighs – followed by rounding and hollowing)
5. Spine arching sequences as on previous page
   (Now could do walking fingers for dropping down and building up)
6. Exploration for the use of opening of pelvis to find a secure grounded base.[41] The tripod feet – aided by opening of the frontal area (pubic area) ('hip fans')[42]

Notes

Most of these exercises are explained and developed in the next chapters.

Folded leaf rest is not in the exercises but is a curved position on your knees with the arms on the floor facing backwards, and shoulders dropping down to the floor.

The diagonal swing is the Arrow Swing in Chapter 7.

What is striking in these notes, if you take time to parse them, is the ease and confidence that Arnold has that the students will follow the work.

The exercises are beautifully broken down, but there are no teaching strategies. A comment like 'stiff spine', 'stiff expression' is left as a truth. Today we would be thinking of ways to open and loosen spines and understand that a student with a stiff spine is not necessarily responsible for that stiffness.

---

[41] This exercise refers to the pelvic rock.
[42] We possibly wouldn't be able to use the word 'pubic' today.

6 First classes

The first Pure Movement class from Trish Arnold techniques: A practice-based technique

The exercises in the next two chapters on 'spine and feet', 'working in 3 dimensions' and 'swings' evolved and developed from my work with Trish Arnold. They are part of my repertoire of Pure Movement.

Laban's more abstract, complex theories of movement are not part of my practical pedagogy. I discussed its historical and cultural context to draw attention to how its connection to the Third Reich, as German Dance, has not been brought sufficiently to light. And to question whether it is now appropriate for drama school training to include it anymore, since the current emphasis on anti-racism and decolonization.

Leeder evolved a pedagogy for dance artists, which Arnold adapted into a movement pedagogy for actors in a drama school. In creating this practical pedagogy for movement training, she was one of our innovative pioneers, alongside Pisk who pioneered the links between physical expressiveness and drama. Both were innovators and committed themselves to teaching movement for actors as an artistic discipline, incrementally and developmentally. Like Lecoq, their understanding of body-based training focused equally on the physical and the expressive. The Pure Movement I teach is in a tradition and is also evolving. It has been considered for actors and, as a technique, has earned its place in drama schools.

When I consider some of the struggles students encounter, it isn't the past that worries them, but the present, which paradoxically is a reason to continue to build on the knowledge of movement teaching for actors, which we already have. A Facebook post by the movement teacher Ioli Filippakopoulou personalizes her teaching practice as part of a bigger picture of how to educate young people in the art of empathy and the understanding of the human condition. Cultivating empathy at the beginning of a movement class, she describes sitting in a circle with her students:

> all these moments we sit together, discuss and hold space for each other in a way that is profoundly Human. What teaching has taught me is that empathy is a skill, it can be nurtured, and we are all responsible for cultivating it … Love hard. This is the art I want to practice and it is a collective one. (Filippakopoulou, 2024)

There is a qualitative distinction between learning about empathy as a vital part of the art of acting and empathy as a heart-felt act of resistance and social justice.

If we build from the original roots of Actors' Movement, we can fortify a practice that is technical but allows for originality both in the students and the teacher.

The heart in the space: Teaching with empathy

Let us reconsider the practice of empathy as a physical skill. Every movement class I ever taught and ever learned practices empathy. The body is opening, the heart is opening, the breath is opening. Actors moving in the space, making room for each other, balancing space, seeing and responding to each other. I see this just as much a way to hold space and create empathy, as talking it so.

Empathy is not the same as feeling comfortable. It can stretch us. Movement brings a creative release to our bodies and quite literally a depth to physical expression. Movements travel up and down, in and out, forwards and backwards, along the diagonals that come from one arm and down to the opposite foot. Within these planes and energies is the possibility of physical development – changing how we move, how we feel and relate to the world and each other. With the actor's imagination we discover why and how the character or role we are playing moves differently to us.

Transformation and empathy are linked.

I will now describe the first Pure Movement exercises that I learned and developed from Trish Arnold and some developments to make the work connect for today's students. The classes offer scope for adaptations and variety.

My description of these first classes presumes there is sufficient time to do this.

Time and the first movement classes: A new way of working

The first movement classes are very important and shouldn't be rushed. As a guide, it takes up to two to three lessons to establish how the classes work and what students can expect.

How to introduce a new way of working

When an actor begins their training, they might not even know that movement is a subject on their course. The classes might feel like dance classes, but the content and pace of a movement class is more exploratory, with precepts and outcomes they might never have encountered. Remembering sequences is not part of the process, but exploration. Nor is performance – yet. It is vital that everyone feels included; no one should be made to feel they can't move.[1] So, the classes are very easy at first.

To recap: here are the skills and new ways of thinking about physicality that Actors' Movement introduces.

- Body awareness. Locating different parts of the spine: the sternum: the pelvis: how shoulders, thighs, arms and legs are attached to the spine.
- Isolation: comes after body awareness – how to isolate and move specific parts of the body and recognize how one movement will lead to another.
- Proprioception/kinaesthesia may be underdeveloped, so making it hard for them to follow simple instructions.

---

[1] Students have often told me this was their first reaction to encountering movement classes, which fortunately changed as they got used to the work.

- The challenge of co-ordination, that it can be practised and learned.
- Learning through doing and observing.
- Spatial awareness: the body in space, and then moving through it. Other bodies in space. Copying your teacher's body in space, if they are facing you.
- Rhythm and tempo: moving to different rhythms or with different tempi.
- Presence: standing in silence to experience stillness and the volume of the body in the space.

These are learned through regular classes and exercises, to discover how your body moves.

Holding space

My version of 'holding space' is to make the playground of a movement class safe and fun, but also somewhere you might take risks, explore and make new friends. That is what the exercises called 'ice-breakers' are for.

I vary the tempo and rhythm in a class, so it feels alive for the students. I like to create a level playing field for students to work together. This shared starting point creates trust for students to explore and transform together. Movement teaching is usually ensemble based: but often students want to work on their own, so there is also time for solo exploration or reflection.

Consistency in scheduling and teaching

There should be space for students to feel a bit lost at the beginning of their training. This is helped when a movement teacher is employed to teach on a two-to-three-year educational cycle. Many tutors today are on short-term contracts, but this means they miss the privilege of seeing students develop, which creates a sense of disconnection and lack of engagement. It also makes it harder for movement tutors to meet each other informally to discuss the work. Managers often deliver class protocols and learning agreements through emails. I worry that this means tutors can't educate their students incrementally – giving a toolbox taster of a practice instead. The development of an organic practice, delivered through a clear pedagogy, is far more nurturing. A mosaic, or modular, approach to delivering training doesn't support students or teachers.[2]

The classes I describe below are part of an arc of development, taught consistently. The first exercises are for the slow-burn approach over three years.

First classes

I always look forward to the first class in Pure Movement with incoming students.

I start with a few words about how to approach the work to encourage actors to explore the exercises without watching others or judging themselves. The approach is **experiential**

---

[2]Many of the movement teachers are employed by the term; there is a precarity to their contracts and hours.

(as described below). The classes are taught without a mirror (so if you are in a dance studio make sure the curtains are closed).

How to set up the first classes

The movement classes are physical, emotional and imaginative. So, before I begin to teach them I set some simple ground rules about what students might expect. At the outset of teaching and learning, students don't need to prepare. They need to show up and be present. 'The readiness is all'. Below I explain some of the ways the classes will work.

1. Experiential
2. Working with a drum
3. Working with touch
4. What to wear in class

The following is what I might say to students in their first few classes[3] – and how they connect to these areas above. I have written this down because often young teachers have shared their concerns with me, that it is hard to hold space for Pure Movement teaching during the first few weeks of teaching. Students on BA courses who come straight from school have rarely experienced learning that is experiential and empirical, which asks them to be curious about physicality.

1 Experiential

- The classes are non-verbal and practical. The approach is experiential. Try it first, understanding will follow, be free to experiment and explore.
- These practical classes are taught incrementally like any other artistic discipline. One class leads to another and doesn't stand alone.
- Unlike some other artistic disciplines like Musical Theory, or Labanotation for dance, there is no theory to underpin your experience.
- You are learning a physical practice.
- You learn through doing and then allow the movement to change you.
- This is a transformative and organic experience that takes place over time.
- There will be time throughout the class to stop and reflect on your discoveries, and time at the end of each term to reflect as a group.
- This is not a dance class, though the levels of energy and physicality might make it seem as if it is.

Movement teaching has better outcomes if taught slowly, rather than looking for instant results. Pure Movement teaching is about specificity – teach the exercises in detail, but don't over-correct. Teaching experientially means they will be trying them for themselves, once you have shown them or guided them in what to do.

The exercises below and in the following chapters are broken down into specialized areas.

---

[3]Working with actors or in workshops, I would use a different approach.

For the actor/student reading this

You are learning how your body responds to weight, breath and different speeds: the way you can expand or contract through the 'dimensions' (and what these are), how to be economical in the use of your energy but have the maximum impact: actor's movement can feel both simple and, also, obscure. You are learning a language and vocabulary for acting! Be playful, be curious, enjoy the journey, and don't judge yourself by others' standards.

(I often find a less poetic way to say this in class, and only after a few weeks.)

2 Working with a drum

On the first class, I arrive with my drum. I teach all my classes with a hand-held drum.

The drumbeat is an invitation to move; Lecoq and Philippe Gaulier would say 'c'est parti' and then bang the drum – 'we're off!'.

I like working with sound and rhythm. The drumbeat offers an impulse for the start of a movement, the momentum of which becomes the actor's. I rarely drum in a strict musical rhythm – though sometimes I might work with simple rhythms, either 4/4 or 3/4. Sometimes I divide 'duration' in simple multiples from 8 counts: 8s to 4s to 2s. I learned this from Trish Arnold, and it is delightful to see how students respond to simple accelerations of tempo in rhythm. Sometimes I use the drum expressively: sliding the beater across the surface, working with different rhythms, or sound dynamics.

Lecoq used the drum like opening a door to the playground. The key reason, pedagogically, for a drum is to give students time and space to move[4] independently without words.

The drum is not a command, but an invitation to move, and part of the language of movement. It helps actors find expression beyond words: but using a drum with words is part of an ancient tradition linking movement with theatre. There is a history to working with a hand-held drum, which Lecoq, and Copeau, Leeder, Pisk and Arnold tapped into.

Greek poets wrote plays in which actors danced, and dancers acted. (Pisk, n.d.)

All dance and movement work with rhythm and tempo. All plays have rhythm. All text has rhythm or tempo. A drum is dramatic. But to work with a drum actively changes the space and as a teacher helps you to work non-verbally.

Teaching inclusively

Inclusive teaching depends on the needs of the students, which vary in each cohort. Accommodating the needs of neurodivergent students, for example, is continuing to develop. In drama schools this takes the form of Learning Agreements, agreed by the student – they might need to step out or leave the class for instance. With a student who is a wheelchair user, and working with a physical disability, there is an onus on the movement teacher to find out how this impacts their physicality and adapt their physical practice accordingly.[5] Movement teaching is not correction or fixing a body to make it 'right', but instead enables the actor to be physically expressive, following the laws of gravity and momentum and space, applied to their bodies. However, working with the spine, or working with balance,

---

[4] I remember sometimes Lecoq or Gaulier saying, as well as the drum, 'c'est parti' – which we took to mean, 'and we're off', time had started.
[5] See below for references to Candoco Dance Company and teaching over sixties.

needs constant reframing in our teaching as we deliver the classes. Where I suggest the spine is upright, this is in terms of direction – up to the sky for instance. Where I say the movement starts from the base of the spine, this can shift to mean the bottom of the spine available for movement. The sit bones can root into a chair, where feet find the ground. These are working adaptations, and, as I say frequently, we need more practice-based research to ensure that pragmatic adaptations like these are part of a sustainable practice that can be passed on. Teaching inclusively is in development, and I am not aware of any research projects that are currently taking place specifically in drama schools.

3 Working with touch

How to help integrate a growing physical/body awareness into delicate shifts of weight, spine, and balance?

Before COVID-19, touch had always been an optional part of movement feedback, though always with consent. The pandemic conflated this respect for boundaries, with a fear of infection and abuse, forcing us to rethink how to deliver this sensitive form of guidance. Touch is part of intimacy, but touch is also changing. A way of teaching what was sensitive and nurturing now must comply with COVID-19, #MeToo and safeguarding protocols. Drama schools now define the ethos of nurturing in an educational environment, through additional classes on Consent or Intimacy for their students. There are courses that offer training in Consent and Intimacy, which can be included in the ethics of your class teaching. I always follow the institution's guidelines, though protocols may vary from school to school.

However, touch is complex and can feel intrusive and inappropriate for an acting student. I rarely teach with touch, unless I have worked with the group for months, and I always ask their permission first. Most students will signal clearly when touch in a movement class breaches a boundary.

Touch from a teacher is about consent and trust and mutual respect. Touch is also part of communication from student to student. A touch will always affect us. I understand the current concerns. Students are often fearful or anxious with touch. But we risk losing the wisdom that can be transmitted from the hand of an experienced teacher to the back of a student, which can by-pass many words.

We can also never ignore how touch is a vital part of naturalistic acting. Characters touch each other; this might not be consensual between the characters – but actors need to be in charge of how that story is told.

The change I record here mirrors how the role of the teacher in drama schools has changed, because the social and cultural context has changed. The way teaching used touch previously veered between guidance and correction, placing the student in receipt of learning. Ideas of learning have changed as well.

But the abuse of touch is different. It is when we force an actor to move or respond in ways they aren't ready to, or insist on a standard that is too exacting. All current teaching now looks at ways to give students agency.

*

Touch was part of my own experience as a student learning movement, as different as the decades and subjects they were taught in. In my ballet training at Phyllis Bedells, it was often a stick placed on the bottom/pelvis to stop the lower spine from arching, and or a hand extending the arms in 'Second'. At Lecoq in Monika Pagneux's Feldenkrais classes, it was to encourage awareness of parts of the spine and the interconnectedness between sternum and pelvis, which could unlock propulsion in the body, and was by turns gentle or dynamic, but never 'critical' like the ballet corrections were.

Lecoq never touched us when teaching 'Analyse de Mouvement' classes, or Expressive classes, instead giving notes about how the movement was 'speaking' in the space. He would always leave a respectful distance between himself and the student. I found this approach the closest to an acting note – you thought you were doing one thing, but the body told a different story. It is an excellent way to guide the body.

I have previously discussed the way touch is used in Alexander classes – sometimes quite a forceful lengthening and opening of the spine when lying on the table, promoted by touch. Often with observations about 'best practice'.

When I worked with Trish Arnold, I experienced touch for lengthening the spine in rolling up and down the spine, and then more forcefully to feel the weight of legs or arms as they swung. In class teaching, however, Trish Arnold found ingenious ways for students to experience the 'sensation' of touch (which I describe below).

Contrary to what might seem like the imposition of physical control, I always found touch a very liberating way to explore physicality in motion. It helped the body, and the muscles adjust technically to balance, weight and flow. Whereas a verbal instruction might flip the student into a more analytical approach.

For the first class I start by saying that touch is a simple way to give feedback but I will be using verbal instructions instead. I hardly ever use touch, but when I do, I ask permission and check in at the end of class to learn if it was helpful.

4 What to wear in class

The first class will also address what to wear. Photographs of movement classes or even workshops for young people in training in the UK show most of them wearing 'blacks': this is a combination of black leggings or tights, with T-shirt or leotard, and bare feet. Why?

When we were at Lecoq we wore blacks to show the outline of the body. To see the 'body in the space' was to see dramatic action in an uncluttered way. But throughout the training, many of us started to wear our own loose clothes to move in.

By the time I had joined RADA in 2015, most drama schools had adopted 'blacks' for movement classes. When I first started teaching at Rose Bruford in 1996, it was a new phenomenon which only Guildhall and LAMDA also required. The teachers at Guildhall and LAMDA, and myself at Rose Bruford, all had training connections to Lecoq. Perhaps this requirement stems from the first wave of Pure Movement teachers' connection to Lecoq.

Clothes that reveal the body's expression go back as far as Jacques Copeau. When Michel Saint-Denis established the Old Vic Theatre School in the 1930s, movement clothes were chosen for students to free them from social restrictions and reveal the body. Yvonne Bryceland, who was a student at The Old Vic in the 1930s, describes how their movement training was designed to reveal everything about them – 'warts and all'. They wore sleeveless tunics and bathing trunks, exposing the body to scrutiny and expression.

> You were meant to be as bare ... as ugly as you didn't want to be. Anybody who had knock knees or pimples had to face that first day as you all had to fail together. You couldn't be self-conscious.[6]

The clothes suggested for movement classes today aren't meant to be that shocking or revealing and I will negotiate with students when I ask them to wear these clothes; I will not use the term 'blacks'.

The benefits are that black tops and leggings allow the actor and teacher to notice critical shifts of physical expression and technique. These shifts are subtle and come from the spine, or a shift in weight or tempo; they help an actor find a transformation that they can feel and inhabit. However, to reveal the body can trigger concerns about body image and enhance a sense of unwanted vulnerability. The objective is for students to be able to move safely and comfortably in the space.

The emphasis on what clothes to wear to class, with no makeup or jewellery, is based on an idea of 'unmasking'. This can be traced back to 1960s' and 1970s' ideas about identity which searched for an authentic self 'untainted' by society. The notion of self is more fluid today. Perhaps the simple way to explain the need to wear clothes which reveal the outline of the body, and help the body move, is that the technique can be more clearly taught and understood.

Feet

Most movement classes, and modern dance classes, are taught in bare feet.

Bare feet also requires negotiation: try this now. First stand in your socks (or even trainers) and rock forwards and backwards through your feet. How much of your foot feels in contact with the ground? Now lift one foot off the ground to balance: you need all the small bones in your feet to infinitesimally shift to stay balanced. Now take your socks/shoes off and shake your feet, trot lightly on the spot, and stand for a moment (eyes shut) to experience how the entire weight of your body is flowing down through your feet into the ground. Open your eyes and shift your weight forwards and backwards, feeling the play of weight through your feet. Now lift your leg and balance again and see if you can feel your balance more easily with your feet bare, than with shoes or socks on?

*

These conversations help prepare the student for transformation. Wearing clothes which are functional and easy to move in and read the body creates important boundaries between the teacher and the student. Working with openness and curiosity is part of the ethos of movement training. It is impossible to convey all of this in the first few classes. The best way to set this in motion is to start the work on the first day that you meet with them.

---

[6]Yvonne Brycland quoted by Irving Wardle in *The Theatres of George Devine*, published by Jonathan Cape (1978).

Tenets of Pure Movement

In Autumn 2023 I taught a Pure Movement 'intensive' to a group of students, teachers and actors. As preparation I revisited the notes that Trish Arnold had passed on to me and came across these 'tenets'. As some of the participants hadn't done Pure Movement from scratch, I read them out and discovered they were surprisingly useful to anchor the start of the work.

	Tenet	Definition	Year training started
1	Release	Relaxation in movement, allowing breath to support every movement, impulse and action	First Year – applied through the swings – needs to be practised regularly
2	Weight	Your awareness of it, i.e. heavy or light, to achieve release, economy and action playing	First Year – applied to all Expressive Movement classes as well
3	Finding centre and alignment	Knowing where the centre of gravity is and the relationship of this to the spine, balance and change of weight	First Year – technically tested in dance classes, and used expressively in character transformation and situation
4	Flexibility	To enable expression and iron out stiffness	First Year – needs to be practised regularly
5	Muscular Support	Essential for support to the skeletal framework	First Year – developed substantially in Second Year
6	Co-ordination	Physical and vocal co-ordination	First Year – develops in Second Year for Dance and Fight – useful for complex text
7	Physical Sensibility	Awareness of Space and Time in relation to your own space and that of other actors and the use of space in creating situation/scenarios	First Year – starts with understanding of the dimensions, and directions in space and then develops into scene work, mask work, character and situation
8	Availability	Listening and readiness	First Year – develops in work on spatial awareness and impulse which is introduced in second term
9	Invention and Imagination	Being able to move from technique to interpretation and improvisation	First Year – develops through every class which will have time set aside to play and respond imaginatively

The spine and the breath

The skeletal structure supports the body, and the spine holds the body upright and the body is in space – alive and responding to stimuli, inner and outer.

The first class that I teach is to introduce how to understand the spine's relationship to gravity and its skeletal function.

First exercise: How movement and impulse connect to the spine
Stand with your feet apart and gently breath in and out.

You breathe in, the spine rises.

You breathe out the spine sinks (these are very small movements).

When you breathe out allow the knees to soften (all these techniques will be much more clearly explored in the following chapters).

Breathe in and feel the body floating up onto your toes, and rise up a little, then as high as you'd like to.

Imagine you are observing something that is important to you.

Someone has scored a goal? A much longed-for person appears through a crowd? What happens physically? Perhaps you breath in (or out) with excitement? Perhaps you step forward, jump up, make a sudden gesture to be noticed? Whatever it is, it is breath, spine action.

*

Trish Arnold would always start with an exercise to wake the spine up: which I will show later.

The spine is the largest part of the body. The most neglected part is the feet.

From feet to spine

Sit on the floor, with bare feet, and feel one foot (then the other) in this way.

- Feel the pads of your feet under each toe, how those go into the little joints that cause the toes to move.
- Place your first finger in between your big toe and second finger in between your next toe and so on, until your fingers are laced in between your toes; this might take a little encouragement, as you begin to feel your toes releasing and relaxing, then move the toes forwards and backwards, encouraging your foot to spread.
- Now use your fingers to feel the bones and muscles on the top of your foot that lead into the toes and up to the ankle and the heel.
- There are twenty-seven bones in each foot: forefoot – phalanges and metatarsals; midfoot – five tarsal bones, cuneiforms, navicular and cuboid; hindfoot – two tarsal bones, the calcaneus (heel bone) and talus (ankle bone); the foot has the potential for much more movement than we often explore, or experience.
- Once you have explored the mobility of one foot, walk around and feel the difference between both feet, then explore the same with the other foot.

Stand up and see how much you can picture the bones in your feet.

Next, picture your foot as a triangle and try to distribute the weight across three points: the big toe, the little toe and the heel. Feel the play of the instep as part of this (in my case my instep is dropped) as you explore redistributing your weight across your foot.

The skeletal experience stacks up like this, like a tower pulling up and away from gravity.

Feet
Ankles
Shins
Knees
Thighs
Hip joints
Pelvic girdle
Spine
Head

As you are standing, move through the 'tower' of your spine with small movements to wake the spine up. Think of an animal shaking its fur, or a bird ruffling its feathers.

First exercise: Rolling down the spine
Stage 1
Stand easily with your feet under your hips.

Distribute the weight across the three points of your foot (or feet) as above.

Gently look from side to side by turning your head.

Nod your head gently up and down, as if saying 'yes'.

Now shake it from side to side, as if saying 'no'.

Let these movements have the unforced gravity of a child, answering yes and no.

Think of them as simple and light, not full of energy, and allow the muscles in the neck to free up and the bones connecting the top of the spine to the ball and socket joint that joins it to the base of the skull to move.

*

Stage 2 Sinking the sternum
Place your hand on your sternum, this is the bony breastbone just down from your neck, where your heart sits on the left.

As you breathe in and out, feel the sternum moving.

Gently sigh out and allow the sternum to sink (don't let your shoulders roll forwards) and the knees to soften, and your head dropping.

This is the 'giving in position' – a position of surrender; Arnold called it the 'depressed position'.

Allow the breath to enter, and unfurl through the upper back, vertebra by vertebra, with the head last, to come back to where you started.

The knees will have lengthened.

*

Stage 3 Find some movement in the pelvis – Gently rounding and arching, when standing
Explore standing easily with the legs long and a sensation of the knees floating.

We are now going to think about the placement of the lower spine or the pelvis.

The lower spine are the five lumber vertebrae that lead into the coccyx.

The fifth vertebra is the last of the lumber region: if you soften your knees and gently round the base of the spine, you will be curving the pelvis forwards: if you soften your knees and gently lift the tail bone backwards, you will be hollowing the base of your spine.

Gently move between these two places of forward and back, gently lengthening the legs between the two points.

Come to rest, with the legs long, and the pelvis hanging loosely on your legs, and the knees floating, not tight.

If you place your hand on at the back of your pelvis, there should be a slight curve: let this curve happen.

*

Stage 4 Dropping down through the spine, finding different suspensions

Start with feet apart, not too wide.

Gently let the head float down onto the chest – think of the head of a flower drooping, hanging off the neck.

Feeling the weight of your head, let it gently roll you down until you are hanging off the seventh cervical vertebra, and soften your knees – the upper spine is lengthening and dropping down in this curve.

Continue to gently roll down the spine until you are hanging off the twelfth thoracic vertebra, with knees still soft – you will now be hanging from your waist.

Gently continue to roll down the spine until you are hanging off the fifth lumber vertebra. Still keep the knees soft.

This is hanging off the spine.

If your hands are on the floor, turn their backs onto the ground so your hands are completely relaxed.

If you can't hang so low, soften your knees until you can, and think of tilting your sit bones up towards the ceiling.

To come up, gently curl the pelvis underneath you, and building up through the vertebral column, roll up through the spine, until you are back up to standing, balanced through your feet. Try and do this continuously.

Stage 5 Variations – With a sudden drop

Roll down the spine until you are suspended and hanging off the waist.

The pelvis is gently rounded underneath you in this position, as though the pelvis is connected to your legs.

Now gently tilt the base of the spine backwards a little, so that the sit bones are facing the ceiling and allow the upper spine to drop to hang off the spine; this drop is dynamic, like falling off a cliff.

Gently bounce the knees up and down with very little movement, to shake out the spine, like a rag doll.

Keep bouncing the knees gently to help coming up through the spine.

Stage 6 Bouncing down the spine

To bounce the knees, find a small rebound in the knees up and down, keeping the rest of the body very easy. This is not a plié as in ballet, or a bend, it is a movement which has as much up as down to it, like bouncing a ball. The knees should feel oiled, but if there is stiffness in the leg muscles or round the tendons this might take a little time to get used to.

Staying upright: bounce the knees for 8 counts on a little double beat – 1 and 2.

Bounce down through the spine until you are hanging off the sit bones: take 8 counts to get there and remember to drop your head.

Bounce for 8 counts hanging off the spine.

Bounce for 8 counts to come up.

*

Bouncing down through the spine is called a shakedown, as the knees are loosening out the spine.

The image that Trish used for rolling down the spine was furling and unfurling.

As you roll down the spine, you are furling like a fern in the forest.

As you roll up through the spine, you are unfurling like a fern in the forest.

Starting a class with silence and then ice-breakers

Stillness by Hierma

> *Stillness holds all action in embryo.*
> *Stillness is an aspect of wisdom.*
> *Stillness is the Mother of gesture,*
> *gesture is the posture of stillness.*
> *I did not move until .... I was still.*
> *The Posture of stillness entails all gesture,*
> *this is the gesture of Love.*

I don't know the poet. This was in Trish Arnold's notes.

Being still is a choice, reflective or active. Active stillness is open to all possibilities.[7] Reflective is meditative, inwards. A gesture can find stillness.

We are looking for a particular kind of stillness – an expectation and sense of connection. It is useful to start a class in stillness, but it takes time to set this up. Stillness and silence are connected and focus on the body's power of expression.

After the Second World War, France created a silent physical expression – expressive mime – that could tell dramatic stories without words. Marcel Marceau, the famous French mime, joined the French Resistance, to help Jewish children escape to the Swiss border through the forests. He would use mime to keep them quiet. The power and

---

[7] Terms like 'neutral' or 'blank page' have often been used in books or discussion about this starting point for movement training, or class. But the word 'neutral' seems to provoke very strong views, which I don't really understand, so I rarely use it, as out of context it can sound non-committal, even like vanilla. Vibrant, alive stillness is the opposite of this.

strangeness of this is remarkable. Stillness can lead to movement. But doesn't always lead to words.

Silence. Stillness. Movement.

You can start a class with stillness or use it as a starting point from which to move, after having played and warmed up.

1 Ice-breakers and exercises to get student actors moving freely before starting the first exercise

These exercises are examples of what I might gradually introduce over the first term's work. Moving together helps the group connect, and finding stillness or still points helps the students come back to themselves.

1 Loosening up as a group

Trish Arnold taught me this when I went to work at the Stratford Festival Theatre in Canada in 2003. It helps a group to let go, using simple ideas.

Start by trotting round the space, with loose knees, shoulders and floppy feet, circling or travelling through space, then lift your arms up high above your head and 'lighten the mood', and from there go around and say 'hello' to everyone, then drop the arms and drop the knees and half trot half slouch and the mood has changed, depressed, demotivated, etc. and saying 'hello' from that place, people will usually be slouching. Then ask them just to walk, looking at the room, at the people in the room, keeping space between you, and aware not to collide. Drumbeat. Stop. Drumbeat. Go. Stop. Go. Get the group to stop and go together. Get them to stop with their feet 4-square, feet in line with their knees, knees in line with their hips. Then get them to repeat this and add a change of direction.

2 Move how you feel today

Ask each member of the group to move round the room 'how they feel today', expressed through the body. Ask them to make the expression bigger. If someone is low in energy, suggest they take that impulse onto the floor. If excited or nervous, ask them to take this to the end of their fingers or toes.

Drumbeat. Still point. Ask them to stop as they are – which will be holding the position they got to.

Drumbeat, change direction, and move 'the opposite of how you feel today'. These opposites are often freer and more playful. Drumbeat. Still point. Stop as they are.

Drumbeat, change direction and move 'how you feel today'.

Encourage them to use as much of the body to express this: arms, legs, feet, hands, rhythm, tempo, posture.

Drumbeat, stop. Drumbeat, change direction.

This exercise expresses feeling but doesn't dwell on its psychology. Sometimes I get the actors to create sequences by combining the two, and then to work as pairs, to teach each other these sequences. Immediately they start to move in ways that are different to how they came into the class.

3 Run. Stop. Go. Observations

This exercise, and its adaptations, is the one I use the most to get a group moving together.

When I first started teaching this exercise in 1989 (I have adapted it a lot since then), it was fun and playful. It relies on group dynamics and didn't present any problems until 2015. From then on, I needed to introduce this differently. Students found it hard to work collectively. There was an anxiety and fear of bumping into each other, and they found it hard to manage speed and distance between them. Spatial awareness, and proprioception seemed less secure than before. We discussed this a lot in staff meetings and thought that it could be that the students hadn't played outdoors much as children, or lacked spatial awareness because of looking at their phones too much. How this might manifest was a lack of engagement, or students not wanting to look at each other.

To move from stillness into walking and then to stop, involves a shift of weight, and a desire to move with others. When you do this as part of a group, you work together to find these impulses. Often it is very scrappy: to get everyone to agree to work together is a negotiation, but when it happens, it is arresting to watch and powerful to be inside of. Run. Stop.Go is an exciting methodology to generate dynamic movement on stage, that also tells a story. It can also develop different energies, as actors move collectively.

How to encourage students to actively want to learn collectively?

*

An article by Melanie Phillips in *The Times* (Phillips, 2024) references a survey by the Onward Think Tank which revealed how the sense of community and belonging for young people

Figure 7 *I'm Sorry For Your Loss* written and directed by Shona Morris at NT Studio 2025. Different energies in the same space. Actors Wendy Allnutt, Leah Muller, Jack Chiswick. Photo taken by Sheila Mars.

has disappeared. Social media is how many young people relate to their friends but is isolating. Jeremy Adams, a Californian teacher, has done research into teenage depression, and discovered that it rose by 63 per cent between 2007 and 2017, a timeline which reflects developments in how we communicate. The iPhone 4 arrived in 2010.

When I was teaching at the Manchester School of Theatre in 2023, an acting tutor told me the only way he could set up an improvisation between two students on the theme, 'breaking up with each other' was if it was by text. 'We don't meet to break up with someone, we text them.' Young people's lack of experience in dealing directly with people in the real world is borne out by Adams' research, which shows that millennials and Gen Z (born between 2000 and 2010) are less likely to take part in group activities, with people under 25 three times more likely to distrust their neighbours than people over 65 were. For young people, even trust of their family was an issue. As Melanie Phillips observes, lack of trust extends to creative activities, as atomized social contact has become the norm.

For many years we have trained actors as an ensemble. We ask them to explore the craft of acting and transformation with each other. We ask them to sense and to feel, as springboards from which to express and communicate action and text for theatre. The intensity of online communication has stepped in to fill the gap of real-life communication and competes with this simple idea of connecting to others in real time and space. The fragility is increased by hours alone on a phone, or a screen, scrolling through life in another dimension. A mistrust of collective engagement makes it hard to deal with people face to face. Running in a room with a group is the opposite to this and asks students to use their peripheral vision, and their senses and their empathy and sense of being part of a collective. But the physical impact of looking at a screen for many hours creates a lazar focus in 'forward space'. 'Forward space' is what we see directly in front of us. Often very disturbing information is taken in this way, as you sit watching a tiny screen. These disturbances setup responses through the body, affecting the nervous system, often eliciting trauma responses. Any action in a real space or real time which might shake this is hard.

*

How to accommodate this change in the relationship to physical activity and real experiences in a simple movement exercise? I need to make sure that the exercises of running and stopping are light and playful. Little and often. Doing the exercises for a few seconds, until stamina and resilience has built up. I am beginning to understand that this fear of connection is like a muscle that needs stretching. Working collectively creates a language from which to make theatre and new possibilities. We need to learn that openness to everyone in the space, as a collective, makes the collective more powerful creatively.

Ensemble playing used to be vital for modern theatre. In 1981 I was in a production of *Cider With Rosie*. It was adapted by Nick Dark and directed by Richard Williams for the Contact Theatre Manchester. This and many other scenes required the acting company to move from specific characterization to detailed company work, in a heartbeat.

In Laurie Lee's *Cider With Rose* his whole village went for an outing to Weston-Super-Mare in charabancs – this was a community event.

> mothers with pig-buckets stuffed with picnics, children with cocoa-tin spades, fathers with bulging overcoats lined entirely with clinking bottles. There was little Mrs Tulley

collecting the fares and plucking at her nervous cheeks; Mr Vick, the shopkeeper ... the two dressmakers ... The charabancs were high, with broad open seats and folded tarpaulins at the rear, upon which as choirboys, we were privileged to perch or to fall off and break our necks.

The vibrancy and specificity of the physical life described, and the focus on the narrative and the character is a gift for actors.

When I first started teaching at drama school, students understood that they were part of a company, learning together to craft ensemble action, as described above. But we can no longer take this for granted, and I have now some thoughts to make this more accessible – and keep in mind the outcome for creative storytelling. To accommodate those that struggle with sensory overload, or who are new to being present in a flowing group of people, remind the group that everyone can move at their own pace. Or they can move on the edges of the group until they feel able to move through the group. They can also step in and out of the flow of movement. This can create interesting interactions and stories.

I will now describe the exercise:

Phase 1

Run. Stop. Go

The group walks in the space, driving forwards and crossing through centre. Ask them to avoid walking in straight lines, to frequently change direction, to move with a sense of purpose, and to keep equidistant from each other. They can avoid bumping into one another by changing direction or moving backwards/out of the way or suspending. The whole room develops a sense of being 'in play' as you remind them to use the whole space.

> If there are levels in the room, and some brave souls step up onto these levels, don't discourage this. It is exciting when someone adds new dimensions to a task, so long as they are working with the group. When you watch the group moving you should be able to see it move as an organism, like swirling water, a collective sense of moving together. Let the tempo find its own level. It might start fast and then find a level for everyone.

Encourage them to connect to each other by making eye contact but ask them not to 'lock on' to one person, but instead keep finding new people to connect to, by moving through the group. The sense is that everyone is taking everyone else in. Not everyone will feel comfortable doing this. The more you do this exercise, the more the players relax. If you have the energy and the inclination, join in with the exercise, modelling how to be present, playful and connected.

- Drumbeat. First stop. Ask the group to stop with their feet underneath them.

This is described as *'Four Square'*, with feet aligned with knees.[8] At first people will find it hard to stop calmly: it is a first experience of grounding. It is also something an actor does

---

[8] The more you do this exercise, in concert with the Pure Movement exercises, the clearer this position will be, as it is the 'stance' position from which the roll-downs and the stretches come.

a lot – to enter a space and then stop. Encourage them to respond to the drum beat and stop as an impulse, not a command. The more 'balanced' the body becomes, the more the group will be able to stop together. The body must be relaxed, not rigid like a soldier, so some people will stop after others – depending on the levels of physical tension. A tense body will stop suddenly. An easy body will flow into the stop. Ask them to find stillness. This is called a *still point*.

This develops into a sequence.

- Drumbeat. *(Still point)*
- Change. Change direction on the spot (180°). *(Still point)*
- Drumbeat. Go.

Continue moving as if the stop was just a momentary interruption but now add the dynamic of running.

- Run.
- Stop. *(Still point)*
- Change. *(Still point)*
- Go.

It is like a piece of music.

Phase 2

Spiral

Now add the spiral as part of the change of direction. This introduces the idea that a change of direction is a change of thought.

Set this up by exploring how to change direction on the spot with the head leading.

*

Stand *four-square* and look behind you, to develop into a turn by spiralling through the body, head turns, which opens the shoulder and travels down to open the hip and the knee and both feet.

- Head. Shoulder. Hip. Knee and you have changed direction.
- Experience the turn because something has caught your attention, with a sense of curiosity.
- As a group, breathe out when you stop and breathe in when you change.
- The breath affects the impulse to make it sudden.
- Ask the group to breathe out as they change.
- The change is sustained – deliberate – as if the player has something momentous or important to do or say.
- Working with the breath is altering tempo and weight.

Observe the different impulses this simple change in breath and tempo elicits.

Working with a spiral in the Run.Stop.Go exercise is a good way to show how the spine moves: there is always a part of the body that leads, or (if playing character) doesn't respond, or is suspended in half a turn, and then turns back.

These are refinements, accidents and possibilities for later scenarios, but this is a dynamic way to set this up. It also introduces the idea of time, and tempo and how breath changes intention.

> Spirals are part of Pure Movement work and body awareness, which will be taught over the three years. Not everyone will be able to do this at first. The hips are where the movement often gets blocked.

Phase 3

Time

All the above you can set up in one session, or two if you only have time for a short warm-up. Still using the drum to set up the Run.Stop.Go.

You now start to play with the 'time' between the 'still points'. You are looking at 'duration' – how long an activity takes. This is very useful as a lodestone for future movement analysis of how people move, or what the movement in a scene might need in terms of tempo and rhythm. Like all these exercises, they are more than the sum of their parts.

1. Run for a short amount of time. Stop for a long time.
2. Run for a long time. Stop for a short time.
3. Run for short time and stop for a short time – a sense of propulsion.
4. Run for a long time and stop for a long time – epic endurance, like a messenger in a Greek play, arriving to tell their story.

Discuss with the group what different stories or scenarios might arise from these sequences.[9]

In all cases the movement changes what is happening to the breath and the muscles. This changes the story and the intention.

Make sure the *still point* is alive, alert, present, that everyone is together and feels it as one.

> The beauty of this approach is that the group can decide and develop their own story and meaning from the elements you have given them. It is a deconstructed way to deliver meaning, and could be (and has been) a way to bypass binary meaning-making that feeds into conventional story-telling and characterization.

The group doing Run.Stop.Go. will then lead themselves with different durations. One person takes the initiative and everyone picks up the impulse. The actors are 'listening' to each other but everyone has a 'voice', because anyone can choose to stop or go, and the group will follow. The only 'rule' is that you offer, listen and respond. The varieties then become infinite.

---

[9]This is also a way to build modern dance sequences and modern music, where the form can be malleable for different ways of telling stories or building sound and movement, but within a given vocabulary.

Especially if you allow people to 'stop as they are'.[10]

Some ways to make this into a group improvisation

- People walking along a busy pavement in a big city, stopping at traffic crossings
- People running for trains, or looking at departure line boards, when the announcements keep changing
- Doctors in ICU tending a sick patient
- People walking along different aisles in a super-market
- Children and teachers going back to class after break-time
- A political rally

After a couple of sessions or days with Run.Stop.Go with the three phases, the running and walking could and should evolve into something more fluent. Ask them to move continuously and in all directions, covering all the dimensions; encourage them to be clear physically. The movements become increasingly individual but within a collective frame of moving and stopping and changing as a group. Moments of possible collisions become suspensions.

You can add jumps to this or travel to the ground and rolling. These additions will be easier for actors/students to do if you have worked on the dimensions (so later in the first term). Keep the space safe by slowing down the continuous movement and make sure that students connect and make eye contact.

Variations

Stop as you are and what do you see?

Stop as you are comes out of Run.Stop.Go and can also be played as a separate exercise.

- Move through the space as above, when the drum stops you stop where you are and find the still point for this, as you stop with immediacy.
- This will be a position off centre, sometimes on one foot, or in a small lunge, or one leg up, sometimes arms will be active, up, balancing you, or out.
- This position needs to be easy, not tense, a suspended moment in time.
- From that position, the teacher/director calls out 'justify it', meaning, what are you doing? Or why are you in that position? Some people move with it, others live it, all is allowed because very quickly you will ask them to move and resume the exercise.

> The 'justify it' exercise reminds actors that movement needs to have intention; sometimes intention frames the movement, sometimes movement gives you the intention. But it can never be a 'shape'. Nor can you demonstrate or comment on what you are doing.

What do you see? helps the actor focus their attention by looking outwards and starting to respond to the space around them.

---

[10]See next exercise.

- Cross through the space, as above, and this time pay attention to keeping equidistant. This means keeping the space between each actor the same. This is not the same as Lecoq's 'Plateau' which I refer to later. It is an easy exercise, asking each actor to be aware of others which at the same time will mean that the tempi of movement will vary as you assess how to keep the space between you and others the same. You are keeping the gaps between you the same and trying to fill the whole space at the same time, so the whole room should be 'in play'.

The focus is on seeing those in front of you, those around you, the room.

- Drumbeat. Stop/*still point*. Stop as you are or *4-square but* planted, whether on one or two feet.
- 'What do you see?'
- Ask the students to breathe out, or in, or find the breath as they 'see' what's in front of them.
- Then ask them to change direction.
- 'What do you see?' What they see will have changed. A new perspective.
- Move on again. This move on could be another change of direction, or they could continue moving in the same direction.

Drumbeat. Stop/*still point*.

- Look up – 'What do you see?'
- Look down – 'What do you see?'
- Look out the window – 'What do you see?'
- Look out the door – 'What do you see?'

They will be reorientating for the last two. To really see, encourage them to change the orientation of their bodies to do this.

Repeat the travelling through space; again, keep the energy focused, open, curious, looking, sharing space, not grabbing it.

- Drumbeat. Stop/*still point*.
- Repeat the same questions as above, what do you see? And this time ask them to use their bodies to answer. To look up they might lift their head, for instance. Then ask them to add a gesture that completes the body impulse to look up – raise the arm maybe – half-lift two arms in surprise.
- Looking down, same impulse, to take the 'look' into the body, they can drop, reach, bend their knees and add a gesture with the arm.
- Looking out the door, they might spiral their arms to see, or lunge to reach to what is outside the door.
- Out the window, maybe they are corkscrewing round to change their orientation.

In one suspended moment of silence there are four different attitudes, with different focus or points of attention in the room.

The movement, its direction in space and the gesture that follows, should come from the 'seeing'.

> The movement and the gestures need to have breath in them, breathing out as you move is allowing for the possibility of speech: and 'suspension', a stillness full of life and what next?, and an impulse, to look, or change direction. The tutor is leavening this, and you, the actor, are living it.

First foot and spine exercises

The next exercises are how I might start the first few classes of Pure Movement. The exercises are simple, and grounding.

Heel ball toe

Start by standing still for a moment, and test the placement of weight through your feet, by moving forwards towards your toes, backwards towards your heels, and sideways towards the right, and to the left. Shift the weight round in a circle, keeping your balance.

Rise gently onto your toes.
Then sink gently by softening your knees.
Articulate your toes, by standing on one leg, and gently pressing into the first joint of all the toes backwards, then pressing them into the ground facing forwards: change legs and do the same on the other foot.
You are now going to take a wave-like movement through one foot, then the other, articulating it sequentially, from the back of the foot (heel), through the arch to the ball of the foot (ball), to lengthen it and stretch the front of the foot by lifting the toes off (toe):
Heel, ball, toe – as if you were a cat gently padding. Mirror this movement with the hands, moving through the wrists to the fingers – then jump and change onto the other leg.
Heel, ball, toe – with wrists as well
Heel, ball, toe
Heel, ball, toe
Jump and change, resting on the heel of the opposite foot
Repeat.
This is an exercise that can be done at the beginning of the class, before the ice-breakers, and after the silence (if you choose to start with silence). It can also be done, like the feet and 'tendu' exercises of a dance class, after the stretches and waking up, which I describe below.

*

Spine and rolldowns: Useful for voice exercises as well

This builds on your understanding of the spine introduced earlier, but is more fluid, freer.

- Sigh out and let the heaviness of the head lead you to rolling down the spine until you reach the lumber region, gently allowing the sit bones to reach towards the ceiling, to finish hanging down from the sit bones.

- Stay hanging off the spine, allowing the weight to drop and release with the help of gravity, with arms hanging and weight through your feet.
- Make sure the head is free and feel the ribs widening and opening.
- Drop the pelvis down, keeping the upper body curved, so you are squatting with heels raised, then lift the pelvis up by lengthening the legs.
- Gently bounce (or soften) the knees up and down so that the head can free itself from any tension.
- Check in with where your weight is, through your feet, as the exercise above, but you should feel the weight is slightly forward through your feet, feel the drop as forward, and not to hyper-extend the knees.
- Unfurl and build up through the spine, until your head lifts up last, as though you have seen something in front of you.
- Breath out and notice the changes in your body.

Bouncing down through the spine

This next exercise should follow lightly from the previous one.

This is a drop down through the spine with small bounces that suspends in the shifts in the vertebral column – neck, cervical spine, thorax and lumber region.

The bounces should be gentle, like shaking out.

*

Start standing and bounce the knees upright for four beats, making sure the pelvis is free, the knees soft, feet relaxed, remember to breathe.

- RELEASE as you now let the head drop, the neck is gently curved and lengthened, like a swan's neck, and you are hanging off the atlas joint in the neck, bounce the knees for four beats. Be gentle, to free the neck.
- RELEASE as you now drop forwards, sternum softened, to hang off the upper spine, the seventh vertebra in cervical curve of the spine – bounce for four counts.
- RELEASE as you drop down hang off the twelfth vertebral curve in your spine, just under your ribs – bounce for four counts.
- RELEASE as you now drop forwards to hang off the fifth lumber curve in your spine – bounce for four counts.
- UNFURL for four counts, to standing, travelling through your spine.

You can develop this exercise to work with duration. Moving from 8, to 4, to 2 counts for each journey, finishing with a jump, and arms open saying, HEY, like a jack-in-the-box.

*

Waking the feet up for trotting, through rising and dropping

- Start on two feet then send the weight to left and gently bend the right foot by resting on the toes of that foot.
- Transfer the weight through both feet by coming up onto your toes and settling on the other side, resting on the toes of that foot.

- Now speed this up, you are treading lightly from foot to foot by rising and lowering with the knees bent.
- Lift the foot now and increase the speed from a padding to a gentle trot, with your arms by your sides.
- You will feel some kind of elasticity through the feet, though we all have different feet, so work just to keep the feet feeling part of the trot, moving through the foot.
- Trot through the space, lightly.
- Find a forward direction in space, by placing the fingertips of one hand on your sternum and pull an imaginary string out of the sternum.
- At the same time, gently blow through the lips, and loosen the head and shoulders as you trot, like a prancing pony.

Take the trot into a gentle walk and come back to place.

Linking the exercises and recap

This might be how to link the exercises together. I include an exercise in the list below, that I introduce in Chapter 7 (Working in three dimensions) on the swings, called stretching through.

1. Stand with feet comfortably hip width apart.

   Breathe out as you roll down the spine to hang off the sit bones.

   Hang down and gently bounce the knees up and down.

   Roll up through the spine, unfurling, vertebra by vertebra, letting the shoulders ease into the upper back.

   Stand easily with knees softened.

2. On a gentle breath impulse, breathe into softening through the spine into gentle animal-like stretches, with gentle yawns.

   Come back to centre and gently shake shoulders and base of the spine, like shaking droplets of water off your spine.

3. Bounce down the spine, dropping through head, upper spine, mid spine, and lumbar (as exercise 3 above).

   Bounce and come up.

4. Move into trotting through rising through alternate feet until you are trotting (as in exercise 4) and gently trot forwards, backwards, circling right and circling left.

5. Gently trot in the space, as if you have woken up, and as your energy lifts see into the space and gently run or move as fast as is comfortable for you through the space.

6. Take this into Run.Stop.Go with a change of direction.

   All these exercises are explored with ease, and openness. Connecting the breath to the movement. The impulse is not intense.

   This is the organic application of the exercises described above.

7 Working in three dimensions

Working with swings: The basis of all dynamic movement

Part one: The spine in three dimensions

Spine exercises work in three dimensions and use the whole the full range of the spine, and the whole torso. All movement starts in the centre of the body and travels outwards and spine exercises introduce you to the volume of your body. They are surprisingly strong, often releasing powerful feelings.

Working the spine is a transformative act. As soon as you commit to it, the body changes and your physicality alters. These movements can be learnt separately and then threaded into a class, after the foot-work and spinal rolls, described previously.

Magic. Let the movement change you.

Spine exercise on all fours: Rounding and hollowing, rippling through, into standing

Place your weight on your two hands and knees and to feel the length of your spine from your tail (the end of your spine before it dips to your legs) and your head (the top, before it ends in your head). Your spine is flat, a table-top, the direction of the energy forward, like a tiger.

Distribute the weight equally across on your hands and knees.

The hands form right angles to the ground, and spread from thumb to little finger.

Your hands and knees support you like four pillars.

'Hands in line with your shoulders, knees in line with your hips', I will say.

The weight is not on the arms, which can lock the spine. This exercise is to loosen the spine.

Head

- Breathe out and drop your head, then breathe in and let it 'float' up.
- Gently move your head from side to side, like a tiger gently saying 'no'.
- Move the base of the spine gently, like a dog wagging its tail.

Spine

Gently drop the tail downwards, by rounding the base of the spine.

Lift the tail upwards, by hollowing the base of the spine.

You might feel the lumber region (the vertebrae leading into the base of the spine) waking up or feeling tight.

Make sure the belly is soft. Stay grounded through all fours. Let the head follow the dropping and rising.

Rippling through the spine

- Join up both ends of the spine by gently rounding from the base of your spine in a ripple, one vertebra following the other, until the whole spine is rounded like a rainbow, head falling downwards last.
- Try not to push into your shoulders or tighten the back: the skin is spreading over a wider area, like velvet. Looking down or through your legs, you have closed the front of your body and opened the back.
- Reverse the movement by arching the back: lifting the tail bone (as before) and rippling through the spine, vertebra by vertebra, until the head is looking forwards, not cricking the neck.
- If the shoulders are tight, try opening the chest as you arch the back and soften the elbows. At the same time try dropping, or gently pulling the shoulder blades (or wings) down your back. The spine is scooped like a crescent moon.
- Repeat rippling through the spine from tail to head, rounding and hollowing.
- TAIL FIRST, HEAD LAST.
- Round (ripple) – Tail to head.
- Hollow (ripple) – Tail to head.

Like electricity. Like a tiger undulating their spine with flowing power.

Rippling with sound

- Send the breath into the resonating chambers in the front of the face and the back.
- Say: mum, mum, mum, mum, mum MAA as you ripple through.
- Feel the back reverberating with the power of this.

The solidity of your four pillars to support you
Keep this continuous.

Changes of impulse in spine ripple

- Speed this up by starting the flow back at the tail as soon as the ripple has reached the head, the movement is continuous – an undulation, snaking through your spine. Think of oil, of slithering, of waves on a lake, of silk moving in air. Try not to rush. Go through every physical sensation.
- Add with surprise Fast, Light, Free by 'snatching' the movement in one motion with a little 'ha' sound.
- Add the gaze – 'what do you see?'

Think of a kitten watching a fly.

Figure 8 Rounding and hollowing – Composite image. Drawn by Peter Shenai.

Stand from all fours

Bring the back to flat spine, turn the toes underneath you, and walk your hands to your feet until hanging off the spine.

Gently unfurl to standing.

Stand, look around you – where are you?

Roll back down with a sigh until arms are hanging.

Gently let the hands take your weight, by sinking your knees and walk yourself out onto all fours.

You have a whole sequence.

(Rolling up and down the spine is the exercise you have already done.)

Variation of spine exercises

Each of these exercises can start on all fours or from standing with incremental journeys. Moving from small to big, gives form a sense of story and musicality, and the experience of scale and expansion.[1]

- **Chewing through the spine**

---

[1] My understanding of the need to move into larger forms of expression, vocal, physical and emotional, from small beginnings, were formed from working on Shakespeare.

Start standing, gently chewing, as though you were softening a toffee. You will let the movement travel down through the neck, shoulders, back, chest, shoulders and into your hips and down into your knees. You are like liquid toffee, viscous, free flowing, but not floppy. The movement is radiating out of the spine.

*

As you chew, sink down through the spinal column (vertically) to the ground, lowering your centre of gravity until you are kneeling, then slide forward onto hands and knees. This might suggest a situation, or an emotional response.

*

Keep the sense of 'chewing' going through your spine coming **up** onto your knees and sinking **down** onto your arms. Think of the elasticity of chewy toffee. You will be exploring **S T R E T C H I N G and gathering** as the limbs respond to the movement in the spine. Like a sea-creature.

End on all fours, and pace like a tiger, moving arms across your front, alternating them, keeping the sense of chewing in your shoulders.

*

Gently bring yourself up to standing by shifting your weight back onto your heels and building up from a crouch to a knee bend to standing, as though recovering from something. Stand.

*

Partner work

- In partners, one person works, and the other guides by gently touching places on the spine to encourage the movements to be fully expressed. You are both standing. The touch is 'waking' movement up in the partner (you will need to ask consent to do this.). This can be done with breath as well as touch. It can be developed into an improvisation – Ariel leading Ferdinand in *The Tempest*?
- Working on your own, add a piece of text and make the movement smaller.

Circling the spine like a cat

This is a circular movement across the spine as it rounds and hollows.

It explores direction and counter direction.

Circle the head

- Hollow your spine, lifting your head, with your eyes directed forward (not up).
- Turn your head to the right and gently start to circle it round from the right shoulder, dropping it across the front of your chest, over to the left shoulder, and up and arcing over the top of your circle as you reach the front.
- The circle is directed by your nose.
- You are like a cat when they groom themselves, the movement is small and light, and focused. The neck is supple.

Add the spine

- As you circle the head, let the spine join in by rounding and hollowing the opposite direction to the head. The spine is in counter movement to the head.
- <u>Head and spine moving in a full circle</u>
  Hollow the spine, lift head up looking forwards
  Circle head to the right/pelvis swings to the left
  As head circles and drops across the chest to the left the SPINE ROUNDS, direction of pelvis to the right
  As head lifts up to the left the SPINE HOLLOWS, and the pelvis is still to the right but suspended and ready to change direction
  As the head circles round the top to the right, the SPINE is still HOLLOW and the direction of pelvis moves to the left
  Continue to circle so the head drops to the right shoulder
  SPINE ROUNDS
  As head moves to left shoulder
  SPINE ROUNDS
  PELVIS is to RIGHT
  Continue circling
  Change direction
  The upper body and lower body are always working in opposition.
  Make sure as you round and hollow that you are exploring the movement through the entire spine.
  You can start the exercise from the ribs and let the head follow.

Animal Drinking and Tortoise in a cave into Undulation on all fours

This exercise is useful for Animal Study and for waking up the upper spine.
   Works with the directions of forwards, backwards, rising (up) and sinking (down).
   There are many playful interpretations possible.
   This exercise has four phrases:

i. Animal Drinking
Start on all fours:
   Hollow the spine
   With a hollow spine, sink the chest to the floor by softening the elbows
   Chest lowered, tail still arched – think of sinking the front of you, but keep the weight equal
   You will be opening out the upper back and feeling a lateral stretch like a lizard
   Add the idea of an animal drinking to this position and start to drink, allow your quality of movement to be affected by what you are drinking – respond, thinking you hear something or see something.[2]
   Go back to the position and check that the spine is still open.

---

[2]These physical transformations and responses are explored elsewhere in the book. All the exercises feed forwards and backwards to some of the basic principles of movement, expression, transformation, gravity, space and swings.

ii. Tortoise

From animal drinking, retreat into an imaginary cave
    Slide the pelvis back, so that you are sitting on your heels, with your back rounded
    Allow the upper spine to round as much as it can with your head tucking into your thighs, you will feel the belly almost retreating into your back
    You are like a tortoise retreating into its shell
    Keep this movement soft and quiet
    You are safe and in the dark, you aren't tense.

iii. Tortoise creeps out into Animal Drinking

From tortoise, lift your head, and imagine you have seen a glint of light outside the cave.
    Slide forward on your belly until you come back to animal drinking.
    The light is bright, it might dazzle you. Keep the arms soft and the back open, don't go into a press-up.
    To see more, lift up, by straightening your arms.
    You are now in hollow spine.

iv. Undulation like a wave in two dimensions, forward, backwards, up, down

This exercise is more abstract and continuous. The movement flows through the spine.
    Direction forwards: the head leads as you slide forwards.
    Direction backwards: the spine leads as you are pulled backwards.
    There is an undulation – like a wave, or the sea or a snake.

The exercise

Start on all fours:
    Round the spine and sink backwards into tortoise (softening your knees).
    Lift your head and slide forward through animal drinking.
    Lift up further with your head leading into:

Hollow spine

Then round the spine, to repeat the journey as many times as feels nice.
    This is an undulating forwards, backwards, lowering, rising, sequence.

Directions

Back, lower
    Forward, rise

Spine

Round
    Tortoise
    Animal Drinking
Hollow

Spine exercises starting on your back

The next exercises look at the influence of gravity when lying on our backs and explore how to move from lying to standing. For this we explore the body spiral and change of direction.

Sometimes the smallest adjustments to what the body does, can 'release' the story and the actor's intention. The detail in spine exercises provides the material, both for the actor and the movement teacher, to work effectively through physicality with a similar detail and awareness, to help create the physicality of a role.

1 Resting

Lie on the floor with your knees up. This position is often called semi-supine.
  Let your muscles relax and the floor support you – sigh out.
  Push the feet away and release your hip flexors, so your knees hang near your chest.
  Bounce the ankles with a little pah, pah, sound to free the breath.
  Release the hip flexors and bring the feet back to the ground, softening them as you go.

2 Conversations with gravity

These exercises 'play' with gravity, using the ground to support you.
  They ask your muscles to let go.
  You are yielding to the space around as you lie on your back or sweep your side.
  The exercises journey through the vertebral column to the pelvis and out into the space.

Shoulders, arms and pelvis and gravity

- Start in semi supine
- Lift both arms up to the ceiling, so that the arms are balanced easily in the shoulders, and the shoulders are resting easily on the ground
- The arms are reaching up to ceiling – a child asking to be picked up – with space between your two arms, palms facing inwards
- Gently release the arms from the elbows so that the hands/fingers end gently on the chest
- And then unfold the arms back out to the side, onto the ground, with little resistance – this is two movements

Climbing arms

- Lift the arms up again to the 'appealing' position
- Alternately lift one arm after the other up to the ceiling so that the shoulder comes away and returns: there are four impulses to this movement
    - Lift one arm
    - Drop the shoulder from the arm lift
    - Lift the other arm
    - Drop of the other
    - Speed these movements up like a rag doll, you will be rocking from side to side, with the head free

- See if they can bring you up, by rounding your spine, to end spine slumped forwards, knees bent
- Flop and sink backwards

Rolling from side to side and opening and closing the arms

This exercise changes direction and works across the body.

The movement and sweeping motion of the arms prepares you for the spiral lying to standing exercise that comes next.

Don't force the stretch.

You aren't being asked to 'stay' in these positions for long.

*

Start in semi-supine and then push your feet away so the knees come to the chest and the feet are dangling as in semi-supine into leg release exercise (starting position leg release):

- Arms are out to the side, palms open, which opens the shoulders.
- Let the legs fall to the right, left knee on top of right.
- Turn the head to the left, and look along the fingers of that hand – you are in a spinal twist.
- Sigh out along the hand, circle the left arm over the top of the head, sweeping it along the floor and following it with your gaze, letting the back and shoulder follow, making the circle as big a circle as possible (like seaweed, or sweeping cobwebs away).
- To end curved on your right side, with the left arm on top of the right and your left leg on top of the right. The back is curved and soft, the shoulders in line, the hands joined.

To return, you have two options. Both require the leg to swing back with the momentum of the movement.

1. Gently pull the left arm along the right arm as if pulling a bow and arrow, stroking the shoulder chest and arm, to return to the arm to the open position, and swinging the legs into the starting position leg release.

   OR

2. Circle the left arm over the head again, opening the arm out – the left leg will also respond with the momentum of the movement.

   Both movements end with you in centre, legs up, arms wide.

Take the movement into rolling

You start on your back with the knees in (as described):

- Swing the legs to right
- Circle the left arm over
- Pull the left arm back/or circle it back
- With the momentum of gravity, the left leg swings open and you roll across your back
- The pelvis connects to the right leg and for a moment you are suspended like an upturned beetle
- Then let the legs fall to the left, look to the right, circle the arm and circle/pull it back

Working in three dimensions

- Let the legs follow back to the centre
- Swing the legs over
- Continue

Continuous, rolling, spiralling, opening and closing movement
Connect to the momentum and the freedom of momentum.

3 Spiral Into standing

The sequence starts on your back and draws you into standing through spiralling and turning through your whole body and a series of positions: lying, sitting, twisted sitting, lunging and standing.

You are spiralling within a cube. The floor the bottom and the ceiling the top.
You spiral from lying to standing.
Your focus:

- first behind you
- to the side
- to the front
- the side
- the corner of that side
- the opposite corner on the other side
- the front

You move in three dimensions while rising and sinking – you connect to diagonals and to flat planes.

You start lying on your back. You are facing the front of the room, with your head directing to the back and your feet to the front.

Your spiral will take you on a journey from on your back, to standing facing the front.

- First journey from lying on your back is to 'mermaid' to one side of the cube – ¼ turn.
- Second journey is from 'mermaid' to the front, sitting with knees up – ¼ turn.
- Third journey is ¼ turn to 'mermaid' on the opposite side of the cube.
- Fourth journey is 1/8th turn to 'twisted sitting' facing the corner of the room/cube.
- Fifth journey is ¼ turn to starter pose/lunging facing the opposite corner of the room/cube.
- Fifth journey is ½ turn to standing.

The dynamic accelerates, particularly over the last journey which is the longest.

```
< corner            corner>
S           BACK       S
```

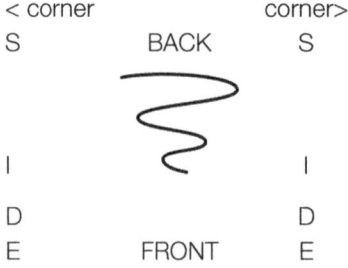

```
I                      I
D                      D
E           FRONT      E
```

138 Physicality and Acting

You are at the centre of the space around you, like the eye of a storm, and spiralling within it, gathering momentum. Where you look pulls you to your next direction. Your focus is outside of you but the spiral is inside of you. The sensation is that of a corkscrew, turning and lifting, finally releasing into standing up.

The new positions are sitting, lunging and mermaid. All these positions open the spine. Try not to tense the stomach or put too much weight on the arms.

1. **Sitting in 'mermaid'**

    'Mermaid' opens the hips and helps direct the spine to spiral from head, shoulder, hip, knee
    - Sit up, with your knees up, and your feet facing forward. You might need to support your back to do this as the knees are hip-width apart, plus sitting means that you need to lift out of your lower back. Think of directing your energy up out of the top of your head, and down into your feet.
    - Bend your right leg in front at a right-angle (the hip will be open and you will be resting on the outside of your thigh and lower leg): and your left leg behind you at a right-angle (the hip will be closed and weight on the inside of the thigh and lower leg) – you will be in a Z shape.
    - Switch legs to
    Left leg in front, right leg behind, by changing direction looking over your left shoulder. To return, look over your right shoulder. Think head, shoulder, hip, knee to help the movement flow.
    - Don't worry if you need to support yourself with your hands to do this.

2. **Sitting upright**
    - This is the position described above. You sit on your sitting bones, with your feet hip width apart, with your knees pointing up to the ceiling, and your feet placed in line with your legs.
    - It is easier to facilitate this position if the base of your spine is rounded a little, but you need to also lift out of the hips, and not sink backwards. Use your arms to support you.

3. **Twisted sitting**
    - Open the left knee onto the floor, so that your weight is resting on the outside of the leg.
    - At the same time lift the right leg over the left leg, with the knee pointing up to the ceiling, and the right foot placed in front of the left knee on the ground.
    Both hips are 'closed', but not tight. You will feel that you are tucking your energy into you. Birds sometimes rest like this.
    Lift up out of the hips

4. **Lunge/starter pose spiralling into standing**
    - Bend your left knee on the ground, with the toes tucked underneath you and the weight on your left knee.
    - At the same time, bend your right leg forward, with your weight on your right foot.
    - Place your two hands on the floor next to your front knee, and direct your gaze forwards.

- This will lengthen your upper back, driving the energy forwards.
- Turn to look over your left shoulder and turn your head shoulder hip knee to create a new front: your right foot and right side will follow in a spiral and you will find yourself standing.

The whole exercise of the spiral

First position: Lying on your back

- Lying on your back arms out to the side, in semi supine
- Push your feet away and let the legs fall into your chest as in 'semi-supine into leg release'.

Second position: First mermaid position

- Swing the legs over to the right, and turn to look over your left shoulder
- Circle your left arm over the top of your head and with the momentum of this sweeping motion, allow this to 'flow' you up to mermaid sitting, facing the side of the room, with the right leg in front and the left leg behind
- The circle and swing of the left arm will also propel the left leg to move behind
- Stay in this position for a while.

Third position: Sitting position

- Turn your head to the left, to the front of the room, and let your body follow: head, shoulder, hip, knees, to finish in the sitting position, both knees directed to the ceiling, and feet on the ground facing the front.

Fourth position

- Turn your head to the side (left) and change position, head, shoulder, hip, knee, to face the opposite side of the room, with the left leg in front, the right leg behind – this the mermaid position on the other side.
  Stay sitting in this position for a while.

Fifth position

- Turn your head to the corner, a ¼ turn of the head, and swing your right leg over to face the corner
- This is twisted sitting like a bird nesting, you are facing the corner, and in a diagonal

Sixth position

- Turn your head to opposite corner – to unwind twisted sitting, to find starter pose
- Your left leg will be behind, right leg in front
- Turn your head left to the front and push yourself up to standing
- Your left side will be opening and pulling the right side after to you.

Seventh position

- Standing.

Return

The gathering momentum of the spiral, from lying to standing, can reverse to take yourself back to lying.

Reverse the journey by looking over your right shoulder to lower to starter pose.

When you get back to facing the first side in mermaid, with the right leg in front, sink and slide on to your back, by looking behind you and sliding your arm directly in line with your right shoulder, to take your weight, and then circle it round to the side, swinging your legs into semi-supine-leg release.

Make a story

Add the drama by working in twos.

One person stands behind you.

As they walk the spiral, you watch them, and they pull you with them until they bring you up to standing.

They then reverse the journey, and you follow them.

The tension between the two of you is a wire or a thread.

*

Part two: The Gravity Swings working in three dimensions

This section looks at the Gravity Swings, which Trish Arnold taught me. The swing for acting is not to a rhythmic beat but finds its own momentum through the natural weight of an actor's body. The swing includes a suspension as it reaches the top of its arc.

The repertoire of swings merits a whole separate book, where they are broken down incrementally and explored for their dramatic possibilities, as well as inhabiting their simplicity. The drum beats I describe are best thought of as accents, rather than a strict tempo or rhythm. The drum is always an invitation to move. This is not dancing.

The property of the swing, 'Drop, Swing, Suspension' harnesses momentum, and develops stamina, strength and optimum placement for each body.

The swings are all different, each one activating drama, weight and tempo – responding to gravity. The further away from the ground the starting point of a swing is, the bigger the arc, the further the drop, the more the weight of the body is harnessed, and the more dramatic the swing.

I look at a selection of swings that start from different parts of the body.

The full torso swings are the most challenging, and I am only including two in this section.

They are here in the order I often teach them (over 2 years):
WIDE SWING
ARROW SWING

LEG SWING
TREE TOPPLE
RAG DOLL
FIGURE OF 8 SWING.

The swings start from one part of the body, travelling out into dimensional space, which gives them their dynamic and specificity. Giving into gravity offers a sense of release and being in the moment, to discover the sequence of momentum into stillness.

I teach the swings in silence, sometimes with the sound of the breath, punctuated with a drumbeat to start the movement. Silence feels exposing at first, but invites a lovely, open and playful way to work. Actors, when they work together, can 'see' each other.

The detail is important to enable the free flow and the placement. There is always an element of unpredictability to a 'swing'.

Preparing to swing by activating the ribs
Before learning the swing, we need to open the ribs.
Here I focus on an exercise called
'Rib stretches in High, Wide and Forward'.

Preparation for rib stretches in High, Wide and Forward
The spine is flexible, and the knees soft.

Teaching point
The direction flows from the back into the ribs, the arms, the fingers and out into the space. Once the stretch has happened you let go, and release, often coming back to where you started. The stretches respond to the breath.

Starting from the ribs
Swinging the ribs from side to side. Stand with feet hip width apart. Lift the right elbow to the side and let it pull you sideways. Drop back to centre. Repeat on the other side. Always soften the knees when you drop the arms.
The stretches starting from the centre like this, increase volume, range and breath.
The rib stretches travel to the dimensions of High, Wide and Forward.
'The Dimensions' is an exercise which Trish Arnold taught me.

Dimensions
'The Dimensions' help with the placement of the swings, and the rib stretches but they are key exercises for story and intention.
Every swing starts its journey in one of these dimensions, travelling to another, through loops and curves. We inhabit space in 360 degrees and in three dimensions.
The exercises below are playful, and easy to understand, taking you to different destinations, which change your physicality and centre, useful for Animal Study and Character Study. You will learn to flow through these dimensions, rather than to think of them as shapes.

The journeys in the exercise for 'The Dimensions'

The dimensions travel up and down, out and in, and forward and back in the form of a cross. The journeys go:

High – Low
Low – Wide
Wide – Narrow
Narrow – Front
Front – Back

The exercises

I introduce the change of direction with the drum, encouraging different movement qualities with different ways of drumming. You can also do this exercise to music.

- High
  Find an impulse to reach up as high as you can with your arms stretched above you.

- Low
  From high, drop down into a low position, exploring how this makes you move. Dropping like a stone, sinking, crouching.

- Wide
  From the ground find an impulse to surge upwards and outwards to open your arms and feet a wide position – as if welcoming someone, or guarding something.

- Narrow
  Step inwards, and cross one leg in front of the other, maybe wrap your arms round each other, to find a narrow position. Gathering yourself in.

- Forwards
  Step forwards with one foot and reach forwards with both hands. Moving into forward space is active. Stay facing forwards, make sure that the body isn't twisting.

- Backwards
  From forwards step backwards, taking the weight on the backward travelling foot.
  This is quite a dramatic position – can you find a way to do this that is natural?
  Travel physically and imaginatively through these dimensions, flowing from one to the other.
  Find different movement qualities to move with, strong and fast, slow and light, sudden, sustained.
  Add jumps and sinking, steps going forwards and backwards (as in a dance).
  Above all find the 'game' and the acting impulse.
  You can work in a smaller register. The journeys through space could be intentions or thoughts.

Partner work

Face a partner and do the exercises as a conversation, with one person leading and one person following doing the opposite

A will do High
B Low
A Wide
B Narrow
A Forward
B Backward
Change the leader and repeat.

Choose a different order of the directions/dimensions, which compels the actor responding to pay attention to what is offered.

Change the journeys to moving off the spot, running or jumping (in high) or crawling (in low), changing the dynamic and using the whole room.

Place the partners, across the room, still able to make eye contact but not directly facing each other and continue the rule of 'opposites' (whatever the first person offers, the second does the spatial 'opposite'), not following the pattern above.

This becomes a different register, and more an exercise of call and response, than conversation.

Rib stretches in High, Wide and Forward: Technical exercise to prepare for the swings and stretch the body with accuracy

Start with your feet hip width apart, that is not too wide or too narrow.

Place your hand on your sternum, breathe out, sink the knees and sink the sternum with the head and shoulders dropped; this is called: 'the giving in position'.

(The 'giving in' position is also quite an emotional position, the giving up or letting go, or just not struggling to stay upright anymore.)

(We have looked at this as a preparation for the roll down of the spine.)

'All movement travels on a continuum between balance to release or letting go and into extension, reaching or stretching' (Arnold, 1997).

1. *High stretch*
   - Start from the 'giving in' position
   - Lift the right arm by travelling through shoulder, elbow, hand, so the arm unfurls with fingers long, up towards the ceiling
   - Allow your weight to shift slightly to the right, the ribs to open and the back to widen
   - Look up, as though you were going to pick a cherry off a tree, or forwards as though you've seen someone (but the arm for this needs to be facing inwards, so not a wave)
   - Release the arm and drop back to the giving in position, with a soft rebound in the knees
   - You will have shifted your weight back to centre
   - Repeat with the left arm

2. *Wide stretch*
   - From the giving in position stretch your right arm out to the side pulling your right foot out into a wide position, slightly wider than your shoulders, so you have stepped out

- The feet are slightly turned out to accommodate the knees going over the feet
- The right knee is bent, and the left knee is straight
- The sensation is of tilting on the side to the right with the torso opening to the right and the fingers reaching the side of the room
- The left side of the ribs and the torso will be stretched lengthways – the head is in a diagonal with the left foot and facing to the front
- Fall sideways to the right by dropping your arm, shoulder, head to hang by the side of your right knee
- Change direction to stretch to the other side by lifting the left shoulder, elbow, hand sequentially to pull you to the left, coming up and over and not sitting in your ribs
- This is a strong sensation in the body. Both feet are on the ground and your front and back are flat along these planes
- After the stretch to the left, drop to the left side
- Send your upper body to the centre, weight on both feet, back to the giving in position, with sternum softened
- Your feet are still slightly wider than your shoulders.

3. *Forward stretch*
   - The forward stretch is through a soft and rounded spine (as in 'round and hollow' exercise) with the pelvis rounded underneath you
   - Your arm is stretched out in front of you, as you look along the inside of the arm and beyond like a swimmer, or tiger pouncing
   - You feel the length of the upper spine travel into the shoulder and out through the arm. The upper spine is long, the pelvis rounded
   - Start from the giving in position as above
   - Unfurl the right arm forwards from shoulder, elbow, hand
   - Soften the right knee and straighten the left leg, bringing it in slightly in line with the left shoulder
   - Drop the right arm and come back to the giving in position
   - Unfurl the left arm into forward stretch on the left
   - Repeat: you will discover the weight will be moving slightly from side to side
   - Make the movement continuous and it will feel as if you are doing front crawl.

These are all reaches, more than stretches, and are useful as part of any warm-up.
Feel the movement in the ribs, and the opening out of the back.
Think of the knees softening, rather than pushing into a knee bend.
You can do them softly, focusing on reach and release. Or flowing. Or with strong impulses.
It is also possible to do these stretches on a chair with the sit bones taking the weight.

Swings

The first swing I teach is 'Swing in Wide' because it is the easiest to feel. Probably the one you will do when testing a theatre space or need to drop your breath and open your back.

Preparation to feel weight: This is partner work

Find a partner, preferably of a similar height. Stand opposite each other. One person holds out their arms in front of them, and the other person places their arms on top, giving them their weight. Stand for several seconds until the person whose arms are on top has surrendered their weight. The person holding them will suddenly take their arms away, so the top arms suddenly fall. This is the drop and understanding of weight, we look for in the gravity swing.

1 Swing in Wide
Preparation to feel the momentum

Stand with your feet in wide, just slightly wider than shoulder width apart. Feet should be turned to a 45° angle, so that when you soften the knees, they track over the feet with the front of the thighs open.

Open one arm out to the side, lifting it up to a slight diagonal.

Make space under the armpit to do this (imagine you are opening a cloak and displaying the lining). Keep the arm raised until it feels tired and heavy.

Drop the arm to let it swing across the body. Let the shoulder go with the movement, and let the arm drop in the swing, to return to its starting point. The sensation will feel: heavy, then light.

Don't bounce the knees yet. This will mean the sensation of the movement is now more across your back.

Do that with both arms, and return with both arms in wide.

Catch the drop with the knees

Open the right arm again to the side – swing and catch it by:

Adding a slight bounce of the knees on the drop and lengthen the legs as the arm swings back to its open/wide starting point.

Swing again and continue the journey in an inwards continuous circle.

Swing In and Out

And

OVER

And OVER

The arm circles over the top in a big arc, then drops/fall by your side.

Lift the other arm and repeat on the other side:

1, and 2

And

OVER and

OVER

If you do this with a drum it might be

1, and 2, and 3, and 4

Keep the swing on the wide plane

*

Do the same swing with both arms and keep the swings continuous:

- Open both arms out to the side in wide and hands facing the front

- You are opening the cloak on both sides
- Swing both arms across the body, with a little bounce of the knees as the arms drop (and cross each other)
- Circle the arms inwards and over the top to open outwards
- Then continue the swing.

Sequence is:
In and Out
And Over and Over
1, and 2, and 3, and 4, and
1, and 2, and 3, and 4, and etc.

Make sure the knees are soft, don't push the swings, let them happen. This will take a while.

You are exploring the drop as the arms fall (not anticipating it) and the rebound as the arms come up.

The movement is continuous, in and out, over and over, in and out, over and over like a mill wheel, steady and stable.

The softening in the knees helps the release. And it is important not to drop into the hips too much – the sensation of lifting up into the circles will open the spine and the front of the body.

After three cycles, finish the arms in wide and flop down in between your legs, with the sit bones facing the ceiling.

Then build up through the spine with arms wide, to see the world.

You are working in the wide dimension, as above, open, confident, easeful.

2 Swing in wide with a drop

Many of the swings develop into dropping and travelling across the space.

The drop from wide here into the centre is the upper spine dropping as the arms swing inwards, arms crossing a little.

The shoulders stay open, not rolling in.

Stay centred through your legs and pelvis as you drop down, so again two forces through the body, down and grounded in the lower half, soft and fluid in the upper half.

- Open your arms wide as before
- Swing across to finish with arms wide
- 1, and 2
- Now drop the upper spine, dropping down on the 1 and coming up on the 2
- As you come up, think of unfurling the upper spine, coming up through the spine
- Drop
- 1, and 2

Add circle over the top

- Swing across
- 1, and 2
- Drop down
- 1, and 2
- Swing across

- 1, and 2
- Swing over the top, twice.
- 1, and 2, 1, and 2
- To continue, swing across in the same tempo.

The suspension is at the top of the circle: when we come to travelling across the space, the circle in the overhead swing is what creates the momentum for travelling. As the arms circle, they find freedom, and this will give you a sense of lightness. As they drop, they will find their release and this will give you a sensation of heaviness. Find these sensations, don't impose them.

3 Arrow Swing with dropping down, circling and travelling

This swing is on the diagonal. When travelling forwards and backwards your 'front' faces sideways, with your arm directed forward, like the 'point' of an arrow.

I teach this in a 'sequence' that travels back and forth and ends travelling down the diagonal.

When I introduced this exercise to Lithuanian students at the Conservatoire in Vilnius, the Head of Acting found it very theatrical, calling the swings 'stage movement'. She could see how it opens the actor's body to develop stage craft. There is something epic and dramatic about this swing.

Understanding the diagonal line that comes from you into the space is key to this. I explore with students how to reach to the diagonal, by getting them to touch the eight corners of the box their bodies inhabit.

The Box exercise

I have discussed my feelings about the Box or the Kinesphere.[3] As I questioned it, Trish Arnold suggested ways to make this theatrical, and less abstract. This avoids the more troubling aspects of the origins of the work, by making it playful.

I describe this here to feel the diagonal stretch of the body in space.

Exercises to understand personal space and diagonals

'The Box' helps students to swing through front to back diagonals, and vice versa.

There are much more detailed ways to explore Laban's Kinesphere.

We are never flat-on, even when facing front. We are moving in space, which has volume. We are changing direction, which is story. But this is a simple and playful way to explore our three-dimensional use of space.

The body touching the corners of a box

Standing facing the front and imagine that you are inside a box.

There are eight corners in a box, four in the front, and four behind you, going from right to left, and high to low, these are:

---

[3] See Chapter 4, 'The need for a system'.

Front
High Right
High Left
Low Right
Low Left.

Back
High Right
High Left
Low Right
Low Left.
  Wherever you face in the room is your personal front.

FRONT
Point to the four corners of the front of your box:
  – Right finger to right sides: left finger to left sides

BACK
Without changing your front (i.e. turning round) but allowing your body to pivot and spiral, point to the four corners behind you:
  – Right finger right side: left finger left side.
  This will involve spiralling your body to reach out behind you.
  Reaching the high corners behind you, might feel like trying to touch something behind you in the dark. Reaching the low corners behind you, crouching and spiralling, might feel like reaching to touch the back seat behind you while driving a car for instance.
  Reaching to the corners, from front to back, creates the diagonals.
  Extending the arms in the High Right or High Left diagonal, you reach to something just beyond your grasp. Reaching the high back diagonals creates a strong emotional response at something coming towards you.[4]

Pathways and diagonal journeys through the Box: Moving in 3-dimensional directions
The pathways are indicated and completed by where the arm/hand/gaze end up.

- Start with feet underneath you, arms by your sides and raise your arm up to
- High Right Front
- Sink down and reach behind you to
- Low Left Back
  (Diagonal Line)

- Travel forwards to
- Low Left Front
  (Straight line)

---

[4] As with all these gestures, the more open the body, the stronger the emotional or expressive response. You can explore these gestures in a smaller space (box) to explore more 'conversational' responses.

- Travel backwards, rising to
- High Right Back
  (Diagonal line)
  Return to

- High Right Front
  (Straight line)
  The straight lines trace the outside of the box, the diagonals the inside.
  Try different intentions for the Box. Hanging washing, the Witches in *Macbeth* (I have used this a lot), partners facing one another to explore an improvisation on hoisting sails on a ship, a spider in a web, painting a room.

Preparing the shoulder for the Arrow Swing

The Arrow Swing comes from the centre of the upper spine, from shoulder to arm
  The arm circles, with the shoulder looping up and down and round and round.
  When you do this exercise, keep the shoulders oiled, and moving fluidly.
  Start the Arrow Swing exercise with shoulder exercises already described.

The Arrow Swing: The set-up and the movement into travelling

The preparation is inherently dramatic. Work with a drumbeat, silence, breath and suspension.
  The arm comes from the body, like a branch from the trunk of a tree.

- Stand and turn your head to face the right diagonal – a diagonal turn of the head as if looking up at a hill some distance from you.
- Step towards the right diagonal with the right foot. Allow the left foot to turn out slightly: your weight should be equally distributed between both feet.
- Raise the right arm up to the high right diagonal as if reaching out to someone you have a relationship with who is far away.
- Take your left arm from over the top behind you to join your right hand, or pulse point, of your right hand.
- Pull the left arm along the inside of the arm across the sternum and out the High left back, diagonal. Pulling an arrow taut inside a bow. There is a diagonal from the right big toe and out through the fingers of your left hand.
- Drop the front arm. You are now standing in an extended diagonal: Right foot and head directed towards the right front diagonal, and left back arm in line with the forwards diagonal – the hips are open, facing the front of the diagonal line.
- Swing the left arm from back to front and then return from front to back, with a soft release in the knees – to and fro.
- You are swinging between two diagonals, releasing in the shoulder but experiencing the power in the depth and range of this swing.
- Forward and Back.
  1 and 2.
  Next add a circle and half a circle to change direction, followed by another circle and half circle to return.

- Swing Forward and Back: then take a full circle and a half circle with the left arm and to suspend in Forward.
- From Forward, circle one-and-a-half times to suspend backwards.
- Travel with these circles, changing the orientation of the body, leaning forwards on forward suspension and backwards on backward suspension, by shifting your weight through your feet.

Adding dynamic to the Arrow Swing

Add dynamic and depth, by dropping down, followed by travelling off the spot, forwards and backwards with a gallop, as the arm circles.

Practice galloping first

This exercise will make more sense if the class has warmed up their feet first. The elasticity of the foot and the muscularity of the body will mean the quality of the gallop will vary.

Start with the weight on one foot, and travel sideways to the opposite lifted foot with a slide and a lift.

Take this forward with weight on the back foot, step/together (with a little rise) slide hop: Gallop and change/gallop and change.

Children naturally gallop. Think of it, as one foot chasing the other.

The sequence can now be done on the diagonal and becomes one of the 'travelling' swings.

When travelling down the diagonal, the front of the body is facing the diagonal line, not twisting or closing the body.

It can also be done with groups travelling against one another on two opposing diagonals.

Sequence down the diagonal in groups of three or four – Arrow Swing

- Forwards and backwards + full circle forwards with a gallop – when you are swinging to and fro, allow yourself to shift your weight forwards and backwards, onto one foot then onto another and do the same on the reverse journey below.
- Backwards and forwards + full circle backwards with a gallop.
- Dropping down forwards and backwards (no circle).
- Four circles forwards with four gallops, with a 'hey' 'hey' 'hey' 'hey' on each circle.
- The last 'hey' is almost a 'throw' into the space – the impulse is often to jump on the last hey – you are lancing the energy forwards as though you are throwing a spear.

4 The Leg Swing: Small and with a lunge

The Leg Swing requires balance, co-ordination and in 'The Challenge' which I describe below, quite a lot of strength and stamina. Once you have understood the technique in the Leg Swing, you can add character to them.

In the small Leg Swing, add a balance in the front, as a suspension over a stream, as if frozen mid-flight. If working on the Greeks (Greek tragedy), this gives a sense of running outdoors barefoot, like one of the Gods or Goddesses, or a sense of the ground and how it changes the way we 'step' and run and jump, hovering in mid-flight.

The Leg Swing is 'strong and free'. The aim is to let the natural momentum of the leg swing, chime with gravity.

Simple Leg Swing

The leg swings simply forward and backwards, with the same principle of the other swings:
Drop. Swing. Suspension.

The aim is not to swing the leg high, but to find its weight and freedom.

The focus is on relaxing the lower leg and swinging it, swishing the foot along the ground. The knee is soft.

When swinging behind, bend the knee more, and direct the thigh downwards. This will put less strain on the pelvis.

There might be more freedom releasing the leg in front, than when it swings behind, depending on how free the pelvis is.

Preparation

Place your left hand on a wall to steady you.

Lengthen the left side upwards and gently scoop your right hand underneath the back of your right thigh to 'catch' the knee.

Your left side and left leg are long and supporting you (not unlike the feeling in the stretch in high left).

Let the leg hang loosely swinging from the knee. The shin is directed downwards, and knee lifted at a right angle. Don't lift it too high.

Gently tap the top of the thigh, giving it a little push, and the leg should start to swing freely and easily in the hip socket: to and fro – foot brushing the floor.

Don't lock the pelvis – the movement echoes walking and not a 'grand battement' in ballet.

The weight of the leg and momentum from the swing allows the leg to lift to its natural height. Do the same on the other leg.

Simple leg swing beats

- Stand on two feet, lengthen the left side, and lifting the right leg and left arm up together, and right arm behind you, parallel to the ground.
- Suspend there for a moment balancing on one leg, as though caught mid-jump looking forwards with a strong sense of direction. You are standing in a suspended opposition.
- Swing the leg forwards and backwards, for 4 beats over 6 counts, balancing with the swinging of the arms forwards and backwards in opposition: suspend step and lift the left leg.
- Repeat to this rhythm: 1 and 2 and 3 and 4 step 5 and lift 6.

Variation to help with balance

- If you find it hard to balance, put your hands onto the shoulders of your partner, or make a row of 4 or 5.

- Make sure your partner can stand up straight (don't press too much). Any group contact like this is about co-operation, each person balanced in their own space.
- There are ancient line dances from all over the world – the Dabke in the Levant, Azerbaijani line dances or the Ashkenazi dances from the shtetels. Holding each other by the shoulder, or taking hands, moving and stepping together in line, stamping, lifting the leg.
- Swing the legs as a group, trying to keep in synch: instead of stepping and lifting the back leg through, you can sink down onto both knees, with the right foot forward and lift the back leg through as you come up.
- This is a strong deep plié through both legs, requiring you to transfer your weight on to the front foot: 1, 2, 3, 4, 5 (step or sink) 6 (lift).
- Going down the room in a straight line – see what story comes from this. The rhythm is the bond between you.

Leg Swing with change of direction/clown swing

This swing changes direction with the momentum of the backward swing, which swivels your torso to face the other way, like flipping a coin.

Lift up right leg in front, swing for 7 counts, swivel and change on the eighth and step on it and lift the left leg, swivel and change.

- The sequence is: 7 swings and a turn to finish on 8 x 2 times
- 3 swings and a turn to finish on 4 x 2 times
- 1 swing and turn to finish on 2 x as many times as you like
- Try to do all the above without counting and justifying the shortening of the 'duration'.

It is amusing if you do it opposite a partner, starting back-to-back, so that when you turn you surprise each other.

The Challenge

Trish Arnold taught me this, as part of my research in how to make swings have intention and story. She formulated it when teaching movement at the Stratford Festival Theatre in Ontario, to keep the young actors engaged. The scale of the movement and the ground it covers are very good training for the physical demands of plays like *Romeo and Juliet*, or *Richard III* or *Henry V*.

There is conflict and drama in this sequence which peaks in the lunge. I ask them to imagine that they are crossing swords in a fight. There is an exit to the exercise. How you enter a room or exit is interesting.

This is done to a 12-count phrase, which eventually you can feel.

The exercise is done opposite a partner across the diagonal.

- Lift the right leg behind and the right arm in front, arms swing in opposition.
- Swing the leg for 5 counts with the arms in opposition.
- Lunge forwards on the right leg in a deep knee bend, arms in opposition, front arm directed towards your partner as if you had a sword. Your back leg (the left leg) is stretched out straight behind you – feel the energy going out through the heel.
- Stay there for 4 counts, keeping the focus and the arm extended.

- Come up on the tenth count, suspending the left leg behind.
- Swing the left leg for 2 more counts, 11 and 12.
- The twelfth count, the left leg is behind you.
- Repeat sequence starting with left leg behind.

Moving out of The Challenge to finish the exercise:

- On the tenth count, slide the back leg up and straighten the front leg to find yourself standing opposite your partner, dropping your arms.
- Make eye contact with your partner. Circle round each other to the right, ending where you started, then leave suddenly, passing each other.
- When you circle keep the torsos facing each other. This will give you the sensation of spiralling when you turn.
- Both exits take you back to the direction you were travelling, towards the opposite side of the room you started from. There is a sequence here, which has a narrative. Find what your story is and connect to it.

5 Full torso swings and travelling swings

These last few swings engage the whole body, or travel across the space. I will introduce them succinctly because the principles of the swing and how you can 'play' it, or 'play with it' have already been explored.

These movements powerfully change the body.

Let the body speak for itself. The movement is a filter through which the intentions, imagination and story can flow.

Drop, swing, suspension: breath, release, balance.

These simple principles allow us to gain access to a pallet of physical expression for our transformative work as actors.

A full torso swing takes in the whole body, a much larger arc on a grand scale.

Tree Topple

The arc goes from high to low, releases backwards to propel forwards, out and up, to return to high. It is a fall from a place of optimum extension. It is genuinely risky, full of jeopardy, like a change in fortune. When we studied tragedy at Lecoq's school, he described this as the fall of the hero, from heaven to earth, and scaling the momentum that took him back up to heaven.

All swings can travel across the space, because a swing, when sped up, gathers momentum and you must catch this through the footwork, through the travelling steps of a gallop. The swing makes the sense of travelling easier and freer.

- Stand, and bring your arms up to high, through centre.
- The back is open, the arms are in line with the shoulders, the sternum is open.
- Look out and down and pitch your weight forward onto your toes – a moment of jeopardy before gravity pulls you over.
- You need to live through that suspension. Anticipation.
- Drop into a full torso swing forwards – as the knees bounce up, allow the body to rise a little so that the arms and torso swing backwards. The arms are relaxed behind your back, almost curving.

- Drop down again as the knees bounce up again – the fingers will lead your torso forwards, almost parallel to the ground, with a feeling of lengthening out.
- Swing backwards again, and on the next forward swing of the torso continue soaring up to the top with arms reaching up high.
- Suspend.
- Open the arms out wide, slowly, breathing out, keeping the back open, the legs long, with the fingers leading, as if your arms were wings.
- Do this opposite a partner and say 'hey' at the end.

The connection at the end of this phrase will often be the most powerful part of it.

Swing in Wide galloping across the space

In pairs, face one another flat on, ready to travel down the diagonal.

Open out into wide, facing each other, with the weight on the upstage foot (away from the direction of travel).

Swing and gallop across the space facing each other.

As the arms travel across (in) the feet come together, and as they open, the downstage foot pulls the feet open.

Clap:
1 and 2 (arms in and out)
And 1 and 2
Or
123, 123, emphasis on the
ONE

Take hands with your partner to focus on the galloping and you will feel the swing in your body anyway.

(Gallops, skips, run, run, jump, are all helped with swinging arms or legs. You will have done something like that as a child).

Rag Doll Swing/Broken Doll Swing

This is a full torso swing on the flat plane.

Stand in wide, with feet slightly wider than your shoulders.

The bending is deep in this swing, the rebound is in the torso.

If the depth of the bend isn't available to you, make the swing lighter and not dropping from so high, the knee bend will be lighter and softer.

- Legs are in wide.
- Tip and drop your torso sideways to the left on the flat plane. Your head, shoulder and arm are dropped sideways, like a broken doll.
- Lift your right arm straight up to the ceiling, as if you are pulled by a string. You are hanging from this string, with the left side dropped (or broken).
- Let the right arm fall across the front of your body (as though someone has cut its string) and it will swing across the body towards the left knee – the arm is almost shielding your face – up into a suspension and then let the arm swing back in an arc to the right high wide diagonal and let the body follow across the flat plane – opening the body.

- Then swing and return to the left (body and head following) with your head following, crossing the body.
- Then let it continue swinging over the top of the left diagonal in front of you, over the top of the arc/circle and descending and falling to the right, dropping down by your right knee. This will lift and then drop the body.
- Lift the left arm and repeat on the other side.
  This is an interesting swing, exploring a sensation of unbalance, asymmetrically, feeling broken, seeking freedom, losing to inertia. You are 'catching' the momentum through the bend in the knees and sensing the swing as it arcs through space.
  Like Petroushka in Stravinky's ballet, which was first performed by the Ballet Russes.

Figure of 8 Swing

- Starts with feet wide.
- Builds from tracing a figure of 8 on its side with your finger.
  The 8 starts as a curve away from you, then travels in a continuous movement:
- The movement builds into the wrist
- Then into the elbow
- Shoulder, the swing still lateral (sideways) with a release in the knees
- Then out into a front diagonal by shifting the opposite leg to arm forwards and dropping down and flicking/arching into backward space as the figure of 8 has changed orientation from side to diagonal inside a sphere
- The figure of 8 has shifted its axis from side to down and up, forward and back, on the diagonal the shoulder and arm will be turning inwards and outwards
- Then decrease the figure of 8, incrementally, returning foot to the side for the shoulder, elbow, wrist, finger
- The sensation is of expanding and contracting. The arc of the swing on the diagonal is over the top of your head and falling over the top of you towards your front knee, and then back up from the front. The curves here are in front and behind you in three dimensions, floating in your 'box'.

As you get more familiar with the sensation of dropping the weight in a swing, and finding balance, placement, as well as joy at the sense of freedom, you might start to consider which 'swing' might be useful for your personal warm-up or for a play, production or rehearsal.

The difference between how these swings are described and offered to acting students, or actors, is that, though they are technical, each swing and exercise also leads to a story, or an interpretation.

At the end of the First Year at both Rose Bruford and RADA, I introduced an 'autocours' based on Lecoq's Twenty Movements. Students were given a list of exercises they had learned in the first three terms, including several not recorded here, and asked to create, in a duo or trio, a scenario with a connection between them, to find drama and relationships and explore their use of space.

*

This section ends the exercises on Pure Movement. There are many more exercises, which are further recorded in books by Lizzie Ballinger and Jackie Snow.

8 In Praise of Play: Pure and Expressive Movement in Praise of Play

The Expressive exercises I introduce in the next part of the book ask us to re-enact the world around us through observation and play. Playfulness is an essential part of how to approach the Expressive Movement exercises in this book. 'Playfulness' provides actors and students the opportunities to discover for themselves, in the way children learn. Unlike the Pure Movement exercises, these aren't pathways, but provocations which open out the body and the imagination, and can, I believe, provide pathways to a changing theatre.

The responses that come from this, can be unique, and original.

Play can lead to innovation and sometimes theatre. Play is the link between Pure and Expressive Movement.

My son's first piece of theatre

One day when my son was about a year old, as I was giving him dinner in his highchair, the phone rang (it was the days before mobiles) and a work call momentarily distracted me.

He had a little plastic spoon and a bowl with a suckered bottom. It was early autumn, and sunshine poured through the window of our top floor flat. I turned to answer the phone, but turning back moments later I was dazzled by the sun. As my eyes adjusted, I saw my son, spoon in hand, enacting a perfectly mimed sequence, dipping the spoon into a ghostly bowl (next to the real bowl) and gently gliding his hand to feed a ghostly child opposite him. He opened his mouth as the spoon moved forward and closed it as it withdrew. Beautifully rhythmic and perfectly enacted. It took me a moment to realize that he was miming me feeding him, but in a very non-naturalistic manner. His gaze was rapt, caught up in sensing and remembering the activity. Time was suspended in a silence, potent and eery.

What was he doing? Playing at being me? Observing and exploring? Missing me?

*

I remembered how Lecoq had asked us to wear the Neutral Mask and to 'print' on our bodies the dynamics and movement patterns of the natural world. The Neutral Mask both observes a space it encounters and simultaneously becomes it. It has an openness, which leads it to discover everything it sees or experiences as if for the first time. A physical curiosity, with actions that mirror what it sees: simple, pared down, essential. Curious, rather than emotional. The actor and the space are one.

> Essentially, the neutral mask opens up the actor to the space around him. It puts him in a state of discovery, openness, of freedom to receive. It allows him to watch, to hear, to feel, to touch elementary things with the freshness of beginnings. (Lecoq, 2002 [1997])

The way into the mask might be as you would play a character, except this is not a character: there is no history, conflict or context. This is physical action.

> On the contrary, a neutral mask puts the actor in a state of perfect balance and economy of movement. Its moves have a truthfulness, its gestures and actions are economical. (Lecoq, 2002 [1997])

The truthfulness Lecoq refers to is a balance between an unembellished action (from the performer) and the moment of recognition from the audience. A re-enactment of life. The Neutral Mask is physically transformed, as they encounter different stories and scenarios, communicated through simple and amplified actions and gestures.

'Neutral', as I understand it, is like the neutral gear in a car, a place of departure from which other speeds, actions and journeys happen. Or a place of rest, or suspension in which you can be both 'alive' and 'ready'. It asks you to be open, to play.

*

My son was exploring action like a 'neutral mask'. He was already in a child-like state of openness, exploring how to be fed, or feed himself, as an act of mimesis.

> Mimesis:
> Aristotle and Plato used Mimesis as the theoretical principle in the creation of art. It is a Greek word and means imitation, not copying life but re-presenting life. Mimesis is the re-presentation of nature.

Play and mimesis are interlinked, as the ghostly mime of my son shows. You play at being, or doing, something else. Animals also 'learn' through play: witness kittens following their mother as she stalks prey.

Movement teaching has shown me how 'play', and the openness and freedom which comes from it, allows ideas to develop without judgement. Allowing for an exploration of form and content, without being rigidly held hostage to tradition. This, paradoxically, might help us lean more into a more original and timely response to the world around us. It might also help us find a pared down and poetic theatrical language, which carries more weight than words. The power of the body and physical expression carries its own resonances and codes of meaning.

Let us consider a set of stage directions as examples.

For many plays, stage directions are as open to interpretation as their dialogue. Stage directions offer a score for interpretation and a window into a time and place – or a timeless, placeless place.

*

Waiting for Godot (Beckett, 1965) is 'a tragi-comedy in two acts'. The play, written in 1952 and first performed in 1953, opens with stage directions (in italics in the commentary below), which seems to suggest a particular world.

> *Estragon, sitting on a low mound, is trying to take off his boot. He pulls at it with both hands, panting. He gives up exhausted, rests, tries again.*
> *As before.*

Enter Vladimir[1]

The setting for Act I is described as:
A country road. A tree. Evening.

And for Act II:
Next Day. Same Time. Same Place.
Estragon's boots front and centre, heels together, toes splayed. Lucky's hat in the same place.
The tree has four or five leaves.

How to 'play' these stage directions?[2] That are set in a non-specific time and place?

The Beckett Estate is clear that they must be played exactly as written. They are like a sculpture, carrying form and meaning through physical actions, meticulously described. But how should they be acted?

What exactly does Beckett mean by saying *Waiting for Godot* is a tragicomedy? Is the space theatrical or real? There is a tree, whose leaves appear in the second act, so is there a passage of time? The stage directions in Act II that follow the description of the tree and the boots show an agitation and alarm – the shoes, the silence, the absence.

Enter Vladimir agitatedly. He halts and looks long at the tree, then suddenly begins to move feverishly about the stage. He halts before the boots, picks one up, examines it, sniffs it, manifests disgust, puts it back carefully. (Beckett, 1965)

Many of the stage directions in *Waiting for Godot* are cyclical: the opening of the second half, the same as the first half, with minimalist changes, which are both significant and insignificant. The minimalism of the world we are in, a no-man's land of limited options. The tree is almost bare, and in the second act, though it sprouts a few leaves, is still bleak. Godot will always come tomorrow.

In 2015 a review of an Australian production of *Endgame* by Samuel Beckett criticized that when only sticking strictly to the stage directions, the play will be stuck in the past (Badham, 2015). This makes it hard for audiences to connect to, and risks it simply being a museum piece. But the impact of Beckett's plays when they first appeared was the opposite of this. The stage directions express the world and the context of the play and can always be relevant if they are brought to life with an understanding of either a context or a specific sense of a time in history.

*

I discovered a haunting possibility of the significance of the tree in Jeremy Eichler's book *Time's Echo*.[3] In 1937, Buchenwald Concentration Camp was built by prisoners who were to be its inmates. They cleared the trees on a limestone ridge in the forest[4] and built the camp through back-breaking labour, day after day, with very little proper equipment. Their guards

---

[1] (Beckett, 1965).
[2] The Beckett Estate is clear that there has to be a strict adherence to the stage directions.
[3] *Time's Echo* written by Jeremy Eichler examines the power of music, by composers from the Second World War, to transform these experiences into music.
[4] This was the forest on the slopes of the Ettersberg Hill near Weimar.

instructed them not to 'fell' a particular oak, which stayed, as they worked around it. This was Goethe's sacred oak tree, the tree he had eulogized in 1827, as under whose shade 'a person feels great and free … the way he always should be' (Eichler, 2024). As Eichler describes, it embodied the views of the German Enlightenment – humanist and European, values which the Nazis were destroying – but the guards saw Goethe and his tree as part of German culture to be preserved. According to Eichler, the camp their inmates constructed was built around the tree, and it remained as a ghostly reminder of a bucolic past in a brutalized present, barely alive. The tree survived, bare and stripped of leaves, over the seven years that saw the slaughter of thousands of inmates at the concentration camp and though it 'stayed standing', the leaves stopped appearing. I was haunted by the meaning of its survival. The Europe and the enlightenment it represented. In a photo taken by 'a prisoner with a stolen camera, its branches appear bare and skeletal, reaching up to an empty sky' (Eichler, 2024).

A bare tree, reaching up to an empty sky. A god that doesn't see. Is this the significance of the tree? Or could it be?

The play was written just after the Second World War as Europe renewed itself, in the shadow of the past. Beckett wrote it in French and lived in France during the war. Two men in limbo, trying to remember, repeating actions ad absurdum, with a sense of playful despair. In the shadow of a tree which holds this memory? Productions often refer to the vaudevillian influences in *Waiting for Godot*. But what is the hinterland, the backdrop, that forces the characters to repeat, to keep going?

Why is Estragon's boot stuck? The repeated action needs a rhythm.

How long does he rest for? (Rhythm).

How is he exhausted? (Attitude).

What does 'As before' mean? The exact physical action, same tempo, rhythm and attitude or a different tempo, more frustrated, angrier, or more despairing?

Though the repetition suggests a music-hall routine, there is a real action at its heart: Estragon wants to take his boot off and fails. And in the second half Vladimir's agitation 'manifests' in response to empty boots and a hat, and a tree whose leaves might suggest hope. A small renewal. But at the end of the play, the characters are still stuck.

Vladimir: Well? Shall we go?

Estragon: Yes, let's go.

They do not move.

These stage directions set the whole play in motion as a physical text. How to make this text have a context for now?

*

In Lithuania I saw a production of *Waiting for Godot* set in a shopping mall, pared down, with abandoned shopping trollies. It was performed in April 2022, just after Russia had invaded Ukraine. Lithuania was in a state of emergency, and all the artists I spoke to were afraid they too would be invaded. The Conservatoire was taking acting students from Kyiv, to help them continue their training. It felt precarious and the EU was dragging its feet to find ways (or not) to support Ukraine.

This was reflected in this production. The tree was a publicity column, as used in European cities to advertise plays and concerts. At the start of each act a new advert appeared (like the leaves) that referred to the current war. One potent one, *All Quiet on the Western*

Figure 9 Image from *Waiting for Godot*, directed by Roger Blin, France 1953. Getty.

Front, referred to Nato's lack of support for Ukraine; the other, *Midsummer's Nightmare*. In this version the two tramps were in a political limbo that we recognized, not the abstract Vaudevillian tramps of tradition. They were young and anguished. Their boots were trainers, and the 'repetitive action' of taking the boots off was translated into them having to work for big corporations by wearing inane advertisements as costumes which they also had to take off. Their economy had been 'colonized' by the West, and their freedom was threatened by the former Soviet Bloc, from which they liberated themselves in 1991. (I am presuming that the theatre had cleared this with the Beckett estate first.) However, Lithuania also has shadows of its own and was the first country in Eastern Europe to convince the Nazis[5] that much of Europe would raise little to no resistance to a Holocaust (Schama, 2025). Plays placed in an updated context can open an understanding of how to view their past as well.

---

[5]See the historian Simon Schama's *The Road to Auschwitz*, BBC Two, which shows the Holocaust as not just a Nazi crime but as a European crime of complicity.

I am not suggesting that productions of *Waiting for Godot* should only ever be staged with reference to contemporary geopolitical events. But the interplay between a context and a text can lift plays into a physical world that expresses the confusion or absurdity of the present. Being held hostage to tradition in how we stage plays or performances can stop audiences from really 'seeing' the importance of the actions, when delivered as part of an agreed canon of dramatic staging. The Lithuanian production was played with the inherent meaning of *Waiting for Godot*, to reflect the sense of anguish that was present at that time. The interplay of an image and an action on stage can carry powerful and resonant echoes of a political reality.

*

I want to consider how critical theory views literary theatre – the idea of character, text and context as outdated, and how this might impact on theatre and drama school training. As the examples above show, however absurd or non-naturalistic the setting is, the actors still need the skills to communicate the world they inhabit.

Postdramatic theatre, according to Hans Thies Lehmann (Lehmann, 2006), has replaced text-based theatre as a way of re-presenting our world, making it more relevant – an art form to reflect contemporary experience. It creates a theatre where 'character in acting' doesn't exist, and plays are replaced by intertextuality – media, sound and images. This reflects the multiplicity of contemporary experience, which is culturally diverse and fluid in terms of identity, and equally politically dynamic, with post-war ideas of democracy and liberal values no longer accepted as a norm. A theatre text is not just words, but sound, movement, lights and video. If this is true, a performance will need to encompass more than a body, a play and a space. So how does actor training respond to this? What are the skills that the performers and creatives need, to make these performances effective. Do the actors still need to have trained in the traditional skills of voice, movement and acting? I am circling back to that same discussion that the movement department had in 2020, when discussing the Student Action Plan.[6] Are these ideas enough to make radical changes in theatre and performance effective, or do we still need to be able to work with craft as well? Training in craft is expensive, takes time and focuses on the individual actor.

There has often been a tension between more experimental performance courses and conservatoire-based training. For instance, when Drama Centre was part of Central Saint Martins, they were often in discussion with tutors from the design course, who argued that the dramaturgy of the design was more relevant than the embodiment of skills that the actors were training in. There is an implied understanding that training that focuses solely on craft denies actors access to experimental work. That actors who come from a 'literary' theatre or one that either represents nature, or stages plays traditionally in terms of style and period, can't work in any different registers. But as I will show, technical craft and expertise don't prevent experimentation or the expansion of form or aesthetic. The dialogue between the artist and the theatre or director is equal, virtuosic skill being channelled through ideas. It is possible to argue that both disciplines are 'minority practices' and coexist with a tense agreement between them.

---

[6]See Chapter 1, Introduction.

> Literature and theatre, which are aesthetically mutually dependent on each in a productive relation of repulsion and attraction, both being demoted to the status of minority practices. (Lehmann, 2006)

The theatre industry is moving this way, with plays, revivals and theatre increasingly drawing on the post-dramatic within a current economic model. By that I mean that productions are staged perhaps without the laboratory approaches of the universities, or long rehearsal periods. But the interest in the experimental productions of Ivo van Hove and the success of Robert Icke's revivals of *Oedipus*, or the *Oresteia*, prove that audiences are open to new ways of telling stories on stage.

Post-dramatic theatre as described by Lehmann considers Epic Theatre (Brecht) and Aristotelian theatre as part of the same dramatic tradition: fables and stories to make the audience feel something or think something, in opposition to the idea of non-theatre theatre – a theatre without drama, whose open-endedness reflects a sense of transition – and perhaps the end of everything that our world has now become. Theatre is or as performance, spooling into the present day, not as 'the representation of a closed-off fictional cosmos, the mimetic staging of a fable' (Lehmann, 2006). There is a making of theatre now, which takes apart the conventions of suspension of disbelief that previously said we are putting real life on stage.[7] And these performances are proving to be very successful and still rely on actors acting.

How does this connect to movement training? The body in the space has always been part of theatre, along with the voice of the actor. Theatre is essentially a sensuous experience for actor and audience. It has never been just literature. Every play text has powerful examples of action, text and character, whatever the setting. Many drama schools see the necessity to include this de-construction of theatre: because on paper it allows for the presence of more voices and identities, whilst at the same time transformation has been seen as denying the actors' the value of their own identities. The pursuit of a Stanislavski-based series of exercises to explore actions and objectives is often seen as too difficult, and extraneous to the pressing ideas of identity, for young actors.[8]

> Feminist theory, queer theory and postcolonial scholarship, as well as the more recent analysis of disability and performance and age performance, have all pointed out that performance has the power to question and destabilize the spectator's construction of identity and the 'other' – more so than realist mimetic drama, which remains caught in representation and thus often reproduces prevailing ideologies. (Lehmann, 2006)

Identity is fluid. We change over time. Our bodies change, the world changes. Our responsibility is no longer to represent reality but to destabilize these representations. Performance needs to question.

How do we find ways to include these different approaches without damaging depth in training? There are surprising examples to test this.

---

[7] *Oklahoma* at the Young Vic, directed by Daniel Fish and Jordan Fein, still used the original choreography of Agnes de Mille, but set the production in a community centre, with actor musicians making the story-telling far from naturalistic, and breaking the fourth wall with the audience.

[8] These observations are taken from my minutes of meetings discussing the SAP at RADA, and the subsequent dismantling of the acting course, at least while I was employed there, which argued that the Uta Hagan-based acting exercises on playing actions and objectives were too hard for young actors.

Some contemporary classical music uses 'play' to explore the synthesis between composer and musician and poses piercing questions about the individual in relation to musical expression. These delve into what might be described as postdramatic performances of music. Dr Laura Bowler's 'composition' for the virtuosic pianist Zubin Kanga entitled SHOW(ti)ME for piano, voice, MiMU gloves[9] and electronics is a multilayered piece that Caroline Potter describes as evoking 'the pressure on performers' for perfection in her online review of 3 October 2023 (icareifyoulisten.com). It interweaves the pianist's obsessive repetition of musical phrases with clichés from the wellness industry pinging in health-giving advice as if from your phone, delivered as videos. The musician is seen at the end wearing a crash helmet in the shape of a mirror-ball to withstand the noise impact of the last movement, whilst sitting at the side of the stage indulging in a self-care routine of tea: a synthesis of wit, self-reflexive critique and musicianship.

All creative expression, when exploring fluid responses to identity and artistic form, still needs technique – the freedom that craft and technique give you to work in any register you want. Pure Movement and Actors' Movement training is a valuable body of work that has its place in contemporary practice as a rigorous technique and syllabus to enable acting and innovation at the same time.

The actor is an individual. You train the individual. There is no aesthetic, philosophy or predetermined outcome, as there might be in ballet training. And this emphasis on the actor in training, rather than on theory, can look at the actor in a contemporary context. Let us call this an 'organic' approach to theatre training and to acting and theatre making. 'Organic' because you look at the body in training (or on stage) as a way into the situation and the scene. You might say: 'slow down' or 'open out' or 'pick up that book as if you hadn't seen it before'. Or 'notice if you are holding tension in your tummy here', 'is that tension useful for the action or the situation?'

The body is also part of any theatrical text. The actor's body doesn't have to be a certain type/person/sexual orientation/race/class/gender to play in the acting space.

Working 'organically' means creating physical text and theatrical staging from the playscript (or stage directions) and then allowing it to emerge out of a rehearsal process with the actors and the creatives that interpret that world, or (in the case of Beckett) respond to the resonances in the stage directions.

Stage directions and social realism

Social realism of the post war placed an important emphasis on the body in the space. The actions were often based on the writer's observations, pared into stage directions. The postwar theatre focus was on ordinary people and their problems, with the detail written into the stage directions, leading the audience to understand the social issues – to think with feeling.

When John Burgess ran his writing course for aspiring writers, he had a 'homework' that he called 'actors have bodies'. I mention this because Burgess himself was in a lineage of

---

[9]Software for composing and performing music using movement, designed/discovered by the musician Imogen Heap. Their use straddles different artists from beat-boxers, vocalists, classical pianists and Ariane Grand on her world tour in 2015. I was fascinated by the synthesis between music and movement which goes right back to Dalcroze and Eurythmy.

the 'body-based training' that Michel Saint-Denis brought to this country. He worked with Peter Gill, who came from the Royal Court, when it was run by George Devine. Burgess had also trained with Roger Planchon in Paris whose Théâtre National Populaire was founded as 'a people's theatre' to bring culture to working-class audiences. Performances at the Edinburgh Festival were praised for a 'physicality' and 'freshness' that was like some of Joan Littlewood's productions. The specificity of the physicality came from Brecht's influence on Planchon and how he approached directing 'historical theatre'. Brecht's idea was that the production of historical theatre came from researching the lives of working people. Something which the Copiaus[10] themselves had done, when living and working in Burgundy.

> The layering of complex social realities produced work that was once historically accurate and intensely poetic. (Bradby, 2009)

There is a balance to be struck between social accuracy and how that distils into poetry. The poetry is expressed as a physical enactment, where the physical text is taken through the actor's body. The body holds powerful information about who we are and the world we live in. If you transfer that 'body' to an imagined scenario it can communicate the details of this without words or exposition and can amplify the text. If you add the creative and interpretive choices of how you move in space, in relation to each other, or the set, with how you might work with objects or entrances or exits, you have a physical text which supports the 'literary' text. The actor is aware of the meaning they are making. The staging, the movement and the text all support one another.

In fact, in a 'social realist' text in particular, the stage directions and the atmosphere created by sound effects, or how an actor creates what they are looking at, are often written into the text. This relates directly back to the run.stop.go exercises I do with students, where I ask 'what do you see?' Actors have bodies, which these playwrights from that time understood. It is a sensibility that is particular to that time, and, as I propose, comes directly from the Michel Saint-Denis tradition. The body is not demonstrative or choreographed, but a tacit embodiment of character, text and situation. For a naturalistic text, with silences and subtext, this is a wonderful resource.

> The sound of the sea pounding against the shore.
> A maroon goes off, it is very loud, the sound splinters and echoes.
> Fifteen seconds' pause. A maroon, as before. Fifteen seconds' pause. A
> third maroon.
> Lights pull up:

This is from Robert Holman's *German Skerries*. Set in 1977, this four-hander takes place at a birdwatching spot on the North Sea in Teesside. Interweaving between friendships and married relationships and death, the play uses the backdrop of environmental dangers caused by industrialization. The extract is from the beginning of Scene Two: the characters are then described as standing together in their best night out clothes. There is a *'slight storm'* and *'the air is damp'*.

---

[10] See Chapter 9 for further comments on Les Copiaus. Les Copiaus were a touring theatre troupe formed by Jacques Copeau in 1924. They worked with physically expressive forms of theatre, including masks and improvisation.

These are the first lines of the scene; after at least half a minute to a minute of silent story telling.

JACK: (excited) Look a' that, there it is, it's a flare – it's the lifeboat
CAROL: Frightened me to death, it's spooky
JACK: Sommat's 'appened somewhere. (Holman, 2016)

The other factor in this opening sequence is time. The time between the maroons. Time enough for us to hear the sea. Sound. The sound of the maroons, the sound of the sea and the wind. The sounds of the words – the s's following one another, ''sommat' after 'spooky'. And space. How the actors, by looking out, tell the audience that they see the sea. Like a piece of music, this whole first minute of theatre creates mood, emotion, atmosphere. All of which will be created together through direction, sound, lighting and the bodies of the actors in the designed theatre space.

Is there space for this in Lehmann's argument that postdramatic theatre has permanently influenced our understanding of postdramatic action, where character is seen as no longer necessary? The naturalistic detail in this play belies all this as it relies on the specific craft of actor, director, designer etc. working as an orchestra to make the 'ordinary' extraordinary, bringing a numinous lucidity to the everyday. Lehmann's seems to be a circular argument, as it is used as a term/descriptor that links experimental and contemporary theatre since the 1970s as sharing an aesthetic. Even though much of this is based on the use of space and intertextuality, which relies on the actor's body to bring this form of theatre to life, there is no mention of the impact movement training has had on postdramatic theatre; even though the discoveries of the dramatic and narrative potential that movement can bring to theatre and as it was developed in drama schools (as I have shown) became a key player in taking acting into the twentieth and twenty-first centuries – all of which in the current discussions about experimental theatre has been ignored.[11] In fact, I would argue that the presence of movement training as it was practised in most drama schools up until 2020 allowed for writing which both broke form,[12] whilst also allowing actors a language to inhabit the detailed naturalism of post-war theatre. This lack of curiosity of the specificity and potential of actor movement training (and by extension all actor training) has been whispering in the wings and increasingly gaining traction in all policymaking decisions about how to train an actor in the UK. While at the same time the expansion of laboratory-based theatre studies in universities, is seen as an alternative to what is often dismissed as 'traditional training' in the conservatoires.

Perhaps the 'academic' practitioners and their advocates have the backing of academia and intellectual theory, which gives them voices that are regarded as more powerful evidence of relevance, than the practice-based approaches of most vocational-based training. In fact, there has often been a tension between these two strands, vocational training on the one hand and laboratory-based 'experimental' training on the other.

---

[11] By this I mean the craft and training of movement for theatre: the names of practitioners are often used as signifiers to different movement approaches and languages.
[12] Sarah Kane and Simon Stephens who write the text to be spoken, for instance, whilst leaving the allocation of lines and production to the director and the actors.

The Theatre Lab at RADA offers a much more practical approach to a laboratory-based training, but again, reading the prospectus in 2023, it appears to set out its stall as an alternative to in-depth training and 'more traditional' training. The Theatre Lab, we are told, encourages students to experiment, and 're-addresses acting as an embodied and exploratory art-form at the heart of the theatre making process', with 'actor-centred' approaches.

However, actor training when it focuses on the body is experimental, in the sense of experimenting with how to bring a text or a character to life, both body centred (actors have bodies) and actor centred.

I want to deconstruct the idea of physical embodiment being unique to postdramatic theatre and argue that all acting is embodied and always has been. I have a proposal to make that shows how an actor in full command of their instrument can work in many different registers, including experimental theatre.

*

In 2002 Caryl Churchill's play *A Number* was played at The Royal Court, with Michael Gambon and Daniel Craig. The play explores whether identity is constructed and interrogates open-endedly what makes 'personality'. There is a father and son relationship, with Daniel Craig playing two versions of one son, or is Bernard Two cloned? The play tapped into the current concerns about cloning, which can (I presume) be now replaced with concerns about AI. The dramatic structure is played with through Churchill's use of language and embodied by two naturalistically and stylistically adroit actors. Lyn Gardner in her review in *The Guardian* refers to their physical clarity: *'Gambon nervously dons a tie and gazes into vacancy'*; *'Daniel Craig, by the simplest of gestures, shows the difference between'* the two sons.

It is possible, I suppose, that Lehmann might argue that this is a fable in a world requiring mimetic drama, as opposed to non-theatre (and non-acting): but the form of the play text is open-ended, and there is no naturalistic detail in the stage directions aside from deliberately ambiguous frontispiece:

Characters
SALTER, a man in his early sixties
BERNARD, his son, forty
BERNARD, his son, thirty-five
MICHAEL BLACK, his son, thirty-five
The play is for two actors. One plays Salter, the other his sons.
The scene is the same throughout, it's where Salter lives. (Churchill, 2008)

There have been several productions of this play since it was first produced at The Royal Court in 2002, which show that the world can be abstract or specific. The actor is embodying the experimental here: using their craft to respond to the demands of the theatre or the text (if they differ from each other).

This is no different to a classically trained musician who can adapt his or her craft/their craft to the demands of the music. Modern classical music may play with form, explode what we might think of as music, but the classically trained musician will be able to play it. The modern composer won't have to recruit players from courses that only train musicians for modern classical music – the musicians may prefer to work in this area, but their training will equip them for all types of music making. In fact, arguably, the better trained the musician the better able they are to adapt elastically to the 'new methods' used in music that modern music demands, which is often seen as intellectually and technically very demanding. New methods comprising the innovative use of electronics and multi-media.

My provocation is that experimental theatre is best served by properly trained actors. And that the so-called tensions between experimental theatre and traditional theatre are less present than immediately assumed. The link across all of this is play and transformation. I am making a distinction between theatre which plays with form, and what an actor needs to be able to do to play in this theatre.

Actors play, and this, I believe, is postdramatic, dramatic, postmodernist, experimental, non-naturalistic. Whatever the score of performance demands, they will and can do. A training that has depth, doesn't mean that the theatre the actor contributes to is traditional.

Michael Gambon is possibly best known for playing Dumbledore in the Harry Potter movies, but his work in the theatre is interesting here: not only his work though, but his presence. When I worked at the National Theatre as a young actor, the older actors were exhilarating and unpredictable and you never knew what to expect when you met them in the canteen or the corridor. Gambon was playful, silent, enigmatic, mischievous, small of voice, large of voice, delicate, mournful, gentle, fierce. He straddles the last century, having started at the Old Vic in Olivier's company and played at the National, morphing (and remaining himself) in Miller, Brecht, Ben Johnson, Beckett, Pinter. He was part of a company of British Actors who worked the repertoire of plays and productions that required the actors to rally the art of transformation like competitive sport played in clowns' noses – both serious and irreverent.

Irreverence also seems to be part of the postdramatic tradition.

You 'play' the character and serve the play or the piece of theatre.

The French for actor is 'comédien' and for acting is 'jouer'.

Play. Play is discovery, exploration, an opportunity to inhabit someone or something that in real life is dangerous, troublesome, unattainable, outside of your experience, is linked to time, starts and ends with a sense of purpose. All actors play. Play is a shibboleth that distinguishes the tribe actor. Actors who really know how to play 'see' one another in the rehearsal room and play at double games, constantly introducing a sense of risk and unpredictability into performance – often they can't help it. When I was at the National, we knew when Michael Gambon was in the building when the water bombs 'whizzed past the dressing room windows'. In a YouTube clip asking how he 'approached' the role of Dumbledore, Gambon describes arriving at makeup looking unprepossessing, crumpled, unready, and as the makeup and the whiskers, wig, costume arrives so the character appears: he says it is like playing a mask, you look in the mirror and see who you are and then you become it.[13] David Jays in his obituary refers to Gambon's physicality as 'A really interesting body

---

[13] This is exactly how you play a mask, and shows Gambon's level of sophistication: this is the Jacques Copeau approach to working with character masks, and there were exercises and opportunities to explore this at the National Theatre, from the influence of Michel Saint-Denis at the Old Vic.

and a will to transform it' with 'the strong shoulders' that 'could sag, the bunched fists drop helplessly by his side' (Jays, 2023). The will to transform is what an actor has.

So, to act, 'jouer', play, is to have a private self, doubled with a metier where you can be different to 'yourself' but only for a short space of time, not for the duration of a lifetime. In 'play' you could dazzle and infuriate as Millamant with a fizz of words and wit to celebrate the end of solitude and half mock your agreement to marry, which can take you dancing right to the edge of fun and then after you have taken off the garments of the character, go home to a quiet cuppa. You do not have to be the part to play the part, you can double and be different to yourself:

> Millamant: Ah don't be impertinent. My dear liberty, shall I leave thee? My faithful solitude, my darling contemplation, must I then bid you then adieu? Ay-h, adieu; my morning thoughts, agreeable wakings, indolent slumbers, all ye douceurs, ye sommeils du matin, adieu. (Congreve, 1999)

Millamant from *The Way of the World* plays all the time, words, attitudes, playing one person off against another, and with her lover, Mirabel.

None of this is at odds with postdramatic theatre. In fact it is (arguably) axiomatic to it. In the introduction to Lehmann, Karen Juers-Munby quotes from Tim Etchell's comments on 'Performance Writing', which explode ideas of what writing for the stage is. He argues that there is a 'rich history of writers in rehearsal spaces doing something quite different' from the narrow idea of what most British theatre considers as writing. There is also a rich history of movement teachers in rehearsal spaces exploring 'writing' with the body, and a rich history of actors who exist in two planes, acting and real life, making something 'quite different' happen every night.

And (positively) here is the double bind; to play at someone else, you need to be in charge of your craft, have ownership of what your body, your imagination (and of course your voice) can do. Play, for the 'job' of acting, is only possible if you have craft.

Part III Movement in the world

9 Chameleon

The drama and surprise of Animal Study

The next chapters explore how actors can work expressively and imaginatively. The playful classes of Expressive Movement give actors space and time to experiment by working with long immersive improvisations. They also hone observation and empathy. Embodying the world around you, you experience 'being' something different to yourself.[1] By playing an animal, or moving like water, you 'stretch' to the edges of your expression and imagination, through a process of analogy – 'moving like something'. There are exciting and surprising links to acting classes and classical text by using physical transformation as a springboard. Here are what some of these creative investigations are.

- **Animal Study**. The study of the physical expression of an animal, and how to take that into a physical characterization.
- **Elements**. The physical form and expression of the four elements: earth, fire, air and water, taking that through the spine, and the use of space and breath. This can be adapted to explore how 'matter' moves, to find it's character, or it's animal.[2]
- **Movement qualities**. Movement qualities are the building blocks of both animals and elements.

By looking at how something moves – a feather or a piece of paper – we can break down its movement qualities. We then use these as springboards for a character or a response.

These transformations are arrived at through observation. Observation is empirical, you can't have a political or social opinion about what you 'see' if you really look. You see, transform, observing how that shift affects your movement and your view of the world. When you change how you move, you experience living as a new entity (animate or sometimes inanimate), empathizing, using your imagination. These classes ask actors to be playful, and to work with a different kind of logic from that of reading a script and coming to conclusions about character or situation taken from the page. The more an actor trains physically, understanding how their body moves, feeling connected to their weight, or their balance, the more they can trust that the body can also speak and make meaning, with as much nuance as words on a page.

*

---

[1] This presupposes that 'being' something or someone else is still part of what an actor does, which seems to cause some discussion these days.
[2] The physical embodiment of the elements is explained in *The Moving Body* (Lecoq, 2002 [1997]). Matter is also mentioned, and can also be explored analogously – moving like something to create a physical characterization, or emotional or physical response.

Real Life as material: Then and now

Real life studies were part of the new body-based approaches to actor training which established themselves in British drama schools. Animal Study, along with Neutral Mask and Character Mask[3] developed from the work of Jacques Copeau in France. Animal Study was introduced to British Drama Schools by Michel Saint-Denis and George Devine in the 1930s, and were non-verbal exercises, described as 'animal pantomime' (Wardle, 1978) – an example of the power of silence. Movement was vital to these exercises on observation, which changed the idea of actors being upright, rhetorical tragedians, or matinee idols, to that of fluid and dynamic expressive artists. Students keenly observed the life around them, using its physical life as a starting point for acting. The search for an actor's physicality which is true and expressive is not new. Even Shakespeare was critical of declamatory and rhetorical performance.[4] Acting always needs a body and a spine.[5]

> Let your own discretion be your tutor. Suit the action to the word, the word to the action, with this special observance, that you o'erstep not the modesty of nature …. hold, as 'twere the mirror up to nature, to show virtue her own feature, scorn her own image, and the very age and body of the time his form and pressure. (Shakespeare, *Hamlet*, 1980)

When I started to teach Animal Study in 1989 at Central School of Speech and Drama, it was already an established part of the curriculum in most schools. But the legacy of Michel Saint-Denis also extended to mask work, which, as I will show, used to be a vibrant part of psychologically based acting – relying as it did on the actor's powers of transformation.

At Drama Centre, Michel Saint-Denis's legacy lay in the mask work John Blatchley introduced alongside Animal Study. This work on transformation through play was very sophisticated and was complemented by the psycho-physical work of Yat Malgrem's 'Character Analysis' and Vakhtangov classes led by Oleg Mirochnikov – which combine psychological realism with heightened theatrical expression.[6]

All these classes gave actors the confidence and courage to know how to observe real life which can be crafted into dramatic expression. When Drama Centre London was at Back Hill in Farringdon[7] there was a street market opposite – Exeter Market – which was an endless resource for eccentricity, originality and real-life studies (as well as cheap costumes and joke noses).

Many schools teach Animal Study, and every school I taught Animal Study at has left its mark on my pedagogy.

---

[3]As taught in drama schools until recently.
[4]Lawyers and barristers frame their arguments through rhetoric: many politicians have been Lawyers, but their understanding of rhetoric doesn't guarantee emotionally connected and alive delivery.
[5]Please refer to Chapter 7 on the spine in three dimensions.
[6]See Oleg Mirochnikov's website for more details. Yevgeni Vakhtangov (1822–1922) founded the Vakhtangov Studio in Moscow. He was a close associate of Stanislavski and a mentor of Michael Chekhov. His work was a synthesis of Stanislavski and Meyerhold, which he referred to as 'Fantastic Realism'. According to Mirochnikov, the work explores the relationship of truth to artifice, and develops physicality linking psychology to theatrical physical expression.
[7]This was in the early 2000s.

Animal Study is based on observing an animal at close quarters, and then realizing its essence, life-force and physicality. Using real life as inspiration from which to create theatre developed both movement training and socially and politically aware theatre. It is helpful to trace this lineage, to see how intrinsic these approaches were to the innovations in British Theatre and to training.[8]

Jacques Copeau

Jacques Copeau has been described as the father of physical theatre. But his research and practice was much more than this. His innovation was to explore how to make a new theatre that put the focus on the author's text, or the playwright, through the actor's truthful and expressive use of the body and the space. This is also the heart of all movement training in drama schools and is why I urge its principals and senior managers to study its history.

Jacques Copeau (1879–1949) was a French theatre critic who, frustrated with the boulevard star system in Paris, decided to start his own theatre and training programme in response to the 'fakery' and exhibitionism of French theatre which he saw as a dying art.[9] In 1918, he founded a privately financed independent theatre company. The work and training would develop a poetry for theatre and work with a 'moral purpose' to train a new generation of (French) actors who were physically expressive and collaborative. They trained in past models: Molière, Shakespeare, Japanese Noh Theatre and Commedia dell'Arte troupes. Copeau was researching the act of 'performance' to determine what all theatre had in common with itself. He initiated practical and technical approaches by working with these historical precedents: the actor's metier as craftsperson and artisan, transmitted through a practice, the old art of theatre, informing a new way of working.

The training was initiated and researched by a young group of challenging thinkers and actors.[10] They also developed mask work. Mask work was part of the twentieth century's fascination with the roots of drama. Copeau's mask improvisations explored ways to reinvent fundamental principles of physical, imaginative and personal transformations to explore how an actor can find the 'roots' of their own theatrical expression. This aspect of mask work, the actor digging into the 'roots' of their own expression, is what I also discovered at Lecoq, and has driven my own research into the Neutral Mask. So for Copeau and his students and later co-creators, theatre was not just literary, it was also ritualistic and physical, and its roots lay in the oldest forms of theatre – a totality of theatre, which needed actors trained for this approach. Movement, or how an actor moved, was a key part of this training, finding a simplicity and unembellished physical language. Copeau referred to the working actions of carpenters or agricultural workers as examples of how to move with economy and grace on stage. He researched 'the body in the space' by getting his actors to cover their faces and then do a series of simple actions – sitting, standing, walking – using

---

[8]My research comes from a number of sources: David Bradby, George Devine, Mark Evans and conversations with Dr Coldiron.
[9]It is useful to consider if this is still the case in our theatre and theatre in Europe.
[10]His followers and pupils were: Michel Saint-Denis, Suzanne Bing, Louis Jouvet, Charles Dullin, Etienne Decroux and Jean Dasté, among others. Michel Saint-Denis founded the Old Vic Theatre School, as discussed earlier, and Lecoq was influenced by Jean Dasté.

just their bodies to communicate with. This was the original research for the Noble Mask, which Lecoq developed into the Neutral Mask. When I discovered the reference to carpenters and agricultural labourers, I questioned this romanticization of the 'working man' as both an archetype and an ideal.[11] Perhaps this is always the intellectual's perpetual ambiguity about their own body's capacity to be expressive. The epithet that a 'worker' will be more in touch with the 'land' and 'real life' than they are.[12] But the experiment and open-ended research is compelling when we remember this was 1918. Very little work of this sort continues in our drama schools today.

Michel Saint-Denis

Michel Saint-Denis developed the detail of Animal Study further, by asking the actors to go to the zoo, and make their observations specific and theatrical.[13] This was like a solo 'etude', which the actor prepared without too much intervention from the teacher, testing their ability to physically embody detail and create a dramatic study. This approach is what many drama schools have inherited and still practised up until relatively recently.

Saint-Denis was also instrumental in developing mask work and physical characterizations based on observing real life and using those observations as pathways to both truthful and comedic acting. Some of this was passed on to John Blatchley, who worked at Drama Centre, introducing play and mask work. This also led to George Devine and then Bill Gaskill developing mask work at the Royal Court. Mask work was also taught by George Hall – who was trained at the Old Vic Theatre School – at Central School of Speech and Drama.

Jacques Lecoq

Jacques Lecoq also introduced exercises that re-played everyday life, with economy. These 'enquêtes' researched, almost anthropologically, the physical life of places – stations, markets, villages – which were re-enacted and crafted as pieces of theatre. The work on dynamics developed a language of specificity on how to physically embody the four elements and how people moved in different locations. This training gave actors a methodology to work as a collective, and an ensemble. Jacques Lecoq also developed the Neutral Mask, and introduced the Larval Masks and Character Masks, while also updating The Greek Chorus and rediscovering the Commedia dell'Arte. He developed his particular innovative mask work,[14] by collaborating with the mask maker Amleto Sartori and has probably had the most extensive impact on mask and physical theatre.

The Royal Court

Under the leadership of George Devine, the Royal Court Theatre championed new writing by working-class playwrights, which foregrounded truth and real life. Bringing real

---

[11] *Jacques Copeau* by John Rudlin (1986).
[12] See below for Michael Elliot's reference to Litz Pisk.
[13] See Lee Montague's description later in this chapter (Montague, 2023).
[14] See Chapter 12 on the Neutral Mask.

life onstage proposed that working-class lives were centre stage. George Devine also developed mask work at the Royal Court. Other teachers too, like Bill Gaskill, would lead classes and workshops on mask work. Many new plays at the Royal Court asked actors to research the working lives of the characters in the plays – for instance Arnold Wesker's *The Kitchen*.

*

This lineage shows how the study of physical life and the observation of everyday life of ordinary people combined to influence a new form of theatre in post-war Britain. Ordinary people and their problems, the life of the street transposed to stage, and the making of dramatic action out of ordinary scenarios. The 'ritual' in theatre was transposed to a new aesthetic – theatre as simple, uncluttered and unembellished, based on observation and an appreciation of real life. A bare stage with an actor telling a story. The actor having the craft and body to communicate effectively in the theatre space.

*

Even as early as the 1930s, Michel Saint-Denis based his training on the direct observation of life.

Here is an example of acting exercises set for students at the London Theatre Studio[15] in the 1930s. They were asked to visit Chapel Street Market and Collins Music Hall, both nearby, combined with visits to London Zoo for the animal study, and encouraged to use this raw material for animal studies, improvisation and comedy.

> In the market and in the streets of Islington they were expected to keep their eyes open and select living models for character improvisation, padding themselves out with bottoms, bellies and hunched shoulders designed by the Motleys.[16] Side by side with formal training, much of the work was based on direct observation of life. (Wardle, 1978)

Real life replaced classical plays and literature, inspiring a more vibrant and lively theatre. The distortion of the body with fake padding might seem inappropriate for students to today[17] – especially if they are seeking a transformation that is more true-to-life.

Markets, life, observation as a way into 'transformation', the small dramas of everyday life are all around us, asking us to re-live them with attention to detail and an analytical eye. There was the market on the Rue Faubourg St Denis in Paris that we walked down every day, near the Lecoq school. From the shouting and jostling and bargaining, we observed the physical rhythms, the different working actions of the traders and the dynamics of different times of day. By the end of the first year, we had enough physical skills and understanding

---

[15]London Theatre Studio was opened in 1938, several years before the Old Vic Theatre School. Some of the staff from LTS joined to the Old Vic Theatre School when it opened in the 1940's.
[16]Resident designers at the school.
[17]Although, interestingly, sometimes when the students are moving from animal into character they often bring these in as physical masks, to enhance their characterizations.

of dynamics to be able to analyse movement[18] – so as to recreate these spaces dispassionately and with playful physical accuracy.

Thus, animal study, alongside observation, in these schools dates to the beginning of the twentieth century when Copeau first began to develop a coherent training for his actors.

*

A critique of the idea of training for a theatre that doesn't exist, and idealism

Theatre training at the Old Vic, shared an ethos and made sure that the classes supported each other. There was also an idealistic belief that the training would change the theatre. This was inherited by many drama schools and certainly was still in place when I started teaching,[19] but equally and arguably was not always welcomed by directors whose focus was on a more pragmatic approach to making theatre. Sue Lefton once described this as 'training for a theatre that doesn't exist'. Training the next generation to carry forward the aesthetic and expectations of its teachers has now given us pause to think and is much harder to do today.

For instance, Wardle (1978) points to an 'impossible puritanism' where nothing can ever measure up, and the idea of theatre being entertainment, or a trade, is seen as being at odds with the purer version of acting and theatre that the training offered. However, it is important to acknowledge how this 'impossible puritanism' positively affected the Royal Court, the RSC and the National, in their promotion of the idea of the ensemble and programming productions that expressed the physical and social truth of contemporary society. And these companies were funded by the Arts Council to work in this way.

> Neither in Copeau's lifetime nor in Saint-Denis's did it materialize,[20] but the idea goes marching on in the community and laboratory stages in the 1970s … Young actors and drama students then were no less idealistic than they are now, but when they looked round there was nowhere to make a living out of serious work.

Wardle's comments are not strictly true, as there were many Fringe theatre companies in the 1970s – often political,[21] and also funded. His criticism is more relevant today. Serious work needs funding. How can you sustain yourself through a desire to make a different kind of theatre without it? As a professional actor, you have a choice: earn a living or take a

---

[18]Analyse de Mouvement was one of the physical classes Lecoq taught, where he would present a sequence from everyday life, like a bartender mixing a cocktail, or punting in a boat, and break it down into movement phrases of pushing or pulling: which we could then transpose to our own observations of physical activity to use when we replayed everyday life. Some of the analysis is quite close to mime, like climbing a wall for instance, or ice skating, and so beyond the scope of this book, but the principles are useful and I cover some of them in Chapter 10.

[19]When I started teaching these were: Rose Bruford, Guildhall, LAMDA, Drama Centre, East 15 and Central School of Speech and Drama. These schools had all inherited body-based training systems.

[20]An idealized theatre company.

[21]Monstrous Regiment (feminist), Gay Sweatshop, Black Theatre Co-Op, the Brighton Collective, Joint Stock, Shared Experience, Common Stock, to name a few.

financial personal risk. Very few actors can afford to do that today, unless they have a private income.[22]

Michel Saint-Denis and George Devine were training their actors to be good actors, making good theatre, to align with their tastes and aspirations for theatre. But were they only the pedagogical gatekeepers to a theatre they approved of? Another, at the time, young actor (Peter Ustinov), trained at the Old Vic Theatre School in the 1930s, went further in his criticism, pointing out how difficult it was for young actors to be expected to carry the mantle:

> It represented ideals to people who were embarking on a profession which in this country has always been linked to the fairground and show business. We were *therefore very vulnerable people who were trying to purify the theatre*.[23]

Teaching is very different today. The well-being and development of the student is at the heart of training, but there is less clarity about the ethos of the training, or even what its common principles are.

It is interesting, therefore, to go back to the 1940s, to see the impact of theatre training on a young actor and gauge what the differences might be.

Animal Study through the eyes of a drama student in 1948

I mention above how the Old Vic Theatre School would send students to the zoo to study animals.

As Lee Montague described it: when you played the animal, you also chose 'how' to show it, the drama should be part of your study. This is the critique Michel Saint-Denis gave of Montague's *Chameleon* in 1948, when I interviewed him in 2023, which he remembered verbatim. 'I like it when you are still, but it would be more interesting if you were still and moved again and then were still. Still, move, still, move, still, then move' (Montague, 2023).

Lee Montague trained at the Old Vic Theatre School after the war; he was in Group 3. I interviewed him in June 2023 to find out what it was like working with Saint-Denis, Litz Pisk and John Blatchley, some of the key figures who shaped post-war body-based theatre training. I asked how he had experienced these innovative methods firsthand, and how he had made sense of them as part of his craft?

There was also a personal reason to interview him. Montague had grown up in the East End and, like my father, his family were first generation immigrants. He was also a close friend of my father.

So I was also curious if being a working-class second-generation immigrant had held him back. Today there is a concern that actors from marginalized backgrounds, like my father and Montague were, will find it hard to identify with a classical training, unless the training is adapted to accommodate this.[24]

Lee Montague describes his experiences of much of his training as a 'stretch'. He understood it as stretching the body, the voice and the emotion as far as it could go. A director

---

[22] It cannot be overestimated how much being able to 'sign-on' when you were out of work helped fund experimental theatre.
[23] My emphasis, because the statement is remarkable, in my view, for its insight to the duty of care actor training requires.
[24] This was discussed in the RADA Student Action Plan which I discuss in earlier chapters.

he worked with described it as: 'You have a painting – you stretch out to all the different corners'. This 'stretch' relied on an openness to training and a willingness to learn a craft and confront your limitations.

Montague's journey to acting is very much a window into post-war renewal, both socially and culturally. He had been posted to Egypt just after the war[25] and on his return went to study Drama at the Toynbee Hall with Maimie Watson, who was also a teacher at the Old Vic Theatre School and encouraged him to audition. His audition impressed Michel Saint-Denis so much that he was offered a scholarship. His group was able to study on the stage at the Old Vic, and he was one of the graduates to be selected to work with the Old Vic Theatre company. Montague was adamant that his experience at the Old Vic Theatre School taught him the value of training to enhance the actor's craft.

Montague emphasized that the training at the Old Vic was a Stanislavski-based training – psychological realism. The teachers he remembered were John Blatchley, Litz Pisk and Saint-Denis – most importantly Michel Saint-Denis. One of his most vivid memories was when he played Konstantin in *The Seagull*, which he described as 'a challenge', because 'I was a working-class Jew from the East End'.

> Michel Saint-Denis said of my work: 'That it was acting'. Coming from where I had come from, to hear that word from him: I floated. (Montague, 2023)

Playing a character well, meant you could move away from who you were. You could transform; you didn't need to stay close to your origins. The classes and the training all helped this. Montague never wanted the training to be different to accommodate his class or his ethnicity. The classes he clearly relied on for most of his career were the Voice classes, which he saw as developing the body for voice: 'you found your voice for speaking'. He remembers teachers like Jani Strasser for Voice Production, from whom he learnt the importance to reach back of the auditorium. He was taught some very strong principles about the importance of speaking 'verse' and his strong views about verse speaking stem from his training: 'I can't bear actors who break up the verse'. He also vividly remembers being told by a member of the audience that he couldn't be heard at the back of the auditorium. 'I always made sure I could be heard' after that, he said.

I asked about recollections from his movement training. It is a fascinating insight into the thinking and the teaching at this school from over eighty years ago, to consider his responses. Not least because I hear so many echoes of students I have taught – not in terms of what they were asked to do, but *because of how actors in training need to expand their understanding of what they think acting is*.[26]

For Montague, movement for actors is 'to be aware of the body and what you can do with it'. Apart from Animal Study, which ended in a 6–8 minute presentation critiqued by Saint-Denis, they were taught mask work by John Blatchley, which he didn't much like: 'you have to come to terms with some things'. He loved the Mime classes though and could see the relevance of the precision they asked for. The mime was clearly based on observation of real activities – an approach which Claude Chagrin later brought to Drama Centre, where

---

[25]As part of National Service.
[26]My italics.

the students were asked to mime a real activity, like sweeping up leaves, or washing the floor.

> I did a shoe repairer, the detail, the shoes would go against the last, to be stretched.

His physical training also helped him to interpret acting notes and staging. He remembers Glen Byam Shaw directing *Henry V*, with Eric Clunes playing the king.

> It was a piece of direction given to the soldiers, who had been lying there all night: 'When you wake up your bodies are hurting, and you are in pain, you need to stretch'. I remember how alive this made my body. (Montague, 2023)

He also stood for half an hour, in another production at the Old Vic, holding one corner of a canopy, which he saw as '*good for stillness*'. These recollections serve as a snapshot into the sensibility and body of an actor in training just after the Second World War. This is rarely shown in films or TV shows that reference the theatre at that time. The recent film *The Critic* with Ian McKellan and Gemma Arteton, is a thriller set in the theatre of the 1930s (before the war). Watching it, you would be forgiven for thinking that there was little experiment or new forms of training going on at that time. You would also not really get a sense of how difficult it would be for anyone Jewish, or working class, to make a career for themselves as an actor. The one Jewish character was married to a Lady and was a successful artist. While this wasn't unheard of, it was unusual, as I will show.[27]

The first tour of Europe after the end of the Second World War

In 1952 Lee Montague and my father were on the first tour of Europe after the war, with the Old Vic Theatre company. I refer to Montague's descriptions of acting Shakespeare in Europe at that time, as they are socially and politically interesting. His reminisces highlighted the complexities of being ambassadors for your country, rubbing against the reality of being working-class Jewish actors, travelling in a Europe that was still rebuilding. For instance, they had very little money, so they often entertained drinkers in bars and cafes, by standing on tables and delivering speeches from Shakespeare to get free drinks. A wonderful image, which I doubt would happen today! They were also expected to wear a dress suit for receptions at the Embassies, which, coming from a long line of tailors, Montague's family had made specially for him. But one of the most striking descriptions for me was a recollection of his realization of what it was to be Jewish in Germany, just after the Second World War.

> I was with Wolfe in 1952 in Cologne in Germany – it was in a terrible state – bombed out of existence. One day he and I were in a shop, a sweet shop, and the way we spoke German with a Yiddish accent, we sensed the proprietor knew we were Jews, it was very uncomfortable. (Montague, 2023)

The last sentence haunts me. This was just seven years after the end of the war, which my father had fought in. So many Jews had lost family in the war in the concentration camps, and Europe was re-building. There is clearly compassion for what the German people had

---

[27] *The Critic*, written by Patrick Marber and directed by Anand Tucker, 2023.

suffered from the bombing and the aftermath of the war as, after all, Britain had won. But I wonder whether this balance of empathy and vulnerability, of being able to understand another point of view, demonstrates what actors are called on to do. It is hard to see the world through the eyes of someone else, but it is necessary, for art and for society. Speaking for my father, he saw himself as a Jew, and as an actor. Not a Jewish actor. Fluidity.

I need to emphasize that neither Lee Montague nor my father encountered antisemitism in their classical and innovative training (at the Old Vic Theatre School and RADA, respectively), nor in the theatre. Nor did either of them ever mention that they felt held back from being able to participate fully in their training because of their culture or backgrounds. Lee Montague acknowledges he needed to 'stretch' to move into different worlds and characters, and my father experienced antisemitism during the war. Both acknowledge the influence female teachers had on their training, though the authority of critique Montague remembers were mostly men. My father, however, was greatly influenced by Litz Pisk and Iris Warren, whose exercises he did all the time, and he passed on that respect for training to me. What is striking in Montague's comments is the European influence on post-war training, which had started before the war in France, and a focus on the body as a means of expression for a training in Voice, Movement and Acting. In both cases, their training gave them their careers in the theatre and educated them in the affiliated arts that actor training embraces. Art, literature, research skills, music, psychology, and political and social awareness. And compassion.

Where does that leave Animal Study?

Empathy gives us the capacity to be able to explore something different to ourselves, inhabit it, and bring it to life. Animal Study and research into movement qualities, as a way of changing the body and the imagination, deepens an actor's craft and stretches and expands their capacity to inhabit someone else, their world and the events that happen to them. It can also help to free us to transform ourselves. An actor can be anyone, no matter who they are.

I now explain how I have updated the study to embrace both a psychological approach and a pedagogy.

Breaking movement down for Animal Study

There are different approaches to Animal Study and different reasons for doing it. The study of an animal as a basis for character or physical vocabulary for productions has developed considerably since the accounts given above. Animal Study is often also used for motion capture for films. *Kingdom of the Planet of the Apes*, for example, directed by Wes Ball, used actors who were taught by a movement teacher.[28]

My first experiences of needing to find ways to study an animal's movement, was because I was frequently cast to play animals in professional productions. This was before I was a movement teacher. Though there were often excellent movement teachers provided for these productions, I still found I needed to do my own research to find the animal's

---

[28]There are also Animal Flow classes, which work more as dance and energy classes.

dramatic life. At Lecoq, Animal Study had only been one class. We were asked to offer the essence of the animal, its rhythm and its attitude to the world. However, as we had already covered the building bricks from which we could create a variety of physical studies, when I played animals as an actor I used the full extent of my Lecoq training to create my studies for production.

Lecoq used this one animal class as a pathway to help us decide on our 'personnages'. 'Personnage' was a character study we inhabited for a week. They attended all the classes (and for some of us, went to and from school on the metro and came home with us). We applied all the work we had already explored in other classes, to the specifics of creating our 'personnages'. How we walked, spoke, moved and used our spine had to form a consistent study that we could physically sustain. The revelation for me came when we had to play the 'contra-personnage': the opposite of our first character. How you arrive at an 'opposite' is open to interpretation, maybe applying a binary, old to young, or something that 'feels' different to your first choice. The possibilities for interaction between the two 'personnages' took off, when two actors improvised their four characters in a scene entering and exiting in pursuit of one another, justifying their reasons through the rapid appearance of a 'plot'. The dramatic possibilities of how characters might interact, we had learned through the dynamic interplay of finding character through the elements, or 'matter': how, for instance the element of air might inflame the element of fire (to become a conflagration consuming everything), or oil might emolliate vinegar (to become mayonnaise). Once you start to play with this in improvised scenarios, you have some very interesting exchanges and powerful changes of stakes and emotion in a scene.

The 'logic' I relied on when playing animals in productions was observation. I looked, analysed and copied the movements I saw, usually at a zoo, and then applied them to the 'character' of the animal. I transformed my own face and extremities by observing the details of their senses and faces, hands and feet. I applied what I had learned about dynamic and rhythm to find their movement patterns and ways of changing direction. I played frogs, panthers, wolves, monkeys, deer, and each one had a character, text, sometimes even songs or were part of an opera to very challenging music. I have also movement directed many animals, but the amount of rehearsal time given to explore this is often limited. To compensate I would suggest simple movement patterns for each animal choreographing the physicality for clarity.

*

There is a difference between playing an animal in a production and learning to how apply it to acting. The application to acting is what Animal Study classes in Drama Schools mainly focus on.

When you play an animal in a production, the audience needs to understand who the animal is. The movement also needs to be dramatically interesting. It isn't enough 'be' the animal.[29]

---

[29]See Chapter 10 for an example of this.

When you play a character which uses the essence of an animal to define a physicality you can sustain, the audience doesn't need to know what animal you have chosen for this, only the character you are playing. The animal is a trigger for transformation.

Although playing animals in productions is the most obvious application of animal study, it is not the reason why we study animals in drama schools. Animals are part of our need to tell stories and contact the unspoken emotional parts of ourselves. Like mask work, something inexplicable happens when we explore the world of an animal through our own body, taking on its breath patterns, rhythm and weight factors.

How to teach Animal Study in a drama school

My approach to Animal Study grew from a simple study of animal movement, informed (probably) by the Michel Saint-Denis approach of 'observe and bring this back to class playfully' into a more complex pedagogy. At Rose Bruford I worked with Annie Tyson to apply some of Stanislavski's 'characteristics' to their animals. This helped students think of ways to 'choose' what 'animal' their character was when creating a role for a rehearsal exercise. Often this was for Shakespeare or for Chekhov – with the animal as an essence or an approach to finding a character, rather than an accurate re-playing of the animal.[30] I would refine the animals in the movement classes, which ran alongside rehearsals and acting classes. This would emerge as an accurate 'character study' emerging from the 'animal study' – like a phoenix rising out of the ashes.

Later I researched how to make my pedagogy more inclusive and broke the subject down even further. Students researched how their own bodies moved, to help them understand what they need to change physically, to accommodate different movement patterns. For instance, if an actor was playing a flamingo, and they weren't flexible enough to show how the animal stooped its long neck low or unfolded its legs to walk, the actor may need to select exercises to enhance their flexibility. They would be developing a bespoke training to help them inhabit the animal more fully.

As I mention in my discussion about student anxiety, and transformation, I don't believe it is necessary to change a pedagogy entirely, especially one so fundamental to the principles of modern actor training. My preference is for a space to research, explore and discover the movement of an animal, not as a course, but as a process to your own creative development. Below I offer what this might look like.

*

The first time I taught Animal Study was in 1989, at Central School of Speech and Drama. I was replacing a teacher on maternity leave and inherited a group of first years who were halfway through the course. I had been given the post of Head of Movement, though I was the only movement teacher to cover all three years. The classes, including Animal Study, were only 45 minutes long. These movement classes were taught in Litz Pisk's tradition, which as I have shown are from the same stable as Arnold's work. Pisk's work was more dramatic in the way the technique played into the bodies. The swings, and drops had an

---

[30]See Chapter 10 for exercises.

inherent theatricality, and there was a strong emphasis on the elasticity of the spine. Sue Lefton has described to me how her classes focused on 'spirit' and 'drama'.

There was a particular swing I remember that wrapped round the top part of your spine on the horizontal high plane in a figure of eight. This involved the whole of your upper body, neck and head, circling in response – very liberating, as if you were a tree blown by the wind. Another movement was called "flicking down through the spine" that took in the whole spine and travelled down into the knees. I haven't included these in my chapter on swings. There are simply too many to explore and explain. But I used these swings when teaching this first group of students, as well as an undulation, which I will explain later. These were all different ways to 'liberate' the bodies. I had learnt these swings from my father, who had shown me some of Litz Pisk's movement as an antidote to my ballet training.

Watching the students for the first time it was clear they didn't need much encouragement to liberate their imaginations, and they all had found playful ways to communicate their animals. This chimed with haunting examples I had seen in the theatre. I recall the powerful transformations in Michael Elliott's production of *Peer Gynt* of the Trolls, the Threadballs and Troll King. They seemed like creatures from another world. Michael Elliott speaks of Litz Pisk's work on these sequences in his Foreword to her book *The Actor and His Body*:[31]

> Perhaps her work is the most powerful when it is concerned with the divine or the demonic. No one who was ever part of it will ever forget the rehearsals for the Troll scene in Peer Gynt at the Old Vic with a large cast of actors … Because her movement is always connected to an emotional intention, she can perform miracles. (Pisk, 1975)

Michael Elliot also describes his self-consciousness the first time he met Pisk, as an Oxford graduate with a theatrical 'consciousness' that was 'largely literary, academic, abstract and physically totally inhibited'. Movement is impulse, bypassing inhibition, with enough physical knowledge to be able to express that impulse. This is how Pisk taught and created work for him:

Always she would work from the impulse. When that is alive then it is possible to find form facially, vocally and physically.

When creating a dance on stage, for Litz Pisk, the step or the movement comes from the 'impulse', which creates the form. This is different to choreography, or a formal dance, which makes a form for dancers to fill. Sue Lefton and Jane Gibson also choreograph dances from the spirit and the meaning of the step, rather than just teaching the structure.

I say 'movement is about impulse' as though we know it to be true. It was Litz Pisk who probably made this 'happen' in the theatre and gave us the idea of what it was. I had certainly seen it take shape before my eyes when the madmen in Act V of *Peer Gynt* appeared in loin cloths, powdered in white chalk, squawking like chickens, with coxcombs on their heads: I didn't know why, but I knew what they felt.

---

[31] Important to understand that 'his' was the generic for 'their', or both 'his' and 'her' at the time the book was written in 1975: but this does not diminish the impact of Pisk's work, as a female artist, on British Theatre, or the importance of all 'bodies' she speaks of in the book.

When I taught my first animal class at Central, I expected an acting exercise that involved the spine – something outwardly expressed, to communicate what was happening inside. I was also an actor, teaching a movement class, so I understood this need for an inner life. This seemed important to me and everyone who employed me as a movement teacher.

I have never forgotten that first class. It has served as a sort of platonic shadow ever since, to chase but never quite achieve. There are classes like that, which burn in your memory and serve as a torch to light duller classes (teaching can also be hard).

The students were quite far on in their studies. The format of the 45-minute class was for each one to get up one by one to show their animals. There was a quiet understanding about ease, breath and a certain relaxation in the class. Though some students were soon to confide that they felt the discipline at Central was lax in comparison to Drama Centre, another more rigorous school. However, the spirit of the ensemble was there.

The first student to get up was an owl. She started in silence and stillness, facing sideways. Then slowly she blinked her very large eyes, circled her head, and infinitesimally ruffled her feathers, shifted her weight from foot to foot. Then settled back into stillness. She didn't 'fly', but she brought into the room the essence of the owl, its uncanny ruminative stillness. She was both animal and character.

I didn't comment.

The second actor was a marmoset: he leapt onto a high table and looked around with nerves and excitement, quivering. He ate a peanut and spat out the husk. Breathed, made a strange sound, then suddenly moved swiftly across the space, scrambling onto a windowsill, up and down the walls, rolling on his back, and then stillness.

I didn't comment.

How you hold a space like this is important: I didn't know what to say, so I said nothing. This was partly because I was amazed at the magic I was witnessing. What I understood was the importance of relaxation as the actors moved. So, I talked about breath. Finding the breath of the animal. It also seemed important that the animals should work together, so I introduced the idea that they were all in an open space, for some of the classes. This was a room with ropes hanging from the ceiling and gym equipment, so the animals could roll, run, climb and jump safely. But nothing could ever compare to the extraordinary moment when a placid young woman changed into an owl in front of our eyes, just through her desire to be someone else.

I learned a lot about how to teach animals and what you could ask for, from watching the beautiful work of these students. It was also clear that they had been well trained through Litz Pisk's work, particularly the fluidity and elasticity of the spine, to be able to bring the animals to life like this.

I also remember students finding these classes difficult even then, in 1989. One refused to visit the zoo because they found researching animals in captivity disturbing. One found crawling on hands and knees as a wolf, too exposing. The adaptations I made over the years were to try and answer these concerns, without taking away the depth or the detail. But most of all, to emphasize that Animal Study is an acting exercise.

The work on the spine, and the work on the animals, is almost the same work. Observation and then the actor's capacity to animate it through their own body. The movement work, how you teach it and what it is, is very important.

So is acting.

Acting and Animal Study

I discovered there are many overlaps between Animal Study as a subject in drama schools with how acting teachers use it. Animal Study is an acting exercise. What movement classes can provide is more detailed and focused work on the specifics and how to make choices more physically alive. Animal Study can be used as part of the 'rehearsal exercises' done in drama schools. These exercises were usually rehearsed over a whole term, often with actors sharing roles. The aim was to give actors the space and time to integrate their voice, movement and acting classes and techniques into a performance. At Rose Bruford and Drama Centre, for instance, once students had found the animal for their character, scenes or entire plays would be 'run' with the actors as their 'animals', interacting and responding with the logic of the animals, to find their impulses.

The activities the animal might do can be transposed into human gestures or actions. A flamingo opening its wings into lighting a cigarette, or putting on a coat. An otter grooming his coat into a fastidious organizing of papers on a desk.

Many rehearsals would use 'the animals' as a warm-up for the scene about to be rehearsed. Acting teachers are very well placed to 'see' whether a student is inhabiting and living a physicality – especially Stanislavski-based teachers. Again, just quietly holding the space and letting the animals play for a long time without too much intervention is beneficial; like watching a plant grow.

I have seen wonderful improvisations led by my acting tutor colleagues. One example, was when a young woman was struggling to find the maturity of a middle-aged woman for a play by Eduardo de Fillipo. She was given a goose to study as a basis for her characterization by her acting tutor and director, Annie Tyson. This was to help her find the redistribution of weight that happens after menopause. The focus on her tail-end and the waddle and desire to sit and rest, with sudden flurries of activity that geese often indulge in when they chase you (for instance) provided an extraordinary opportunity for transformation, both physical and in terms of characterization.

These are examples of how an ethos of 'joined up thinking' in drama school can benefit both students and teachers. As Lee Montague reminded me, Michel Saint-Denis critiqued his animal study. The difference now in the schools is that 'Animal Study' has become a subject 'belonging' to the Movement Department. Other departments often take it less seriously, when watching the animals, than they do the plays or voice presentations. This could shift if we understood that it is an approach and not an end. Any movement tutor, teaching animal study in a drama school, probably needs to have worked as an actor to understand its purpose, or to be trained in the acting techniques the students are learning.

The Michel Saint-Denis approach trusts your actors to make the connection between a physical study and the physical life of their character, without too much guidance. Actors will often talk about the need to find the right shoes for their character as this will give them the walk or the stance. Or how an activity, something the character does physically, brings the character into focus for them.

The descriptions above are all 'versions' of Animal Study taken from the Michel Saint-Denis tradition, through Copeau, to the Old Vic Theatre School and onto Central School of Speech and Drama, Drama Centre and Guildhall, as I encountered it as an actor and as a teacher. These experiential and improvisatory approaches to working with 'animals' placed in rehearsals and movement classes, so they can find a physical transformation, without over-correcting, can allow the mysterious and deeper transformations to appear in a quiet and un-pushed environment.

*

Animal Study as a subject

Once Animal Study is placed in the curriculum alongside the demands of timetables and competing classes, the parameters and expectations of the classes change. A scheduled subject of 1.5 hours a week can make the work appear as a 'module'. But there are many constraints when students are working to a very packed timetable. When do they get time to work alone or in small groups, to refine and explore discoveries made in a class? This will be easier when students are given a consistent methodology. The movement techniques and approaches that underpin Animal Study – release, breath, easy work of the spine and strong and free use of limbs in the swings, to help move through space – are Pure Movement. The class could come out of a Pure Movement class and needn't be scheduled as a separate class. In fact, most of the warm-up exercises will be Pure Movement.

However all restrictions offer opportunities and the result of having to teach 1.5-hour Animal Study classes led me to develop a pedagogy composed of various elements that expanded students' physical techniques and imaginative expression. One of these different elements was Movement Qualities. The other was Registers, exploring different ways to use the study for different styles of playing.

Movement qualities

When I was working at the Stratford Festival Theatre in Canada, one of the directors asked me to think about movement qualities for some of the characters in his production. Movement was well regarded at the Stratford Festival Theatre, with a history and legacy of movement coaches working across all productions throughout the season. Trish Arnold had worked there, and a movement director called John Broome was resident for years, whose practice combined Historical Dance with Laban, and whose movement work on productions was legendary. The relationship between voice and movement was strong, and there was also a resident Alexander teacher, Kelly McKevenue, whose work, like all the coaches, flowed between working on productions and individual coaching sessions.

When I was asked to consider 'movement qualities' the term seemed to refer to Laban, though not specifically the 'Effort Actions'. These were principles to help someone identify how they might want their character to move at different times in the story of the play – physical activities or improvisations – to build a 'vocabulary' for the character. Our physicality and movements respond variously to external events and internal states throughout our lives. Working with the actors (at the request of the director) I discovered that Pure Movement techniques, plus weight, speed and flow, mixed with imagery and observation, helped actors to 'settle' on a palette of movement for their character they could then use in rehearsal.

Some examples

Hamlet: To find a physicality that gave a sense of aloofness and entitlement.

To explore this, the actor and myself, imagined how he would carry himself, when riding a horse. His spine lengthened, and he lifted out of the pelvis. He retained this posture which helped his physical characterization of Hamlet as a Prince. This was something the director was keen he developed. We then used real life princes as examples from which to model more specific choices. We looked on YouTube at the diffidence and athleticism that Prince Harry manifests in his physicality in public. We observed that his gestures were contained within Narrow and High, as if he were holding onto himself. We noted the carriage of his head, slightly inclined as if seeking approval and contrasted this with Prince Charles, whose head position seemed more 'direct' – moving in straight lines, to show certainty as opposed to needing approval. We mixed both physicalities to find 'Hamlet the Prince'. We specifically referenced the wedding between Prince Charles and Kate Middleton, as we were interested in how formality constrains impulse: what you choose to show and what conceal.

We explored the idea of a stallion with a high centre of gravity, to find a false composure (horses are easily spooked), and a skittishness when Hamlet is mocking the courtiers.

The actor was naturally grounded and dynamic, an excellent fighter and very free in his movements – very good following his emotions and impulses. So, we were looking to find ways for him to inhabit the opposite, for the more introspective scenes and to explore a diffidence, having to rein himself in. A form of 'gliding' was helpful. Smooth, sustained, but with weight. For the more internalized anguish: 'Oh that this too too sullied flesh could melt' – we looked at containing the energy, compressing and turning the spine, like a coiled spring, so that later in the speech it could be released on 'just two months dead'.

Ophelia: The mad scene. This is always such a difficult scene to explore. How do you express madness? Forensically deciding on what kind of breakdown Ophelia is in the grip of? Working with a conceit (she's on drugs?).

The director wanted to start from the text as a way in, manipulating the seemingly innocent nursery rhymes, to highlight their lasciviousness. He also wanted the actor to explore the unpredictability of a child and the jeopardy of being left to fend for herself, in a world of Machiavellian statecraft. The actor had the image of a little girl dancing on her father's shoes and suggested this might be a memory of her childhood with Polonius. She wanted to embody this memory on her first entrance in the mad scene. This took the form of reaching up to someone taller, then being moved around like a puppet, her feet on the shoes of her dead father. The steps she explored were staccato, with quick sharp movements like a bird and her body was a mixture of loose and tense, as if thrown and then suddenly pulled back into place. She then wanted to find a quixotic change with more sexualized movements for the words 'the owl was a baker's daughter' so that she could sit on Claudius's lap with her legs open. We explored doing this with a loose and free physicality in the wide dimension: both as a five-year-old and then as a chimpanzee.

The chimpanzee image gave her images of exploring Claudius's face as though for the first time, a clumsiness of touch and an invasion of space, with looseness and abandonment, winding her limbs around Claudius's body. The most difficult action was how to climb onto Claudius's lap, which the idea of the child and the monkey combined could provide a sudden and dangerous physicality, but in the end was choreographed along the lines of intimacy co-ordination, to make it safe.[32]

Working with different movement qualities and images gave a structure to the unpredictability needed in a scene that tracked the darting images of a mind disturbed. The actor and I worked together a few times, as she had been a dancer, and was apt to fix the movements, whereas the director wanted her to move with more impulses that were psychologically driven. 'Never move without thought' is what underpins all movement. To search for this, we worked on the swings as a way into freeing her body, before we explored the scenes and the scenarios we created as ways into them. I worked with the actors separately in an improvisatory space on these movement ideas; they were able to go back to rehearsal and integrate these ideas with the director. Occasionally he might ask if I had worked with them – when he noticed a difference – or request I see them again, if he hadn't; or I might offer what I had been working 'for' with them. We preferred it when I wasn't in the room when creative decisions were made on the rehearsal room floor. I believe this is fundamental to the craft of helping actors shape their physicality: you aren't telling them what to do, you are helping them find a movement language to inhabit and work with, both in rehearsal and then performance. They have agency: they are the artists.

This is the fundamental difference between movement and choreography, so often not fully understood.

*

Registers

My methodology for Animal Study has now developed to include the addition of movement qualities and how to break these down so as to physically embody them with detail. This is then applied to our skills of observation, when researching the movement of the animal. The movement qualities can then be used when the actor explores how the animal moves. A creative way to find the physical and emotional life of an animal. My methodology was structured over two to three terms of animal study and provided an arc of learning.

It is interesting how some of the exercises I most recently developed were with students working at home on their own during lockdown, when I was teaching on Zoom. Some of the most amusing improvisations were when the 'animals' went about their 'daily' tasks in 'their' bedrooms. Navigating sofas, and cushions, and opening and closing doors brought the real world into the centre of the improvisation.

---

[32]It is worth saying that all three actors had worked together for years as part of the regular company at Stratford. I am aware that now there are intimacy co-ordinators and directors on most of their productions and that when I was working there in 2017 they were already employed by outside directors who brought their own practitioners with them.

Once the student is able to sustain the Animal Study for several minutes, I introduce the idea of playing the animal in different theatrical registers.

1. Living the animal: through the breath and the spine, small, detailed movements in the day of the life of the animal. Finding variety of movement through a combination of base rhythm, dimensions and leading points, and working with the senses. Often finding ways to sustain the study with the use of music, which can help amplify the scale of the movement and the intensity or speed of the movement. Building a linear narrative, by setting an exercise called: 'the day of the life of an animal' – dramatic time.

2. Smaller version, maybe 50 per cent or 25 per cent animal, to find a character. Using the essence of the animal to sustain a physical life that is consistent, or to focus on an aspect of the animal that will help with transformation to a character, physically or psychologically completely different to the actor.

3. The most released version asks the actor to embody the animal in 'real time' – rather than dramatic time. This is a powerful transformation as the actor is using their imagination. It is conducted without any prompts from the teacher and is in silence, with the only sound being the breath or the noises the animals naturally make. The breath and the spine are vital to this. The actor is living the animal.

4. Heightened version or the cabaret version. Choosing the music of your animal and finding an outfit, or clothes for them, and creating a piece of movement to music that expresses the animal as a theatrical character, perhaps even with a political satirical point of view. The musicality of the animal can also be expressed without the music, in silence – but using the beats and the character of the music heightens the playing like a cabaret version. With a tiny push it can become satirical and so, political. One example was a boy who was a flamingo, choosing his music as a track from the Boy Band 'Take That', and performing to it as though he was at a concert. His 'outfit' was a shaggy short jacket and very tight jeans, enhanced his 'flamingo' moves. Another example was a llama who was a theatrical agent. He wore platform heels and a tie that he kept swinging over his shoulder, and his tongue kept on emerging with delight if he saw an act he enjoyed.

All of these 'registers' ask the students to work as actors. The hardest and most powerful version is version three. Perhaps the most useful, version two. The version that is the most exciting in its theatricality, perhaps version four. Version one is how I delivered Animal Study in a systematic methodology, specifically for students at the beginning of their training and is what I will mainly be focusing on in the next chapter.

The next chapter will chart the exercises and the pedagogy I developed for 'Animal Study' and 'Animal into Character'.

10 Animal Studies

Exercises for the craft of acting

Physical imagination drives all aspects of Animal Studies and illuminates an actor's understanding of the craft of acting. By imagining they are an animal, then physicalizing its impulses, an actor experiences what it feels like to be in the moment. This develops intuitive playful and embodied responses, which can complement a psychologically based training.

In a drama school, I teach Animal Studies in two phases.

1. Animal Study, where the actors choose an animal and study how it moves.
2. Animal Into Character, where they take the essence of the animal and create a character from it.

In the first, the actor disappears into the animal. In the second the animal disappears into the character. I teach Animal Study over a term, which completes as a 'sharing'. An event, where the actors realize the physical life of their animals in front of an audience. The second phase – Animal Into Character – might be delivered in tandem with rehearsal exercises, as described previously, or simply focus on the creation of a character suggested by the physicality of the animal.

Both phases are about transformation, but if there isn't time to deliver the work over two terms, it can be compressed into one 'swathe' of work. The study is designed to connect to an actor's process. Living as another creature, looking at the world through their eyes, draws on the senses – the heat, the earth, the air, the sound of leaves – all the elements of the environment which affect its quality of attention – a completely different emphasis to how an actor might play an animal in a production. Focusing on the senses takes the actor into sensation, and the imagination, as well as physical dexterity.

The exercises in this chapter combine ideas for physical training, with suggestions for how to approach playing 'different' species. The actor's imagination brings them to life, through working with sustained improvisations.

Most of the exercises in this chapter help with physical expression and stamina and strength. However, it isn't necessary for a student, or an actor, to have a dancer's agility, or the athleticism of a martial artist, to bring an animal to life. All it needs is an actor willing to transform themselves, to be different. Finding the life force of the animal is a much more interesting process than simply imitating its movements. Sometimes the transformation from animal into character can be astonishing.

Warm-ups

Though Animal Study is a solo exercise, actors need to socialize, and warming up together frees the body and the imagination at the same time. I always start class with actors playing and responding together, where everyone finds their own space and works at their own level. The warm-up will include a proper Pure Movement warm-up to ease the muscles and get the juices flowing. This helps actors move creatively and with full body awareness.

Teaching points

You are helping actors to develop their observation skills, as well as their ability to express themselves physically. Most drama schools used to arrange student zoo tickets for unlimited visits, so they can see the animals close up and get to know the animal they have chosen to study.[1] I usually revisit the zoo before each set of classes myself, to refresh my understanding of the animals we cover. Each time I watch an animal in depth, I always discover something surprising to add to the classes. A squirrel bounds lightly across the ground – forelegs pulling the rest of the body – but what is the most interesting part of their movement? The small steps they take when less active, little rotary movements of legs and arms, nose and ears alert – where their rodent characteristics are visible. These details lift the work out of a generic study that you might see in a cartoon to a character study that embodies its 'characteristics'.

The more I am familiar with details of each animal's movement, the more my feedback helps actors to inhabit these transformations as acting exercises. I can give suggestions about how a head might move, a paw strike, corresponding to an action or intention from the animal. This develops an animal movement text – its form and content creating something meaningful and alive.

How to lead and embed transformation in the classes

I lead the animal classes with structured exercises, often physically demonstrating to the class how an animal might move. It is rare for students to be able to transform as effortlessly and without guidance as the student who explored the owl. The fertile space that I happily encountered in 1989 at Central School of Speech and Drama derived from the elasticity of Litz Pisk's movement work, and the legacy of the Michel Saint-Denis tradition at the school. The Animal Study exercise was born from a particular view of how to explore transformation and observation with ease, passed on to the teachers still working at Central. Teaching in drama schools used to work like this. Teachers were part of a family, sharing and pooling their knowledge, and practice with an understanding of how all the classes connected, and where the exercises came from. As I write this, I am aware of how 'intrinsic' and unmeasurable this might seem, but many of the schools had Teachers' Training courses attached to them or were already BA Hons Acting Courses. It is possible to share with each other an artistic understanding of how and what to teach.[2] This also ensures that the work is transparent, and not dependent on one teacher alone. Animal Study is part of a 'school' of work in the tradition of embodied teaching techniques this book discusses.

---

[1] I don't know if this is still the case. And as I mention in the last chapter, some students object to going to zoos, for political or conservation reasons; though zoos function today very much as contributors to the conservation of endangered species.
[2] Rose Bruford had a BA Honours Acting Course. Drama Centre ran Teacher Training Courses, and Central School had courses in Drama Teaching and Voice Training.

The desire to physically transform with a fearlessness to explore physical expression is at the heart of this exercise. The drama schools and tradition I refer to above, understood this. So if this is not at the heart of the drama school you might be teaching in, you will need to tread lightly to get students to trust the subject. However, even without this, sometimes there might be a context elsewhere, for instance when Animal Study is part of the acting classes. This was the case for me at Rose Bruford and Drama Centre, and helped motivate the students to explore their animals, knowing they would be asked to use it in their acting class.

From body to the imagination: Working with the spine and understanding the animal's use of space

The easiest pathway for students into animal study is to focus on the spine to develop its freedom and vocal ease with the use of breath as they move.[3] Animal Study requires you to move your body entirely differently, learning new physical patterns, working with a different distribution of weight. This in turn affects how you move through space. Whether you gallop striking the ground, or slither along the ground, or move from High to Low in leaps and bounds. The animal can move round the edges of a large space, or dominate the space, or zig zag across the space. It asks you to be as interested in the body as much as the animal. It asks you to explore how the animal relates to its environment, discovering physical pathways different to yours, and to be curious about how this makes you feel as an actor.

It is a physical acting exercise that combines imagination with technique, and it should always be interesting and enjoyable.

Snapshots of how Animal Study and acting connect: Anatomy and action

1 Working on productions

When I was working at the Stratford Festival Theatre as the Movement Director on Aristophanes' *The Birds*, the director asked me to lead movement workshops on the various movement qualities of the 'different' birds in the play. The actors were wearing masks, so the body would need to animate the face, whilst distinguishing the different birds from one another. I taught one of these sessions with the Alexander teacher Kelly McKevenue,[4] who offered anatomical insights into how to embody the tiny movements of a bird moving its head in all directions, by locating the small movements possible in the atlas joint. This is the ball and socket joint on which our head balances at the end of our spine – like Atlas holding up the world from ancient mythology. These tiny movements can help move the nose, like a beak, and are even more alive when you understand that a bird often needs to tilt its head sideways to get full vision.

All these activities ask an actor to observe, transform and bring these discoveries to life with specificity and flow.

'I am moving as the animal; I am not choreographed like the animal.'

---

[3]In my classes, I encourage the actors to use sound and use their voices.
[4]See below – Mckevenue was the resident Alexander Teacher at the Stratford Festival Theatre Ontario.

2 Specificity and flow

The young actor playing the eagle in *The Birds* had to make a dramatic first entrance, so he studied how an eagle landed from a height. Its sudden rush onto the ground, an appearance from air to earth, was like magic[5] to him. He had studied an eagle land outside the theatre, where he was keen to rehearse, to find its truth. He took me to the exact spot. We went under some large pine trees outside the Stratford Festival Theatre – with old pine cones abandoned in the grass, pine needles, shade and other birds – and he created this beautiful entrance. Disappearing for a while, he suddenly ran out at speed from behind a tree, decelerating rapidly to give a sense of having dropped from the sky. As the eagle landed, the wings half-closed in a right angle and his legs, powerful and grasping the ground for purchase, shot out in front, with the body catching up, continuing the momentum until he could safely slow to stillness. He then settled his feathers back into his body and wound his head in, to look with a dangerous intensity in my direction. It was another powerful moment of transformation, but unlike the owl,[6] it was his physicality, momentum and creation of an animal's body that had made this so alive. Though this entrance didn't make the final cut into the production, when he first offered it as his entrance to the play, it electrified the rehearsal room. It perfectly expressed the physical life and point of view of his character, which informed his performance thereon in.

The actor's interpretation

Another example: I was employed both as a movement director and to play Raksha (the mother wolf) in an adaptation of *The Jungle Book*. The director wanted me to create animal movement for the production, and the designer's drawings showed long pieces of thick ribbon, for freedom of movement, allowing for the development of the specific movement patterns for wolves, monkeys, hyenas – a somewhat uniform solution. The actor playing Baloo the Bear was a large, witty actor, with a tendency towards Coward. He witheringly objected to playing the Bear *as* a bear. He managed to secure a long fur coat as his costume, announcing that he had based his characterization on Noel Coward. He even imported the iconic cigarette in the long holder. Begrudgingly he conceded a few bear-like moves (very funny in fact) saying his was the vaudeville version of Baloo. He studiously ignored input from all the experts, including a visiting zookeeper who made some astonishingly lascivious observations about the length of a bear's tongue. He was brilliant, bringing the house down when he danced, getting all the good notices, and leaving those of us moving authentically in floppy costumes, looking flimsy and under-characterized.

3 Animal into character: Snapshots from the classroom

A penguin becomes a ten-year-old little girl

An actor playing a penguin decided the essence of the penguin was an enthusiastic little girl. She had a shambling gait, with her arms flapping against her sides, not always in opposition, and her head leading, looking up and out (as penguins do). She had a low centre of

---

[5] I explore dynamics later in the chapter.
[6] Described in Chapter 13.

gravity, and clumsy feet. She would hop with enthusiasm, and 'transposed' the grooming actions of a penguin, to suddenly curling inwards to read a book. I was delighted by the originality of the choice – so often an actor will move a penguin into their cartoon archetype of waiters or butlers. This is an excellent example of the inner and the outer life of a character. It is also useful as a reminder that although we will be taught in a movement class the need to balance the arms in opposition when we walk – there are many times and examples of human movement where we don't do this. The actor sustained this character over several classes, and it was a brilliantly achieved transformation.

A small kangaroo becomes a middle-aged church-going matron

An actor playing a small kangaroo made the astonishing transformation into a middle-aged woman. He padded his stomach and wore very formal clothes (twinset and pearls), and was obsessed with her handbag, which was a transposition from the pouch. Her hands (as I will call them now) were delicate and she carried her weight high. At the same time there was a strong sense of gravity in the lower half of her body – the kangaroo's tale. A kangaroo is capable of sudden powerful fast moves, which can be quite alarming to witness. The woman would move with passion when disagreed with, or going to church. There was an extraordinary mixture of vulnerability and aloofness, and single-minded obsessiveness. The actor had tapped into something powerful and original, and I have never witnessed such an original transposition of a kangaroo into a character, before or since.

No amount of animal detail will work, unless it is backed up with story or character.

These examples show how studying an animal, either its essence or its movement, can lead to interpretations that are original and exciting. There must be room for the eccentricity and the unique imagination of the actor.

*

Physical preparation

Warm-ups

I begin each Animal Study class with a strong warm-up. I often explore weight which will take the form of moving strongly or lightly through the space – as if the actor was clay or a feather. I will introduce games using rhythm and tempo and the dimensions. These introduce the playful possibilities available in our bodies for transformation, before even moving as an animal. Essentially the warm-up exercises will be asking the actors to play with 'movement qualities'.

Initial warm-up exercises for Animal Study

These exercises are already covered in the book under Pure Movement.

- Rolling down the spine, using the breath.
- Animal stretches from yawning into stretches in high, wide and forward.
- Spine work: to include rounding and hollowing, sensuous circling of the spine and animal drinking into cobra, pushing back into downward dog.

- Swing in wide into jumping. The swing in wide might also change into swinging across the space in wide, feet galloping, like a travelling monkey.

Throughout most of the warm-up I feed in ideas of how to link this with animals. If we are focusing on the locomotion of the animals, I will add leg stretches, and balancing exercises.

Group work

The warm-up might start in complete stillness. I bring the idea of an animal's stillness into the group warm-up and explore why it is still. If an animal is grooming and hears something, it will stop momentarily, then continue. Sometimes its sense of smell might lead it towards its prey, to wait, stock still in alert. Many of these stops and starts can be felt through dynamics – which I will explore later in an exercise called 'acceleration, deceleration'.

I encourage the actors to use the dimensions, as many animals will use these dimensions instinctively. A cat reaching on its hind legs to scratch a tree, a squirrel lengthening out as it darts forwards. The students can then see how the animals move through space, not always linear, but up and down, forwards and backwards and in and out. These changes of levels or dimensions come from changes of impulses that travel through the body. This can help the students build changes of rhythm or tempo (like the Eagle that landed) or work with a high stake's scenario. As the actors become more familiar with their animals, they do the group warm-up with the 'essence' of their animals. They are upright but moving with the quality of movement, or motion of their animals – gliding, galloping, plucking, slithering, adapted to a more human equivalent.

The spontaneousness of these responses is not the only way to focus the actor's imagination. More structured improvisations and exercises focus on one specific idea, to build stamina and imagination.

These group exercises are much easier to do when students have done the balancing the space games in ice-breakers.

1 The waterhole
Move in the space, stop with the drum. Then form into groups in shapes: a square, a triangle, a circle. Move on when everyone has found their place. Up the stakes by forming groups as if they were being chased, and the shapes were 'home'. Then suggest they move away 'suddenly' from the shapes, as if alarmed, then resume their journeys calmly. Suggest that the 'shapes' are the edges of waterholes that 'animals' gather round to 'drink' at as their animal, using the different 'levels' of their animals. The waterhole has become a truce between the animals.

2 Reaching out: How that changes the body in space
Gliding in the space – with a low centre of gravity – almost as if you are skating; keep the movements fluid and curving (flexible) in the space. Stop with the drum and reach out to connect to groups of people naturally clustered near you – through your fingers. Develop the exercise so that you try to touch only with elbows, then knees, then with both elbows and knees. These points of contact explore stretching the spine and limbs into balances (fingers), spirally (elbows), sinking or opening the hips (knees).

3 Senses into activity

Moving in the space, any way that feels nice, galloping, or skipping, sliding on the floor, adding jumps.[7] Drumbeat, still point. What do you hear? Respond as your animal. What do you see? Respond as your animal. Smell? Feel?

Still point. Response. Activity.

Move through the five senses: smell, touch, see, hear, taste. Each sense will trigger a specific activity or a response: Hear: they might be scared or growl. See: move towards something. Touch: they might scratch. Smell: sniff then scrabble for food.

4 Moving and dimensions

Balance the space with fast and free movements. This is like the balancing the space exercise previously described. On the drumbeat ask the actors to stop in a high shape, then to find ways of moving in High – leaping (like a deer), long and leggy (like a bird), leading with the upper body (like an ape). Different dimensions are called out with each drumbeat until the movements feel instinctive and natural as the group moves from one to the other. Low: slithering, crawling, rolling, lizard like. Wide: travelling forwards from side to side like a goose with its wings out, or a gibbon. Narrow: like a ferret, or a bird. Forwards: could be like a hippopotamus, or a horse. Backwards: backing away. Some animals circle backwards when they change direction.

*

Strength, stamina and flexibility exercises

Below I offer some additional strengthening and flexibility exercises for Animal Study. Many of these exercises are familiar from other movement or dance classes, but I am more interested in the process and story that flow through these movements. You can also do them quite small, not with a full extension, and just as expressively.

Building flexibility and strength is useful for those students keen to explore their animal as closely as possible – how it moves on four legs, or when flying. There are always ways to adapt the exercises, to accommodate your own physical needs, by doing the dog leg, very low, supported by a chair; or bird, holding onto something in front of you.

The key is learning how to distribute your weight through the various points of contact that ground you. Strength and flexibility contribute to agility, once you understand how to work economically. Working with an 'inside' understanding of the spine can make the movement easier to do, so focus on ease, rather than results.

Pure Movement centres around the idea of release and rebound – letting go of tension and giving into gravity and the momentum of your weight, followed by a recovery back to a starting point. For Animal Study you will need to use some core stability: the question is whether to actively engage the stomach muscles or not. So long as the focus is on allowing the spine to move with ease, the stomach muscles engage naturally. If you round the spine, there may be a sensation of the muscles gathering inwards: if hollowing the spine, the stomach muscles will naturally lengthen and stretch.

---

[7] When jumping, make sure that feet and ankles have been properly warmed up. Refer to exercises for feet in Part II.

Students often ask me if they ought to go to the gym to help them become stronger for these classes. Working out at a gym might be necessary in some cases: rehabilitation (from injury), resilience training and keeping up fitness levels. But it is important to make sure not to build up so much muscle that it inhibits physical expression and makes the body tight. This will limit your creative activity or possibly stop you from being able to drop the weight in a swing. After each session at the gym, and after the cool-down, loosen out, making sure that you keep flexible. We are looking for a combination of ease, flexibility and strength.

Strength, stamina and flexibility and body physical awareness exercises

1 Dog leg

This exercise can be applied to your studies of dogs, lizards, cats and frogs. It explores the actions of rising and lowering, and the impulses of stretching or hiding.

The exercise is brought to life by working with breath and flow and focus (where you are looking), which is very important for this exercise.

- Start hanging off the spine, feet hip-width apart, head and upper body hanging free.
- Walk your hands out until you are in 'downward facing dog'. Sit bones pointing to the sky, weight distributed equally between hands and feet. An upside-down V, with four points of contact to the ground.
- Pad the feet gently, by shifting the weight from foot to foot, and resume the position. You might need to raise the heels a little if you have tight Achilles tendons if this is hard, or bend the knees slightly. You might feel like a dog wanting to play.
- Lift one leg up behind you as straight as you can (you will have three points of contact with the ground) and shake your foot, bend the knee so the foreleg is floppy, the foot in the direction of your hind quarters. Then lower the leg, keeping the leg very relaxed, until the foot returns back to the ground to the starting position of downward dog. Repeat on the other side. No need to lift the leg too high.
- Next, lift the leg up as before and bend the knee slightly outwards, opening and lifting the hip: look under your arm – like a dog cocking its leg – release the leg back down to the ground.
- Both movements are a little dog-like in their impulses: up, shake, down.
- Next, lift the leg up straight as before, then bend it outwards again (the same way as before) and, keeping the knee bent, lower your centre of gravity by sending your weight forwards (you still have three points of contact with the ground) and bring the bent knee to the elbow on the same side. The key is how you distribute your weight, which is forward and along the length of your spine. You are lowering and lengthening. Send the energy out of the heel of the supporting leg, to keep the weight distributed through three points. Like a lizard with a flexed foot and the knee bent at right angles: agile, ready to move.
- Look to the side and track the foot and the leg out straight, then raise the leg but tracking a semicircle, out (from low), up to high, and feeling as though the foot is pulling you up high. All this is done with three points of contact to the ground.
- Release the leg back down, to have four points of contact with the ground.
- Repeat on the other side until you bring your second foot down, to downward dog.

- From downward dog, bend the knees to bring you onto all fours.
- Then send your sit bones back to be sitting on your haunches, with the upper body long and weight on your arms, like a dog (or a cat) sitting upright.

2 The Bird

I have adapted this exercise from Lecoq.

When you are studying a bird, you will need to find a way to embody its flight. This exercise of The Bird gives actors a template for how to embody 'flying'. It helps develop balance and flexibility. You will need to work with dynamics for the take-off and landing. I explore dynamics, and their exercises, later in the chapter.

- Stand with feet in first position (heels together and toes pointing at 45 degrees). Lift your arms up high and wide above your head, like the upper part of a starfish.
- Take a step forward on one foot, and pitch your body forwards, tilting like a plank, lifting the other leg up to balance, like an arabesque, and sending the arms out in front into parallel. You are like Superman.
- Keep tilting forwards, to go as parallel to the ground as you can manage (tilting at 45 degrees is also fine), feeling yourself streamlined through your finger tips and the toes of your lifted foot. Geese often fly like this, the body straight, lining up arms with the raised leg (or neck with legs).
- Open your arms out to the side, like wings, and 'fly' by moving them down and up. As the arms move down, bend the knee of the standing leg, and as the arms rise, straighten the leg. Make this movement continuous, following the movement of the arms/wings.
- When the arms are lowered and your knee bends, you are resisting the air, and when the arms rise and the leg straightens, you are carried by the air. Find the rhythm and the momentum of the flight and add a movement quality, tempered by how you use your breath and imagination, and you will be 'flying'. Look out or down depending on why you are flying. You could be floating on thermals, or flying direct to a destination, or looking for prey.
- To 'land', bring the leg in and straighten up. At the same time swing both arms through High, Forward and Back behind you with dynamic (maybe even folding your wings), and drop the knees. The dynamic is of acceleration to deceleration.
- Explore the moment of take-off, with the arms moving from their High and Wide position into the open position of the wings spread into Wide as one movement, and sink on one leg as you breathe out.
- Work in partners, with one person flying and the other person moving past them like the air or the wind, see how this changes the movement.
- You can also extend this into a scenario: Mercury, the messenger god or a Marvel character (like Superman) flying over a city or terrain, to land upright.

3 Undulation

This is the undulation that Lecoq refers to in his book *The Moving Body* (Lecoq, 2002 [1997]). It is part of what he sees as three natural movements: undulation, inversion and eclosion.

He links them as pathways to masked performance, with undulation an 'analogous pathway' for the expressive mask. As Animal Study is probably one of the most expressive movement experiences in an actor's training, this exercise is perfectly pitched to locate different leading points to express whether the animal is pushed or pulled into space. Understanding where movement comes from in the body and playing that to tell a story gives meaning to a movement. If, for instance, you break down the movement of the head into tilting to the side, or moving forwards, or backwards, these could be interpreted as 'I listen', 'I look', 'I'm frightened' (Lecoq, 2002 [1997]) (try it, it works!).

The task with animal study is to create the 'illusion' of the animal, as well as inhabiting it, and living truthfully inside it.

There are always these two pathways in transformation: 'I believe I am this person/being different to me: I have crafted a simple, economical and lively physical way to communicate it.'

Undulation starts from low down in the body and gradually travels upwards until it reaches its apex, to fall back down. It is like a wave starting at the knees and moving through the spine. We learned this exercise at Lecoq, starting upright and undulating through the spine. Others start it hanging off the spine. The best way to describe the initiation of the movement is lifting away from the ground. I am describing this exercise starting from standing, not from hanging off the spine.

- Start with the knees bent and upper body hunched, and head dropped forward (like an old man).
- Ripple up through the spine, until the pelvis is forward, and the weight pitched backwards, rather like a middle-aged person with a large girth (Lecoq amusingly coined this 'leading point' as 'the age of digestion'. The time of life when you prefer an early night and a good meal).
- Continue rippling up through the spine, ending in a suspension with the chest the focal point, with legs long, with the upper spine slightly arched.
- Then, with the head leading forwards, lead out and arched, as if being 'led by the nose'.
- Finally release the knees and drop the upper spine back to the starting point.
- You are accenting a journey through knees, hips, chest, nose and sink. To help find these points of expression, think of each one as a landing post, or accent.
- The movement is travelling upwards and then over the top (like a wave) with the nose leading forwards.
- Each of these positions can remain as 'still points' and in mask work, they are like attitudes, a point of view or a time in your life.

Lecoq suggests each placement tells a story or a time in a person's life. For example the forward position is like a child, the vertical position he sees as a Neutral Mask, the digestive phase is when the pelvis is forward and 'makes us incline backwards on the vertical' and then we drop back into old age, with knees and upper spine sunk down.

I use the undulation as an exercise to introduce the locomotion of animals. When a large animal like a giraffe moves, there is an undulation that travels from the hooves through the neck. A tiger will be undulating along the spine, lengthways. Otters undulate in a sideways movement. There is, as you will see, always an interplay between animal and character, time and place, body and leading points.

This exercise is also fun to help actors find a centre for a character.

*

Motion/locomotion/rhythm/tempo=movement qualities

Studying how an animal moves in detail and underpinning it with a mixture of technical expertise and the release and openness of working through the prism of the gravity swing and a fluid and flexible spine, takes time. To be able to go as 'far' as the actor playing the eagle, to find a depth of characterization through a physical study, asks for curiosity, commitment and daring.

To do it fully, the actor and the student need guidance. 'Movement qualities' is part of this process. How you move. How you move tells the story of who you are.

There are exercises which form part of a methodology for students to examine how the animal they are studying moves. All movement expresses who we are, or why we move, or what we want. 'Words without thoughts never to heaven go'.

Many of the reference points have been covered in the previous movement classes already. I describe the ones not already covered. The Animal Study will express both the animal's locomotion, and its quality of movement. Here are some of the ideas that might help take this further.

1 Suspension
The turning point of stillness before a change of direction in a swing (more a suspended animation).*[8]

2 Direction
Forwards, backwards, sideways – all in relation to the front (where your body is facing).*

3 Dimensions
High, low, wide, narrow, forwards, backwards and the interplay between them (not just their opposites).*

---

[8]An asterisk refers to the fact that these exercises have been covered elsewhere.

4 Pathways

How you travel through space:

- Straight lines (the shortest journey from one point to another – Direct in Laban).
- Direct and Indirect are Laban terms, and part of the Free Dance movement vocabulary
- Curves: arcs, figures of eight (the longest journey from one point to another – Flexible or Indirect in Laban).
- Spirals:
  Spooling and unspooling like thread on a cotton reel. You circle from an outward point to a still point in the centre in ever-diminishing unbroken circles: then reverse the journey by circling outward from a still point in the centre in ever-expanding unbroken circles, allowing the pathway to accelerate or decelerate. The wider the arc, the faster you travel, with the momentum sometimes spinning you to a stop. Think of a whirlpool or a twister.
- Zig-zags:
  Travelling directly on a diagonal for a short space of time, then changing to the opposite diagonal – a short, sharp, staccato motion.
- Crossing over:
  Changing direction by one limb crossing over the other and following the path of the crossed limb.

5 Tempo

- Rate or speed in relation to activity: pace, velocity – as in quick or slow and can be set musically, e.g. 'largo', 'presto', 'allegro', to a metronome or beats per minute: how fast something moves. But for acting we don't set this to beats per minute (bpm).
- Also an inner tempo: fast or slow heartbeat, breath, thoughts, emotional responses?

6 Rhythm

- A clear repeated pattern of movement which can be sensed, counted or felt, often called metre, or a measure: what is the timing for the movement?
- Rhythm of movement of a person: what is the rhythm of movement as they walk, do different tasks? You could for example repeat the same rhythm, but in different tempi. Or change the rhythm but keep the same tempo.

7 Crescendo and diminuendo: Accelerate and decelerate

- The combination of both is movement dynamics, gradually getting louder or softer with an increase or decrease of intensity, through the speeding up or slowly down of movement.
- The intensity and gathering speed of movement is strong/loud/fast.
- The slowing down and diminishing of movement is soft/quiet/slow.
- Like a leaf blown off a tree in a gust of wind. Or a bird landing and carrying the speed of its flight into running, then gradually slowing down to a stop. These are examples of movement dynamics.

8 Weight

- This is how the body relates to gravity, as well as the weight of the body itself.
- This is logic based on combining sensation with observation. A giraffe has density, so when it moves its body, it has 'weight', but conversely, when it turns its head, the weight factor will be 'light' (against gravity). These are two different 'movement qualities'.
- You sit down heavily with exhaustion (weight – slow direct) which you 'feel' (as in 'I must sit down') and flutter your hand as you look for your medication (light – fast, flexible).
- No one animal or person has one fixed weight or pattern of movement.
- To understand this more clearly, we can replicate this in our bodies, often through identifying with the movement of natural objects and exploring their movement pathways and patterns to help us understand these distinctions.[9]

9 Breath[10]

- Being on the breath means breathing with the movement. Releasing with the breath; for instance, you could sigh out with relief which takes you down to the ground. Working with the breath like this is not the same thing as making a conscious effort to place the breath in different parts of the body to help embody an animal's movement.

Two ways of working with the breath, both useful

Therapeutic

To make sure you breathe as you move and the breath is dropped a bit lower in the body, so that you are not carrying tension: this can also help develop your breath capacity as well as keep you centred and grounded.

Interpretive and creative

The other is to understand where the breath is coming from in the body of the animal you are studying.

- What kind of breath, fast, slow – and in some cases this is surprising, and can change.

    An example: an allegator as it moves rapidly towards its prey will be working with a long slow breath, even though it is moving fast. It will be working with acceleration/ deceleration (as above), but with one single sustained objective and focus – to kill. The tension between the outer physicality and the inner physicality is something that Stanislavski-based study addresses: the difference between an inner attitude and an outer attitude.

---

[9]This is explored more fully in Chapter 12.
[10]The use of the breath can be for relaxation and well-being. The two examples referred to above are either for technique in Pure Movement, or as part of a physical interpretation in animal study. When applied to physical choices for acting, the breath always needs to support the voice and the activity so that actors don't hurt their bodies or their voices.

10 Locomotion and co-ordination and pathways

- We can use the movement qualities explored above when looking at various ways of moving for interpreting the animals.
- The pattern of movement, combined with its silhouette and its tempo, rhythm, weight and pathways in space are often the simplest way to start our study.
- The various ways of moving are complex. They involve co-ordination whilst moving through the different dimensions, and require us to shift our weight, working with or against gravity, while moving in complex patterns through the space.
- If this is too physically demanding, there remains the option to contract the physical study, to do the animal standing.

*

How to introduce Animal Movement

If I have two terms to teach Animal Study and Animal Into Character, I introduce some of these movement techniques offered above, as independent training exercises. This gives students a vocabulary to work with and helps them 'analyse' the movement patterns of the animals they study and take agency when creating their studies. If this isn't the case, you can introduce these ideas in classes that introduce different animals.

In either case, you can break the movement down into a combination of weight, and dynamics, co-ordination and leading points, which you then select to be applied playfully to specific groups of animals. This is a movement vocabulary.

*

I help students 'research' the different ways animals move by breaking down the weekly classes into generic species: big cats, big birds, little birds, monkeys and so on. Such 'research' helps introduce the students to a range of animals perhaps not thought of. First to set this up, I run a couple sessions on Animal Movement, moving from one animal to the other with rapid changes. The teacher can lead this as an exploration. I was once led by a brilliant movement practitioner at a Lecoq workshop hosted by LIFT,[11] through all the various movement patterns of multiple animals, which she had fully embodied. It was a two-hour session of follow my leader – thrilling to experience the manifold movement possibilities and animals available to all of us, in such a short time.

I won't analyse every animal's movement in detail, but by using combinations derived from this vocabulary you will be able to work this out for yourself.

Ways to explore this
Combine weight, tempo, breath, and dimension – and ask the actors to explore this and then create an animal e.g.: fast, low, light, breath. The animal might be mythical.

*

---

[11] London International Festival of Theatre.

Animals move in a combination of patterns

- Opposition: opposite arm to leg, as in walking – or the body balancing the forward motion in opposition on all fours, as in front left leg and back right leg travelling forwards in opposition.[12]
- Ambulatory: same arm as leg, with the weight shifting from side to side – camels and ducks move like this.
- Plucking or pulling from the ground: birds, and some mammals.
- Plucking two legged: often in opposition: birds with a complementary movement backwards and forwards with the head (chickens for example).
- Hopping from two feet: birds.
- Hopping from back to front with four feet: small mammals do this, with a little lift of the pelvis, and with a sense of travelling forward (often called a bunny hop).
- Lizard motion: close to the ground, long – either slithering on your stomach or in a semi-press up, ambulatory with the back leg, propelling the front leg forward.
- Moving from high to low: large animals, when they sit or lie down. For a cow or a goat, think of sinking the front legs first, then folding the back legs to follow, and collapsing the weight to the side. Dynamics are useful here.
- Moving from low to high: large animals, when they stand up – a giraffe for example, will push its back legs up first and unfold its front legs afterwards; while a big cat might gain momentum in its version of low to high, by rolling from lying on the ground, onto all fours.
- Leaping: a deer or ibis might travel forwards, lifting front legs first and be momentarily airborne before landing.
- Springing: some deer might leap by springing up from all four legs – an ibex.
- Striking the ground: small dogs might strike the ground lightly, horses clip the ground, deer the same but with an upward impulse.
- Trotting: this is a fox, whose head leads forwards, pulling its long body and luxurious tail (if it isn't mangey) – almost tacking sideways.

Using these templates I often run an introductory session on how to approach the different animals: breaking it down into birds, cats, lizards, giraffes, camels, deer, mice or squirrels, eagles and meerkats. Then I ask students to select one to try for themselves, without having fully studied it yet, as a 'taster'. This is helped by having the technique of Pure Movement to refer to. At Lecoq, our movement vocabulary travelled effortlessly into the physical life of our work, which is another example of what good teaching practice needs – to lay in a body of movement work on an acting course that students can rely on across all their projects. The study begins in earnest when students visit the zoo, or city farm, to finalize an animal to study; this can take time to decide. When I started teaching this subject, the criterion to make your choice was often an animal the opposite of

---

[12]This is front left leg forward, balanced by back right leg forward: on all fours you can practise this by stretching the left arm out at the same time as the back right leg out, and feeling the diagonal across your body.

your own movement qualities. I would probably still suggest this, but the choice needs to inspire the student. Choosing the opposite of your own movement qualities, in a big class, can ensure that there is enough variety for the group work to be helpful for learning. Students will be watching each other as well, seeing as many different animals as possible, while playing their own.

Guidance for different animals

Once you have gone to the zoo, chosen your animal and watched it move, you will then start to find ways to put this through your body.

The exercises below are a way in to this: and refer to all the work previously covered in the book.

By adding movement qualities and pathways, dimensions, breath and weight, you start to realize its physicality.

*

Four-legged crawl: For tigers or big cats, dogs, wolves, apes, monkeys, moving in opposition or ambulatory

Pathway: Direct and crossing – to change direction

Big cats

- Crawl forwards on hands and knees (you might need knee pads). Sense the length in the spine by letting the back leg drive the front forward. Feel the head pull you forwards. The animal is driving forwards but is pushed from behind.
- As the leg comes forward the opposition arm answers with a slight delay – the spine therefore undulates.
- You are pushed and pulled at the same time.
- To change direction, let the arm cross over, turning you in the opposite direction – your spine will flow in a curve to follow you.
- You can do a little figure of eight dance, looking forwards and tacking sideways as you cross from side to side, as though pacing or stalking prey.
- If you are very flexible and strong, you can crawl through feet and hands and a low centre of gravity.
- You can also crawl through hands and feet, or hands and knees with the same arm as leg driving you forwards (ambulatory). But if you do this let the hips and shoulders dip and rotate so there is fluidity in the spine. This is very difficult!

Canines

- Straighten your legs a little and lift your tail a little, taking the weight onto your toes; you can move as dogs, trotting.
- Trotting is usually in opposition, but sometimes, depending on the speed, it can be ambulatory.
- A fox trots with a maintained tempo, very light on their paws, almost silently. This is a springing step.
- If you are strong enough you can take the weight onto both arms at the same time, throwing them forwards with feet following, to gallop, like a wolf or a big dog. This is called a quadruped movement.
- If you increase the weight factor, you will be expressing a stronger intention or want.

Small animals

- Reduce the distance between arms and legs by rounding your spine and squatting down; you can move or scurry like a squirrel or rabbit by sending the weight forward onto your hands and doing little handsprings.
- If you move very quickly in opposition and lengthen and lead by the nose, maybe you are a rat.

Primates

- Apes and monkeys alternate between moving on all fours and moving upright.
- They alternate between moving in opposition and in ambulatory.
- They change direction by crossing their front limbs over each other.
- The upper spines of apes are long and broad, and their leading point is their forehead.
- When they are upright, they are ambulatory.
- Primates will all have different movement qualities. The ape will, for instance, punch the ground as it moves forwards, a chimp is more wiry, fast and elastic.

Bears

- Bears' movement is ambulatory when walking on all fours, with their rear swinging slightly; they gallop when chasing to kill.
- When they stand up (grisly, that is) their weight is back, with a high centre of gravity.

*

Two legs for four legs: Moving between dimensions – Camels/giraffes

How do we 'channel' and create the physicality of a large four-legged animal? If we play a large animal on all fours, we diminish its power and presence. If we rely on props or masks we move into 'puppetry', a separate and beautiful discipline all its own.

It is even common now to play primates with the use of crutches to elongate the forelimbs. But the aim of Animal Study is to capture the essence of the animal, so the study can transform our own body to that of our animal.

Acting a four-legged animal, through two legs

- Stand on two legs, and using your two arms as the front legs, and moving them in the sequence, rhythm and pattern of the animal on the ground is the simplest way to do this. This gives a sense of its size and weight.
- Giraffes, as described above, have weight and flow, and their movement is ambulatory; there is a ripple through their long necks, through which the locomotion is registered.

- Camels are long and lower; they are carrying their humps, and their feet are floppy, as if they are wearing carpet slippers: their movement is also ambulatory, but their heads are dominant.
- Explore this by bending your knees, rounding the base of your spine and tipping the spine forwards a little with the arms out in front. Your spine is curved because it is balancing at the peak of it a wobbly heavy container of water (the camel's hump).
- The sensation is of trying to keep your balance as you manage all this 'weight'. As you move forward, the head is leading you, and the feet and hands on the same side mirror each other, padding softly.
- The camel turns in a spiral. We have already looked at this in the movement classes. The head leads, crossing arms and legs and twisting to the opposite direction (try this, closing, turning movement, standing up – losing the camel. Someone powerful, squeezing into a tight space?).

- Goats climb, so their walk has a little sharp hiccup in it, as they dig into the slope.

The approach is the same as with the studies on all fours: is the animal pushed from behind or pulled from in front? If the animal moves in ambulatory, the back leg and front arm will be on the same side. The hip, or knee, will initiate the leg: the shoulder or elbow the arm. If the animal is hooved, then the 'striking' of the foot on the ground will be mirrored by the movement of the wrist. Much of the relationship between foot and hand (and its connection through the spine) has been explored in the foot and wrist exercises in the previous chapters.

*

Locomotion of birds

The movement on the ground of birds has as much variety as mammals and the four-legged animals already discussed. The smaller and lighter the bird the less body weight is dispersed when it is hopping or walking on the ground. A small bird is almost ready to fly, so doesn't need much effort to get airborne, but a big bird needs a lot of effort to get off the ground. You reflect this in how you move: light or strong.

Large birds when on the ground will often seem ungainly. A vulture will be permanently hunched, managing its large wings and long neck. It will move in ambulatory and occasionally opens its wings to lift itself up from level to level.

Ravens and crows also hop, or strut, quite forcefully to move their relatively large bodies, from side to side, like shouldering a door open, to disperse the density of their body weight. Like a pushy person trying to get to the front of a queue.

If a bird is a predator, their claws are lethal, their legs have enormous power and their beaks are like weapons. Being aware of this gives a context to the physicality. I often wonder why Richard III has never been channelled through a vulture!

Birds which travel through the three elements of earth, air and water, such as ducks and geese, will move differently in all elements, and their bodies change and acquire more freedom in the air and water than on land.

Birds with webbed feet

- The legs and webbed feet of a duck or goose will determine the gait of your study on land.
- A swan even more so; the grace and power as it glides through the water, surveying all seemingly calmly, is in contrast with the effort of propulsion of the feet through the water. But once out of its element, it is a graceless and lumbering unbalanced creature that reminds us of its links to the Jurassic age.
- If you realize the swan in water, it will be graceful and strong. You can't do both things at once, but it is useful to know the effort that goes into the grace. And once on land it is as if the swan is unmasked.

This raises questions that are useful for acting. What do we show? And what are we hiding? How hard must we work behind the scenes to make our public face appear serene? What happens to us when we are not 'in our element'?

Long-legged birds

- A long-legged bird, like a flamingo, has a short body and a long neck; the legs unfurl, with a flick of the foot backwards, to step forwards. This is like a dancer doing a 'développé' in ballet.
- When they stand, with their wings folded, it is for us as if our arms were folded behind our backs, and the ease of the head as they look round allows them to watch for shrimp, and I believe they often stand still to cool down.
- These 'attitudes' are positions which suggest flexibility, and a certain kind of confidence in your own environment.
- An ostrich is another long-legged bird. It has a rounded body and long neck, and as a flightless bird, it has immensely strong legs which power it forward when running.

An animal: A body with a story to tell

Each animal has its unique physical set of circumstances that they live with to move through the world. Animal myths and fables reflect our own difficulties or fantasies – like Aesop's Fables. We learn from animals what jeopardy there is in the world for us and how to save ourselves, with an animal instinct and cunning. Or how to carry ourselves to impress or outwit others, or how to care for others, particularly our young. Or how easily our show of confidence can be unmasked. We identify with our tribe and are wary of others – just like animals. These physical stories are often expressed in fairy tales.

Many of the movement exercises I describe, including Animal Study, lead us to making interesting creative observations and choices that go beyond the original remit of simply bringing the life of the animal into the studio.

*

How to show flying in a bird

Flying, how a bird takes off, flies and lands, can be explored using acceleration and deceleration (explained below). But what about the wings?

- Start with your arms wide and feel the air with the ends of your fingers – the tips of your wings.
- Turn one arm and shoulder inwards, bend the elbow and place the upper side of your wrist against your back and do the same with the other arm, either together, or one after the other. Allow the spine to be involved, rounding or arching it, like the spine of a bird. This is a sudden to slow movement, following the lores of dynamics I mention in this chapter. See the exercise on acceleration to deceleration below.
- Open the wings by unfurling one after the other, or at the same time, allowing the body's weight to shift with the movement.

- Explore with 'smaller' and 'larger' wings: this affects the tempo and the weight factor.
- Explore different intentions – a fast flap of the wings, or a swift opening of the wings to fly away fast – or opening one wing to clean it or to cover your head as you sleep.

*

Final technical explorations and observations

The approaches and exercises described above are my methodology to help break down what an actor or student needs to understand when they are creating an 'Animal Study'. The expectation is for them to study one animal in depth, and then to apply their study to creating a character.

The exercises are delivered in a classroom teaching environment with several students, perhaps exploring different animals at the same time, so these common principles help accommodate everyone.

The exercises can also be reduced to be played or explored sitting down or standing up. This is why quality of movement is important, as it can inform the smallest movements. The last exercises are about intensity of movement.

The end result is for the actor to find a freedom and a specificity in what they do, to be able to live these transformations, moment to moment. The next and final exercises help the actor move within space with changes in tempo and use of space.

*

Pathways and intention

1 Acceleration, deceleration and method

This exercise helps organize your use of space and understanding of tempo at the same time.

- Start at the corner of the room: you will be running down a diagonal.
- Focus on the opposite diagonal across the room and get a sense of where the midpoint of this line is.
- Start by running and building up speed; once you have reached the midpoint start to slow down, in the same ratio as you sped up.
- When you reach the opposite diagonal, you have slowed into stillness.
- You will need to organize your body to do this without crashing into the opposite diagonal – the movement has a purpose.

2 Stories with acceleration, deceleration

- Taking off and landing as a bird. This is a 'story' in 'motion' led by the body: you are almost 'taking off' as you pass the midpoint, and are airborne at the end: or you are landing from the sky, like a bird, landing at the midpoint, and colliding with the force of gravity until you come to a stop (think of a plane bumping the tarmac as it lands).
- A wave crashes on the shoreline. The movement could be a wave that peaks at the midpoint and then disperses by opening out so that when you reach stillness, the density of the water is disappearing.

- Do the exercise again and this time and add different stories to it: a bird taking off and flying, and a bird landing.
- What kind of bird will determine the weight and manner of take-off, and landing and flying. A big bird hovers, glides, wheels, plunges, a small bird takes off faster with quick wing movements and then can often coast on the air.

Character and shadow moves from the animals

To choose an animal that is 'opposite' to your personality is to 'work for' qualities that extend your playing range. Someone finds it hard to play high status and could explore a tiger. Someone who is naturally introvert might explore an exotic bird: someone who is serious might explore a marmoset or spider monkey. These studies are creative ways to help a psychologically truthful actor be able to play 'many parts'.

The study of how each animal moves for grooming, eating, marking its territory, when it is young, or protecting its young, or is predator or prey, is transposed into a human activity for some of the 'character' movement. Smaller movements can be transposed into gestures, that 'shadow' or reflect who you are, and your inner life. How you comb your hair, or look for your keys, is transposed from your animal character grooming or eating perhaps.

Every gesture you make as the character is a transformative act.

My work at Drama Centre London elaborated this, as the students were studying mask work with me, alongside Animal Study, and the work of Vakhtangov with Oleg Mirochnikov. The reference points of mask work and the students' work on fantastical realism allowed me to take the work further into a fantastical and musical approach to transformation. One of the most exciting developments for release, imagination and political commentary. I have described this already in the previous chapter as the cabaret version of animal.

But my starting point is how to take animal study into simple transformation for naturalism.

Working with different animals in a group of students creates different dynamics and energies, moving with individual movement patterns together at the same time. We have a diverse group of individuals. Very exciting!

Animal Study classes: Exercises

Here is a list of classes I might set or run over a term. The actors would bring their 'study' to class from going to the zoo.

1 Rest and spine

- How does the animal sleep and wake up? Focusing on the senses and the breath.
- To standing up as the animal. To be still as the animal, while surveying its environment.
- What is your silhouette in this stillness and how does it transform your own spine?

2 Spine and locomotion

- What is the base rhythm of your animal? How to move that can identify it as the animal: this includes rhythm, leading points, tempo, undulation, weight and whether opposition or ambulatory.

- The base rhythm will be the movement you go back to, when travelling through the space.

3 Locomotion and dimensions

- How does your animal move between the dimensions.
- What are your animal's versions of high, low, wide, narrow, forwards, backwards?
- There may in fact be several versions of these, to take in flying, or swimming, tunnelling or hiding?

4 Shadow movements and psychological gestures

- How does the animal groom itself? And display itself for mating rituals or dominance?
- How does it eat: and hunt or catch its food?
- I often suggest taking in food for this class. Lettuce that can be attached to walls for giraffes to eat as leaves: sweets for meerkats to dig up as scorpions: carrion-eating birds would place food on chairs to lift food with their feet to their beaks. You don't need a lot of food for this exercise. And it needs to be fresh and placed on paper towels for hygiene. Also be careful of allergies.
- This class develops into creating the animal's environment, to make a nest or a habitat.
- It marks the transition from exploring the physical life of your animal as an exercise, to placing the animal in a high stake scenario, with strong wants.

5 Stakes

- How does it play and how does it mark its territory?
- How does it protect its young?
- Feed its young?

6 Impulse

- Journeys: how does it go on long and short journeys?

A development of a narrative

Each class would start with a warm-up and then private practice to explore solo the exercises set. Then often sharing this with a partner.

Through studying the movement of an animal in its environment, a narrative emerges. This sets the study up to move into acting.

Acting exercises

1 The last class in this group of exercises is 'A Day in The Life of Your Animal'
The actor imagines a day, in its natural habitat, and creates an Animal Study for about six minutes. I ask students to find ways to thread these elements into their story, moving through the dimensions, change of tempo and dynamics, and bookending it with waking and sleeping. I will ask them to pay attention to what the animal's rhythm throughout the day

is: when are they most active? When, if ever, do they siesta? And where do they travel? It is an exercise that is both close-up and cinematic in scope.

2 Finding your character from animal study

When I was teaching at RADA, the Animal Into Character classes coincided with the first-year realist project. This project explored either Russian or American playwrights – Chekhov, Gorky or Miller or Lorraine Hansberry, for instance. The Acting and Movement departments collaborated to help students choose an animal for their character in the play, which they then used as a springboard to refine into a believable characterization. 'The character' had a life outside of the play and the physical life could both inform and respond to the imagined scenarios explored in improvisations.

The choice was based on identifying three adjectives to describe the character you are playing,[13] to then choose an animal that might embody that.

The exercises below are Animal Into Character. You can use the same approach when working with the animal you have chosen for a play.

- Travel from the movement of your animal (say on all fours), to standing, to discover leading point, tempo, centre, weight, rhythm. This will give you a sense of how you move, and who you might be.
- Explore the details, from grooming as your animal, to exploring how that would translate into a gesture, not necessarily linked.
- Eat as your animal, and see what that translates as, not necessarily eating: it could be arguing, worrying, threatening.
- Explore sitting, lying, moving through the dimensions in animal, then the more human version. You begin to get a sense of how you move, so who you might be.
- Gradually a person emerges: this is a secret, for the actor, so they can mull on it and refine it for the next week. Never ask them 'who they are' – they will know.
- Then ask them to come to class in the garments of their character.

Extended improvisations

The invention and creativity and sophistication

Let the actors find their personal ways to express their characters. Here is an excellent example:

An actor had been studying a heron. He had found perfectly the mournful aspect of the long feathers closed behind him, and the stillness as he watched for fish in the pool. He opened his wings, and became elegant and graceful as he soared into the sky. He arrived at class in a raincoat, an umbrella and a dog collar. He was a priest, looking for lost souls. The umbrella was his wings opening out.

Solo exercises: A day in the life of your character

I ask them to explore their day as their character, and then select a scenario to dig into further. This must have a problem and a want in it.

---

[13] This is based on Stanislavski's system.

- One actor was a librarian and she had lost a book and had to look for it. Her animal had been a goat. The looking was a kind of foraging.
- The emphasis is on the physicality of the character expressing wants and solving problems, and the refinement of the animal movement into 'character movement'.

Improvised interactions with other animals/characters

- Two or three animals interact. This is 100 per cent animal back in the 'wild'. Predator and prey: mother caring for her young.
- Replicate the same responses but place the animal characters in a lift, or a waiting room and see how the 'animal behaviour' translates into a similar smaller version of fighting over territory: in small shadow moves, glares, stillness, getting up, reading a book. They are their characters, wearing their garments.
- Scenarios, based on social situations: a Parent Teacher Meeting for instance. Focus on interacting truthfully with each other, using the animal as the way to find your naturalistic responses.
- Two-handed scenes. You can take this into a job interview, where the interviewer might have high social status but physically be intimidated by the interviewee: for instance, a character based on a mouse interviewing a camel.

Looking for a text and speech patterns that match the physicality of animal into character

Most of the exercises above have used minimal text. These next ideas focus on the actor combining physical and emotional and vocal life, from animal into character.

- Hot-seat the character, by asking them questions about their life. Their relationships, their problems, their hopes. The answers are generated from a character created from the physical life of the animal, not from a literary text.
- Speak the text of your rehearsal exercise or scene in the physical life of your character, found from the animal, and see if that shifts the text.
- Stay connected to the sense and structure of the text, and make sure the breath is engaged: but see if the physical life of your character changes the depth of emotional connection, or makes the language more embodied.

*

The exercises above show you how you can 'create' a character from an animal.

Many of the examples show the phenomenon of 'let the movement change you'.

Once you have explored the richness of bringing the life of an animal into a character, you can choose an animal for a character you might be playing. The animal is an inspiration for the life force of your character, and you can select, from its movements and its responses, how to shape and craft your performance.

11 Mask work

Neutral Mask work: What is it? Is it still relevant? Can it be taught?

Wearing the Neutral Mask explores 'acting' in a unique and innovative way. The mask asks actors to embody essentialist dramatic action, with the simplest and clearest of gestures in improvised scenarios. The impact of its expression is enhanced by working in silence, on solo exercises, to create a physical text in front of peers, played fully from the imagination. Yet working with the Neutral Mask is often seen as a 'movement class' rather than part of a methodology to expand an actor's craft. Expressive Movement, Mask work and Animal Study still struggle to consolidate their central position in drama school training[1] (Morris, 2017). Drama schools still prefer to give more value to voice and text classes, continuing a long slow journey to give as much value to the dramatic training of the body – with psychological realism, or truth, as the potential connective tissue between the two. If drama schools committed themselves to working with masks, taught not for superficial transformation, but as an opportunity to let the body speak, the results could be very exciting.

For many years, mask work was taught very effectively for Drama GCSE, with companies like Trestle Theatre offering workshops for schools.[2] At school age, the impact of mask work to develop imagination and creativity is invaluable, and I have found the students who have already explored these techniques are often the most adventurous in my mask and movement classes. Sadly, this is less and less likely to be the case now. As the 'National Drama's Response to the Arts in Schools Review' reported in 2023, Drama is under-resourced and undervalued in the school curriculum. There is a danger that the imaginative creative work of mask and drama will only be available to the privileged fee-paying schools, and the impact for education is worrying.

> National Drama regrets the fact that economic and party-political policies should be a reason for the marginalization of children and young people's learning experiences in developing imaginative thinking and creativity. (National Drama, 2023)[3]

Through its playfulness and powers of transformation, mask work develops the imagination and opens our creative thinking in ways it is impossible to quantify.

---

[1] I am offering myself as a source for this information as I have taught in drama schools since 1989, and have recently encountered a certain unease when teaching both Animal Study and mask work. This wasn't the case when I started: possibly because the schools I taught still had teachers who had trained with Michel Saint-Denis.
[2] Trestle Theatre Company specializes in masked performance and leads many mask workshops. Also sells masks. Théâtre de Complicité used to offer Neutral Mask workshops in the 1990s as part of its education programme.
[3] Nationaldrama.org.uk

The context of mask work, and the mask as an artefact which can affect dramatic action

I learned Neutral Mask at Jacques Lecoq when I was at his school from 1976 to 1978 and have been exploring it ever since – teaching all forms of mask work since 1989. My practice is informed by a 'search' for a depth of physical and imaginative expression and builds on the physicality of the movement classes.

I ask the actor to inhabit the mask, by applying the techniques from their movement classes, as acting precepts. It is easier for students to understand the Neutral Mask once they have learned to be still, listen and respond, and work with the breath. In fact, it is virtually impossible to teach mask work at professional level, unless the participant has had some form of movement training which addresses these techniques. Embedded alongside voice, improvisation and many other acting techniques, mask work could become an essential part of theatre training.[4,5] In fact I was able to teach both Neutral Mask and Character Mask at Rose Bruford and Drama Centre London, alongside Commedia dell'Arte, in just this way. As improvisation, transformation and stagecraft are vital to this work, my classes were viewed as physicality and acting classes, and their techniques were actively sought in rehearsal exercises and public productions. I taught Neutral Mask at RADA as well, also momentarily introducing Commedia dell'Arte to a young theatre group of RADA graduates, but with less curiosity from the faculty (not the students) about how the work connected to an actor's journey or could be used in productions.

There are some challenges facing us when working with masks, whose function will always ask actors to submerge their own identity. The actor 'carries' or 'wears' the mask, bringing it to life by embodying it, but the artefact of most of the Neutral Masks available to work with will be described as Eurocentric. The Neutral Masks I work with are Satori's, which I describe in more detail below, but I acknowledge the problems concerning their ethnic features – and there are added difficulties, as they also divide into male and female Neutral Masks. Inevitably this raises questions about what a 'neutral' facial expression ought to be, perhaps challenging the concept that this is even possible, and certainly raising the question of what, or who are we being asked to embody. Sartori's masks are reasonably generic and abstract in their features but are Caucasian in type. So, there is possibly a need to consider African, Asian and East-Asian Neutral Masks, which neither Lecoq's nor Copeau's Noble Masks encompassed.[6] This has yet to be researched properly, especially if Neutral Mask continues to be taught, and I don't dismiss any concerns this might raise. I have never encountered a resistance to the form of the Sartori mask, but I have encountered a fear of transformation. The apparent ethnicity of the mask has never been referred to – though its abstraction has.[7]

I work with six leather masks, designed by Amleto Sartori, three male and three female. I now ignore the gender of the masks. Smaller faces (male or female) will 'carry' the

---

[4]Meisner work is now offered as a regular part of actor training, as is Michael Chekhov's work.
[5]Most drama schools taught Movement, Acting, Voice and Scene Study/Rehearsal Exercises, as well as Dance, Music/Singing and other subjects like Film and TV, Fight and Radio.
[6]This was the reference for Copeau's 'Noble Mask' above.
[7]Though I am mindful of Mackinnon's comments about compliance – see 'The Need for a System'. See Chapter 4 for more details.

smaller female masks, and larger faces (male of female) the larger (male or female). Gender does not determine the size of a face. The features of male and female are the same, with the exception that there are two lines for the eyebrows for the female and just one for the male. It is possible that the male mask appears stronger, but once the mask is 'carried', it is the wearer who determines the specificity of the physicality.

My provocation for students and drama schools is to explore what Neutral Mask can teach us about theatre, the dramatic moment and the use of the space. I have developed a way to teach the exercises, inclusively.

When I taught in drama schools from 1989 to 2023, I witnessed mask work wax and wane.[8] Part of this is a resource issue; masks are expensive, and the schools which encouraged me to teach Mask either had their own or were able to buy them. When I taught Neutral Mask to the BA Acting Course at RADA, it was the first time it was officially included in the curriculum – though it had been taught on its other courses. I brought my own masks to the school, as there were none there. Rose Bruford had many masks, as did the other schools I mentioned.

What is 'neutral'?

'Neutral' is a state of mind, a readiness, an openness which affects an actor's powers of expression and is not a particular gender, or ethnicity, or racial type. Perhaps we can consider it radical, that 'neutral' means we can express anything, and are not bound by our identity. But perhaps its origins in modernism and cross-cultural references, limit the scope of 'neutral'. The next descriptions seek to interrogate this.

Neutral is also the actor unadorned

As previously mentioned, my teaching of Neutral Mask comes from my training at Lecoq. I have developed my own pedagogy for text-based drama schools, and the exercises I describe don't refer to other practitioners, except for David Latham.

Lecoq's Neutral Mask is not about psychology or character. The mask has no 'character'. The transformation the actor encounters in the Neutral Mask is their own – how they transform physically when they interpret the scenarios the mask encounters. This is a form of renewal for the actor, which mirrors the transformation that psychologically based acting requires, but is quite different. You transform your body with an imaginative idea, you expand an imaginative muscle. Without the mask on, this can contract to more subtle and naturalistic transformations. However, the Neutral Mask does have a 'point of view' – of curiosity and openness. This point of view is expressed through the actor's body, making it open and balanced, and responding to the movement of the natural world, which, crucially, the actor imagines and brings to life in front of their audience. What they 'see' is invisible and is only communicated through the detail and passion of their movement.

---

[8]Christian Darley at LAMDA, John Blatchley at Drama Centre, Joe Blatchley, Trish Arnold and Wendy Allnut at Guildhall, and Rose Bruford and E15 all taught vibrant mask classes on their BA Acting Courses.

In Mask work, the actor is at the centre of the space, working on their own. This is often a new experience for an acting student – to be the architect of dramatic action, making their own text, not reliant on a writer or director – and can have professional benefits. Today actors can no longer rely on the repertory system to give them a grounding in stagecraft or playing a variety of roles. And today stagecraft stretches to many skills. Stand-up comedy, devising, listening and responding, stage action, the ability to hold a space and deliver a soliloquy, even rapidly pivoting to record self-tapes at a day's notice. Neutral Mask is useful for all these as it trains the actor to be physically present, and work with immediacy and creativity, and an awareness of how to use the space available to them with clarity.

Transformation as challenge to identity

An actor who wears a well-constructed mask with skill and connection can bring the mask to life in surprising ways. As the body moves, with different impulses, its expression will seem to change – a remarkable thing to behold. How much information the body carries!

When a mask is in play, we understand exactly who the mask is, and what they are doing, because we can see all of them and the (imaginary) space they are in:

$$Mask + Body + Action = Space$$

For this the actor needs to let go of how they might move in a naturalistic space and find a simpler and more direct physical response, propelling them out of their comfort zone. To make stronger, more expressive and clearer physical choices can feel very exposing, particularly as they aren't choreographed. Actors can feel they are losing their identity – the part of their physicality that defines them as an actor and as a person.

At Lecoq, I remember his instructions to us, not to work with small 'quotidian' gestures. He would often comment on how moving very fast, with tight short steps, was not neutral but an urban tempo in a crowded space, carrying too much of the identity of the actor and their view of the world.

I mention this, to deliberately provoke some thoughts for the reader, on how to unpick these responses.

When we inhabit the mask, with our own everyday gestures, it will come across as a 'petit personage'. This was Lecoq's way of saying a 'type' – but also that the actor lacked focus and presence. The small gestures would draw the attention to the mask and what they were feeling – rather express a response to the space they were in. The neutral mask asks us to find clear, epic responses.

Sometimes actors find that they are blocked. Their own physicality, speed of movement or tempo can't change; or there are personal problems that impede a direct response. This is why it is important to find different ways, at times, to teach the mask work to accommodate these fears.[9]

Perhaps it is not so much losing our identity we are afraid of, but becoming something different.

---

[9]See later in this chapter for ways to do this.

Masked physical expression for dramatic action

Any dramatic mask, worn in theatre or by an actor in training, asks them to release into an amplified form of physical expression and characterization: to move away from themselves towards something different. The masks, for instance, designed by Jocelyn Herbert that were used in Peter Hall's iconic production of *The Oresteia* at the National Theatre in 1981, called for a non-naturalistic style of acting, which Peter Hall went on to use in all his subsequent productions of Greek plays.

This is a form of non-naturalistic acting that distils movement and gesture into its essence, but the mask still needs to reach the audience and touch their imagination; the actor is still acting. The actor must amplify *inside* as well as outside, to meet this intense and essential demand. Masks need very little décor, as the act of wearing a mask makes the space theatrical. Following this practice, the Neutral Mask also creates the space that it too encounters. Their space is the dramatic narrative of nature: trees, sea, sky, mountains – and can feel ancient, linked to ritual, the worship of gods and goddesses, who are the embodiment of nature – pantheism.[10]

Finding ways to consider our place in nature is also a current preoccupation of many theatre makers today, who search a theatrical language and discourse to express our relationship with the non-human world and tackle the major preoccupations of climate change.[11] The Neutral Mask uniquely dramatizes this through its identification with matter and nature, and today there are pockets of research and thinking on how to expand this vocabulary theatrically. As an example, Dr Michael Pearce,[12] who trained at Lecoq, has been researching how to make theatre from an 'ecocentric perspective' by using these techniques with drama students at Exeter University. He explores this in some detail in his article 'Embodied ecological awareness and the pedagogy of Jacques Lecoq' (Pearce, 2024).

What we can learn from wearing the Neutral Mask

There has been some discussion about the open-ended teaching of Neutral Mask – a 'via negativa' – where the actor's offered response to an improvisation will only be met with a 'no', to guide them, or a yes! It is a philosophical way of teaching, leaving the actor to make their own discoveries, rather than providing answers or side-coaching. But in a drama school this can be very unsettling, as actors are training, as much as developing their artistic sensibilities, and often respond with more confidence to practical suggestions than if left to find out for themselves. The Neutral Mask is a teaching mask, not designed for performance, and will always reveal how clearly someone has played the exercise. They might, for instance, feel very strongly that they have fully thrown the stone into the lake (one of the exercises), but the body has told a different story. Instead

---

[10]The study of Neutral Mask is an excellent reference point for Greek Tragedy.
[11]RSC's recent play *Kyoto*, written by Joe Robertson and Joe Murphy, directed by Stephen Daldry and Justine Martin.
[12]Associate Professor of Drama at Exeter University.

of just responding with a 'yes' or a 'no', perhaps the teacher or student can ask, 'did we see them throw the stone?' and if we didn't see this, the actor will be prompted to find ways to play the story more clearly. The difficulty is to create generous teaching spaces for such frank observations to work. But we still have the problem of the 'body never lies'. By this I mean that it often tells a different story to what we imagine we might be saying. One of the first things many actors say, when watching the Neutral Mask is how much it reveals about someone's physicality. As a teaching exercise, it helps actors understand how much information is transmitted physically, which in a process of 'reverse engineering' they can apply to character work. The actor's sternum might be sunk as they see a tree in front of them, which tells the audience they are scared or shy, instead of 'look how tall the tree is!' These adjustments, and observations, are not solely technical; they are also imaginative and interpretive.

I teach the Neutral Mask as a solo exercise. The actors watch each other, and I always ask them to watch empathetically, as if they were also doing the exercise. It is easy to watch critically, but much more interesting to watch with engagement. I use the analogy of running for a bus or a train. In those moments of intensity, we are gauging the speed and momentum of what we are following – so we can jump aboard. This is how we should watch the exercises. As though we were doing them ourselves.

In Neutral Mask, the body needs to amplify to express the world outside. The macrocosm of the world around us enters the microcosm of the space inside us. The mask and the space are one. It can be counterproductive to give technical feedback[13] when the actor doesn't meet this demand, because then the actor will tend to self-correct as they improvise, going back into their heads, and losing their freedom to express themselves. This is where a common set of principles is helpful, in the form of good physical preparation in other movement classes. In my pedagogy these are the Pure Movement classes but they could be any classes which have increased physical range and expression. The Neutral Mask might then reveal the difference between you thinking your body is balanced and open and what is really happening, which the actor will work on to improve in the Pure Movement classes.

- The place of feedback on how to open the body is in the Pure Movement class.
- The Neutral Mask class is where you explore how to put this into practice, using your imagination, and your connection to the dramatic moment.

The feedback would be more about the story: What did we see? Was it alive? Did it reach us? Could it be bigger? I like to think, that this is a 'via positiva' – assessing the benefits and creativity that can be taught through really 'looking' at a body moving in space.

How to approach neutral

Neutrality has often been seen (and written about) as a negative attribute to ask students to aspire to. Lisa Peck in her book *Act as a Feminist: Towards a Critical Acting Pedagogy* identifies both Mark Evans' and my caveats about 'Neutral' as a twentieth-century trope.

---

[13] I have seen this done: but I don't agree with this. Neutral Mask isn't a technical exercise to get right. However, at the same time, if it is too ineffable it risks being mysterious and without detail. That is why I prefer to ask questions.

Evans identifies two 'types' of body that movement training aspires to make available to the actor – the 'natural' and the 'neutral body', both of which are understood within the context of 'the efficient body', a specifically twentieth century trope. (Peck, 2021)

'Neutral' or being ready, as I see it, is a place from where each actor's *own* physical expression can start. Technically, all bodies can find an alignment and balance which suits their physicality. And as all bodies are unique, the same mask will look different on different people, which actors will wear with their *own* neutrality and their *own* identity.

The idea of the 'efficient body' has never interested me. When you move in a Neutral Mask you are working with gestures and movements that are clear and uncluttered but still filled with your genuine responses and passions. It is fascinating to witness how different imaginations respond to a bird, or the sea: some will be delicate, some tempestuous, with a world of possibilities in between. The 'effective' alignment that both Neutral Mask work and Pure Movement teach us is the result of the work of 'expression-in-action', not of correction. Think of how we learn to ride a bike, by navigating speed, distance, balance and co-ordination as it happens to us. Effective movement in theatre is much the same thing: we discover if it works as we do it in a theatrical context. We learn how to recognize it, in classes like the Neutral Mask.

The effectiveness of the Neutral Mask as an artefact

The artefact of the mask itself projects a sense of inner calm and was originally designed by Amleto Sartori and Lecoq. They are still handmade in Sartori's mask workshop in Padua.[14] The form and idea of the mask to express openness and harmony derived from the initial experiments of Jacques Copeau and Michel Saint-Denis. There are no specific movements encoded in Sartori's Neutral Mask, and the expression is both abstract and specific. Sartori's Neutral Mask is made of dark leather, and the form derives partly from Oriental Noh Theatre,[15] and the noble expression on Greek statues. Sartori had rediscovered the original techniques for making the leather masks of the Commedia dell'Arte, and he and Lecoq designed the template for the 'Neutral Mask' from leather. Leather breathes and is the best material to convey the life of the body. Plastic masks don't breathe and always look a little uncanny. Sartori and Lecoq worked together to conceive this expression, which the actor then takes on as they inhabit the mask.

The expression on the mask

The balance of the eyes and cheekbones on each mask is deliberately asymmetric, to make it human, more mobile and less 'perfect'. The eyebrows are lifted, the eyes slanted upright and open, the mouth and nostrils open. The expression is of wonder and calm. The mask is abstract, almost like an image from a Picasso painting.

These masks are not a reinterpretation ancient or traditional masks; instead, their form is an entirely unique design – to express openness and looking at the world as if for the first time.

---

[14]For a more detailed understanding of the work of Amleto Sartori, refer to the Centro Maschere e Strutture gestuali http://www.sartorimaskmuseum.it/centro-maschere-e-strutture-gestuali/.
[15]More on Copeau's interest in Noh Theatre later in this chapter.

Lisa Peck is correct to say this is a twentieth-century trope, but the trope comes from an interesting and exciting tradition of experimentation and renewal. The actor's body making meaning from nothing – a new beginning – from a place of calm and balance, both inner and outer.

The body and the mask

Let us see what happens if you explore that expression of the Neutral Mask now. You don't need to have it in front of you to experience this. Because when an actor looks at a mask, they transpose its expression onto their own face – and the body responds. These physical changes can be determined by prompts, described below.

The Neutral Mask that Satori (and Lecoq) designed has an expression with:

Eyes wide open
Eyebrows raised
Nostrils open
Mouth slightly open
Face relaxed

Try to take this expression into your own face. Does it change the way you feel and relate to the world around you and your breath?

The neutral expression on Sartori's mask has been carefully considered to produce an internal sensation and action and responses in the wearer, in much the same way that playing a piece of music, its style or mode of expression comes from the notes on the stave. But, unlike music, the notes are only written once the actor starts to play, and the Neutral Mask prepares the actor to play. The Neutral Mask carries within it the potential for movement.

Is the Neutral Mask and a state of calm therapeutic?

The state of readiness and calm that you need to start to work from, for the Neutral Mask, often creates respite and calm for students. The artefact of the mask, with its facial expression, conveys a 'neutrality' where there is no 'inner conflict'.[16] The Neutral Mask has no past, so no 'back-story'; every moment is new and different, time is moving forward and creates a state of readiness with which the actor responds. Lecoq mentions how finding 'perfect balance' helps actors come off balance or into conflict.[17] He means balance as a sense of equilibrium and harmony with your surroundings: not fighting your surroundings, but instead mirroring them, embodying them. The space and the mask are the same thing, but this means that the mask is ready to encounter all things, some of which are turbulent, some of which are calm.

To mirror our environment is a way to understand it and is a form of mimesis.[18]

If you watch a cat stalking prey, it will take the movements of what it watches slightly into its body. Embodied mimetic action is the aim, from a place of ease, but often actors have told me that wearing the Neutral Mask has surprised them with its therapeutic effects. I stress that these exercises are dramatic, asking us to respond to imagined scenarios with

---

[16]Lecoq (2002 [1997]), *The Moving Body*.
[17]Ibid.
[18]See Chapter 8 'In praise of play'.

a totality. Often students have asked me if they could borrow the Neutral Mask to prepare for a role, to start from a place of stability.

> And for those who, in life, are always in conflict with themselves, with their bodies, the Neutral Mask helps them find a stable position where they can breathe freely. (Lecoq, 2002 [1997])

It is wonderful to work with an exercise which has such a wide and creative impact on actors.

Some obstacles to teaching mask work

To understand its place in today's culture, I am reminded of how Neutral Mask was taught at Lecoq. I have adapted my way of teaching in response to different cohorts and individuals, as there is a constant need for change, which I navigate, to reappraise mask teaching.

At Lecoq we were taught Neutral Mask in the first year (of a two-year course), for two full terms. The use of the mask took us into Elements, Matter, Dynamics,[19] and the Neutral Mask journey.[20] The Neutral Mask was then used as a basis for everything else we studied: from Commedia dell'Arte to the little mask of the clown's nose: from balancing the space exercise for Chorus in Greek Tragedy, to creating the body masks of Buffons.[21]

Neutral Mask at Lecoq introduced us to how an actor is both an individual and part of a bigger picture and story. An actor can't hide when working as part of an ensemble. Every player is important and when you are doing an improvised exercise on your own, every action and gesture you make is fully visible. In drama schools, however, I didn't introduce teaching Neutral Mask until the second year, and my delivery of it has evolved considerably. Despite my earlier advocacy for the importance of mask work, students of acting at British drama schools haven't elected to be taught mask work, or even the creative work of an ensemble,[22] so teaching it had to chime with the aims of the course and the aspirations of the students.

Neutral Mask holds a unique position as an outlier to the main journey of acting training, often catching students unawares and resulting in some surprising revelations. I remember an actor taking off the mask after an exercise on the sea, and bursting into tears. He was overwhelmed to be speaking with his body, which he felt for the first time, and the exercise reminded him of a piece of music about the sea by Sir William Walton. He said he never knew he could move with that amount of expression. When an actor genuinely works off their own impulses, following their imagination and the scenario that has been set up for them, what happens can feel like 'flow' – an intense sensation of connection and joy. The moment of release and the strong feelings that can occur when you connect to the mask is part of its power and creativity, but this is hard to quantify.

---

[19]Elements of earth, fire, air and water: matter, as in physically embodying objects or matter that flow from the elements, i.e. oil and vinegar from liquid (water), a lightbulb (as in fire), butter (as in earth), a feather (as in air): dynamics (see the description of this above).
[20]See these described in Lecoq's book, *The Moving Body* (2002 [1997]) and my own version of this in Chapter 12 of this book.
[21]Ibid.
[22]As opposed to warm-up exercises, or games.

Neutral Mask is experiential: How to teach this as part of an academic curriculum? And how can it be assessed?

Much of my experience with young actors recently is a nervousness to expand beyond naturalism and beyond themselves. I try to encourage them to think of the Neutral Mask as expression, but it can still be difficult to shift the actor to want to even explore the world of the mask. Neutral Mask occupies a unique position, as it is not a 'subject' that is obviously necessary to an actor's commercial success.[23] It is exciting and challenging, but it isn't naturalistic. Part of the resistance to it comes from a fear of the unknown and a mistrust of its purpose in a drama school setting.

If the culture of an Acting Course embraces other challenging subjects, it is much easier for students to accept working with the Neutral Mask. When I taught at Drama Centre London, both Annie Tyson and Vladimir Mirodan[24] actively encouraged the students to view new experiences as an essential part of their training. From listening to modern and early music and using 'difficult' music as stimulus for theatre making, to researching different forms of theatre for their analysis projects, their view of the world was constantly being stretched. I remember one striking assignment was to create a piece of theatre to the works of the German Russian composer of Jewish descent – Shnittke.[25] Their rehearsal exercises were plays by Schiller or Lope de Vega, or obscure Jacobean tragedies, and running through the school was the psychological transformation work of Yat Malgrem's movement psychology.[26] Though this was still Eurocentric, it was also not familiar to most students, which meant they were all as equally unrepresented as each other when tackling this new material.[27] The wider implication of training like this is that the actor is essentially being asked to expand their points of reference, and to explore a more playful, deeper, embodied way of responding to stimulus – non-conformist and culturally diverse.[28]

Lately, there has been a perception that to open new possibilities for a student is to 'break them down'. The argument has been that it isn't inclusive to offer exercises that ask us to move away from our identities and enculturated expression.[29] Any amount of stretch, physically, vocally, imaginatively, cognitively, will involve a sense of distortion for a while, until the concepts or the exercises become familiar.[30]

However, the 'premise' of the Neutral Mask is neither old school nor contemporary. Instead, it offers the actor the possibility to create their own work in ways that haven't been conceived of yet, so a school or a course that introduces actors to the unknown is often fertile ground for them to want to explore this.

---

[23] Which is also one of the reasons it isn't a staple on actor training courses.
[24] Course Director of BA Acting and Principal of Drama Centre respectively.
[25] Shnittke: described as 'a composer who has no home country, who is a foreigner everywhere'.
[26] See Dr Vladimir Mirodan's book, *The Actor and the Character: Explorations in the Psychology of Transformative Acting*.
[27] Another culturally stretching project at Drama Centre was The Opera Project. Second Year Directing students chose a piece of opera, which they staged using the newly arrived First Years, whom they directed over the course of the term in 1.5 hour sessions.
[28] These exercises were also delivered alongside the personal improvisations derived from Uta Hagen. See her book – Uta Hagen, *Respect for Acting*.
[29] As raised by students in the SAP at RADA.
[30] This doesn't suggest that there isn't a need to decolonize the curriculum. It argues that some subjects will be equally challenging for everyone.

How to teach Neutral Mask

I was fortunate enough to take part in a Neutral Mask class at the Stratford Festival Theatre (so not at a drama school) by a teacher-director from the Michel Saint-Denis tradition. The teacher was expert in creating a kind and playful space where everything was permitted. He never judged an offer from the actors or closed it down. In this class he linked the mask's journey[31] with emotional and psychological expression. I personally experienced how transporting this was. I was both 'wearing the mask' and playing a scenario as though it was a naturalistic story.[32] The scenario was walking in the desert in the hot sun, as though we were lost, then seeing a mirage that we thought was a caravan, and then finally sinking to the sand as the sun set. We were asked to take a long time doing this, to live and breathe it. His knowledge of the mask and how to guide the actors was deep: it flowed from him to us, and we understood how to approach the exercise, without him ever overexplaining. This was the result of years of working with his masks, and his feedback was tellingly sparse. The interaction in the rehearsal room between the actor and the teacher was one of guidance, kindness and wisdom. In a mask class, the teacher is witnessing something unique and powerful. To support this, the theatre or the drama school needs to understand how the work helps an actor's development.

*

Recently, I was teaching Neutral Mask in a school where the students had so many issues of their own that even putting the masks on was a challenge. The school itself was very good at working with naturalism and TV work, but wasn't consistent in working with transformation. My strategy had to change, as unlike my classes elsewhere, these students found it hard to trust working with Neutral Masks in front of each other. After some reflection I decided to teach most of the students as if they 'were masked' without them ever having to put the mask on. For this, I asked them to take the expression of the mask into their faces, to connect to its openness and sense of calm and let that make their bodies more balanced and simpler in their gestures – even this many of them found challenging. I then asked them to move not wearing the masks, in silence, while *verbally* guiding them through the scenarios, almost guiding them from action to action. I 'held' them with my words, as they entered these non-naturalistic spaces and epic stories. Though they had read a lot of epic plays in their theatre studies courses, the silent guiding of physical expression in an epic narrative was body-based and a new experience. They told me that moving silently, to tell a story that was bigger than them, was very different and exciting for them. However, I was aware of how the culture and self-consciousness amongst them made it impossible for them to make discoveries in silence, while wearing the masks, without my input to guide them. As the weeks progressed, more students were happy to wear the masks, but even watching the masks, for some of these nervous students, was disturbing. I understand many drama schools and students share the same concerns about transformation today. When courses feel they can only tackle naturalism, using approaches designed to support students' personal experiences, this leaves them with very little spare vocabulary with which

---

[31] I will refer to the mask as a character, to prepare us for the exercises to come. The actor wears the mask, and the mask has an identity separate to the actor.
[32] The theme was an adaptation of the Mask's Journey, which I will describe in Chapter 12.

to explore playing anything different. Despite this, many of these students were very talented, with a politic and a passion for theatre. I think I managed to give them a sense of how to work physically in silence to tell a story, and an insight to working outside of social realism. But we never tackled this final act of transformation, wearing the mask would ask of us.

There is nothing to fear in working with the Neutral Mask. It is a conduit for student development, and the students don't have to get the exercise 'right'. It takes students into a space that is epic, poetic and metaphorical. Sometimes a student who struggles to be imaginative in acting exercises can suddenly take flight in a mask class, and find deep artistic expression. This value-added experience can flow back into their work when they take the mask off. Learning is non-linear, and teaching mask work is delicate; it is important not to be too mysterious, and one way is to identify its unique place in the curriculum, where it can enrich other experiences for the students.

*

Character Mask: A development from Neutral Mask

I have taught Character Mask in several schools, as a development of Neutral Mask. As I describe earlier, Character Mask work has a rich lineage in this country, from Michel Saint-Denis to George Devine, to the Royal Court, and Joint Stock, the new writing company run by Max Stafford-Clark and Bill Gaskill. Directors like Di Trevis have used it as imaginative and creative exercises, and many actors of a certain generation have experience of its liberating and creative possibilities. Like Neutral Mask, it has receded from our attention. The Character Mask work I describe below, like Animal Study, is to help actors develop their capacity to find the physical life of a character, and to work with each other, through impulse, action and gesture, physical listening and play.

Lecoq (2002 [1997]) introduces the 'Expressive Mask' as showing 'a character in its broad outlines' expressing physically 'essential attitudes ... filtering out the complexities of psychological performance'. When I was at Lecoq's school (1976–8), he had yet to introduce 'Expressive Mask' to our mask study classes.[33] However, the work on animals and elements, as well as psychologically based improvisation, can be equally applied to character mask work.

Character masks have a physiognomy that is immediately recognizable. They convey and carry a particular attitude 'printed' into a fixed expression. Though the masks are fixed, their expressions can change, as I will show. They are usually half masks, but, as with all masks, the expression changes as the actors move. If a character mask carries two expressions at once (most do), this makes for many possibilities of physical and emotional expression – more than just two for example.

Consider one with eyebrows raised, to show surprise or wonder, with a downturned mouth to show sadness or disturbance. When one expression is more dominant, a downturned mouth for instance, this might be the most dominant characteristic. But the 'contra-masque', or the opposite side to the mask's outward personality, is expressed in the less dominant expression when the eyebrows are raised. The actor might interpret this

---

[33]This is a good example of how research and pedagogy can develop a practice.

mask as a disapproving person, suddenly expressing tenderness when feeding the birds. If the birds fly away, the downward mouth could convey sadness, reflected in the attitude of the body. If a park attendant appears to tell the mask that they need to pay for the deckchair they are sitting on, the raised eyebrows might signal worry or anxiety. The interplay between the two contrasting expressions of the mask creates many stories. Character masks prompt actors to create, bringing out surprising personalities they might not have explored before.

All the character masks I work with are half-masks, which introduces the possibility of improvised text.[34] As the lower half of the face is exposed, the mouth and lips of the actor need to balance the face of the mask. The mask can talk, or make noise, but the words and sounds need to be embodied and support the action. A mask using verbiage, words for the sake of speaking to keep our attention, leaves the body behind. Mask work requires the actor to be 'on action', playing a clear intention, just as they need to be when speaking naturalistic text. They are creating a physical text that is more fully expressed through the body.

Stories of character masks at drama schools

The way into playing the physical life of the character mask is to distil its inner attitude into simple, clear gestures and actions that reflect its personality. The character mask is one level up from naturalism, but the actions need to support the emotional and psychological life of the mask. We need to believe what is happening and be drawn to the mask.

Before you do this, you need to find out, for yourself, who you are 'taking on'. The approach always needs to be physiological – through the body.

The character masks I work with are not archetypes or stock characters. The clue to who they are is in the expression on the face, which, as I have shown, in a good mask will have two or three competing expressions, and as many ways of playing them as the actors who encounter them.

Who am I? A quick way to bring the mask to life

Look at the mask briefly, then put it on. Next glance in the mirror and make an intuitive leap, and you are someone different. A miraculous transformation has happened. The next stage is to bring the mask to life, sustain it and create theatre with it.

I don't often use a mirror for the masks I own – but each has a name.[35] I seek a balance between the form of the mask and often might suggest its name or character to the actor, and a structured sense of play, for them to bring this to life and make their own discoveries. This helps the actor sustain their discoveries and create scenarios independently, if they want to work with them outside of the class.

*

---

[34] These were designed and made specially for me by Finn Caldwell.
[35] The puppet-maker Finn Caldwell made them for me: each one has a name – but actors rarely embody the name of the mask and always find their own characters from them.

Rose Bruford 1997

When I worked at Rose Bruford I inherited some character masks, commissioned by a previous movement teacher. I worked with them for eight years, developing a rich pedagogy, inspired by Lecoq's work on 'personnages', animal into character and the elements,[36] which I linked to my own understanding of how to build a character from a set of psychological and situational circumstances. The students would devise scenarios with the masks, using Lecoq-based approaches to find narrative and conflict, from character-based interactions.[37] From this, they might find a richness of expressive characterization – responding differently according to their circumstances, or who they met. The playing was truthful and alive, but the triggers would be phenomenological and physical. For example, if one mask was a bartender and identified with the element of the air, and a mask entered that was like a stone, and refused to leave, the bartender's efforts to ask them to move on, and the punter's resistance, would create a very interesting dynamic (and scenario). The scene doesn't need to be overly physicalized, because the aim is for the masks to distil the physical responses, into intention. Consider, for instance, how the punter (earth) holds their ground, as the bartender (air) becomes more insistent, losing their centre to try to move them.

I focus on helping actors find a detailed physicality from which to structure their scenarios and stories.[38] The mask is working analogously, as if they were air, internalizing it, but letting the movement come through the body. This work on character masks provides a useful counterpoint to acting classes based on psychological realism. But the physical detail can almost provide a point of concentration, that allows a physical life to both emerge and be present.

*

When I first discovered these masks at Rose Bruford, I was told they were 'probably archetypes' but no identifying instructions could be found. The students and I went on an archaeological dig, unearthing the specific characteristic of each mask, which refined itself the more we worked with them. They had lain dustily in a cupboard waiting to be brought to life and emerged as we took their expressions into our own faces. We started by gleaning their 'leading points'[39] by looking[40] at the shape of the mask, letting that change our bodies. If you open your eyes wide, for example, this might give you a sense of surprise that lifts the spine and opens the arms.

A leading point is the part of the body that pulls you through space, informed by the undulation exercises. It can be exaggerated: being led by the nose with such extremity, that you are pulled onto your tip toes. Or very subtle: being led by the knees just to the point

---

[36] The elements of earth, air, fire and water were explored at Lecoq. They can be used as 'qualities', character or situation, or emotional dynamics. The elements also form part of other acting systems – but I only refer to them as I have encountered and developed them.
[37] See Chapter 13 for reference to work on the elements for this. Or how animals interact, see Chapter 10.
[38] Students are happier if there is a sense of structure and development to their classes: there always was at Lecoq, and there always is in a rehearsal process. Actors have an inbuilt sense of what is useful.
[39] Each time you wear a mask, you look at it, and take its expression into your own face.
[40] See Chapter 10 on Animal Study, the exercise on undulation, on where a body might lead from and who that therefore might be. Undulation is 'knees, hips, chest, nose'.

that your knees are sagging, rather than fully bent.[41] The degree of expression would mirror the internal life of the character, and the extremity (or not) of its outer expression. We also used the dimensions of high, low, wide, narrow, forward and backwards to find out how the masks walked, again through taking the prompts from how the masks expressed themselves in the little 'body' of the face. The connection between the body and the mask helped us find their characters. These were emotional, even psychological expressions, printed on a physicality, very much as you would develop a character for a play. A mask with beetling heavy brows and a downturned nose had a sense of pressure downwards, so that might suggest a sunk spine, mirroring a depressed personality.

Once an identity for the mask was found, we needed to find a tangible backstory. This followed Stanislavski-based prompts of who (are you), what (are you doing), where (are you), when (what time, or point in your life). Gradually the masks revealed themselves, and often, miraculously over the eight years I worked with these masks, the same masks took on the same characteristics from class to class. A mask with a very pointy nose and wide eyes like an owl, always burrowed into the imagination of the actors as a spy, or private detective, or Ofsted Inspector, but with an inner life of surprise or curiosity. This clearly was its inherent and essential 'character'. While a mask with a wide face, like a Cheshire cat, often became a self-satisfied teacher or private secretary who secretively undermined their boss, exhibiting a compulsion for neatness and preening.

How the actors 'discovered' the identity of the character masks was through their intuition. They would look at the mask by holding it in front of them, then they would take the shape of the mask into their faces, and allow that to travel through their bodies, altering their spine and postures. Once wearing the mask, and having found the way they moved, they went on to discover more about them, through a series of games, interactions and exercises. Some of these I describe below.

As 'Character Mask' became embedded in the timetable at Rose Bruford, I made a dressing-up box for the actors to source their clothes. I scoured the props department for umbrellas, typewriters, stethoscopes.

On the way to their discoveries of who they were, the masks would find their job, their costume and one significant prop. The mask's relationship with their 'prop', how they handled it, endowed it with importance, expressed through what they did with it, often showed the inner attitude of the mask. I was told by the students that these exercises were very useful in learning how to handle props – particularly in classical plays, where a 'prop' might inform the meaning or the plot.[42]

Other exercises were hot seating,[43] going for job interviews and making a distinction between the mask at home and the mask at work – the mask in private and the mask in public. There were group improvisations of masks at the theatre or in a doctor's waiting room, or even at times implementing stage directions. The arrival of the townspeople to meet the Government Inspector, in Gogol's play of the same name, for instance.

---

[41]Try these leading points to see how different the sensations are.
[42]The handkerchief in *Othello*, or Prospero's staff, or the 'cords' that the Nurse carries to Juliet after Mercutio has been killed.
[43]Hot-seating is an acting exercise, where the actor-as-character is interviewed, on back-story, etc. With the mask, the responses would also require the physical life of the mask to respond. Also mentioned as an exercise in 'Animal Into Character'.

The physical practice of acting with the whole body expands what the possibility for a physical life on stage can be and helps actors feel connected to movements that aren't their own habitual responses.

Masks and their and psychological emotional life

Two lonely people find themselves sitting at the same table in a pub. Beat by beat, they discover a connection and fall in love. One of them has brought his shopping to the pub in a plastic bag.[44] He is so rapt, and embarrassed, he dares not put it down, though he clearly wants to take the woman's hand. Every time there is a strong feeling of attraction he scrunches the bag with embarrassment, and every time he feels ashamed of his own lack of courage, his arms and the bag hanging loosely by his sides, the handle tightly wound round his fingers. His plastic bag expresses his feelings perfectly. Each time the bag scrunches, the woman leans forward expectantly: every time his arms dangle, she goes back, limply, to her lemonade.

The meeting is unresolved, and the woman stands, pauses, then leaves very quickly.

Neither had the courage to take each other's numbers and she had so wanted to meet him again.

This was an improvisation between two masks, all conveyed through gesture, movement and physical acting – specific and truthful, silent and poetic. The audience laughed and cried as they watched. Masks can be incredibly touching when the playing is true and specific, and the responses happen through a real ability to listen physically to the other character on stage. The action arising can be surprisingly sophisticated and surreal. This improvisation had no input from me. The students were following a simple rule of dynamic and presence, action and reaction, while allowing themselves to be seen.

Masks at Drama Centre: Make sure you know when to take the mask off!

At Drama Centre the energy and dynamics of the school and the classes were very rigorous. I was teaching Character Mask work in the Third Year, at the same time as they were working on their solos for Character Analysis and preparing their third-year productions. One day, I brought in balloons and set up a children's party. The masks were delighted. They grabbed the balloons, burst them, whacked each other over the head with them, and then formed a conga out of the classroom and down the corridor into other classes. Fortunately, the other teachers were momentarily amused at the disruption (luckily, they all possessed a good sense of humour) until I corralled them back into the class. The next class I reminded them they would each need to take the mask off when asked.

Working with a mask must always be professional, even when the mask-character becomes anarchic. The mask needs to be 'true' to life in some way, not just an excuse to let off steam. That is down to the teacher though, to set this up, hold the space and, when needed, bring the actors back to themselves. Not easy!

---

[44]It was his personal prop.

There are no words to describe moments like these, when the world of the mask takes over a world that is unmasked.

Masks often unmask the control and restraint that society and culture teach us. Physical life tells stories that words can't, which go deeper than we can imagine. Sometimes this takes us to very emotional and unfettered ways of responding.

*

'The terrible difference between knowing something intellectually and feeling it emotionally'

What is the language of theatre that jolts us into the realization of what is happening in the present time? I write this at a time when the world feels like it is entering an unprecedented time of conflict, when the post-war order is breaking down. To find a language of theatre that can make us feel 'emotionally' seems very urgent. To watch theatre is to see, feel and understand what a story can mean in its context.

> Defenceless under the night
> Our world in stupor lies;
> Yet, dotted everywhere,
> Ironic points of light
> Flash out wherever the Just
> exchange their messages:
> May I, composed like them
> Of Eros and of dust,
> Beleaguered by the same
> Negation and despair,
> Show an affirming flame.

The last verse of 'September 1939', written by the poet W.H. Auden in New York on the eve of the Second World War, captures the sense of hopelessness and confusion. And how we might take strength from seeing the slant of events in a different light, to connect to others, and illuminate the darkness.

I have written elsewhere how movement, mime and (therefore by default mask work) developed in France after the Second World War, as a response to 'how' to express the inexpressible – through silence, movement. I was reminded of this, reading a particular testimony from Janet Teissier Du Cros' memoir *Divided Loyalties* of living in occupied France during the Second World War. She describes witnessing antisemitism for the first time, when on a visit to Paris from the unoccupied territories in the south. French Jews suffered the same fate as Jews elsewhere in Europe where the Nazis were in power. Forced to wear the yellow star, not able to work, and eventually forced onto trains, into labour camps and concentration camps. She describes this as an incident, then checks herself.

> It was not in fact an incident: it was a man … It is not till he was close upon us that I saw the man. He was little and elderly with bowed shoulders and poorly dressed. I doubt whether I would have noticed him at all if it had not been for the sinister distinguishing mark on his left breast, the yellow star with 'Juif' printed across it. It was the first I had seen it: in unoccupied territory the star was not worn, and in occupied territory only from

1942. I stopped dead in my tracks stunned. He passed us without looking at us, but it was a full minute before I recovered the use of my legs ... the terrible difference between knowing something intellectually and feeling it emotionally. (Cros, 1962)

It was a man. She describes him succinctly, and his distinguishing feature, the yellow star. By the time the book was published, he would no doubt be dead.

The difference between knowing something intellectually and the shock of feeling it emotionally will involve a physical and visceral response: 'I see it feelingly' as King Lear says. The act of seeing human movement on stage and understanding the historical context – the facts – changes our physicality and can make us act to change it. Or could.

I have spoken elsewhere in this book, how movement teaching for me has always felt 'political' (with a small 'p') and how my impulse to train actors physically comes from a desire to make theatre a vital, not just a literary pursuit. The development of movement and mask training sought to capture a contemporary urgency and sensibility. The shift that Lecoq's practice brought to a movement and theatre training used the microcosm of everyday experience as a reference book for creating story and narrative; while the Neutral Mask asks us to use the natural world as a source from which to create drama. Both give students an understanding of how to work with an epic approach to telling contemporary stories.

Jacques Copeau, Neutral Mask and Noh Theatre

I wrote to Dr Margaret Coldiron, who is a specialist in Asian performance, in August 2024, to find out what the link between the traditions of more ancient forms of masked performance, and the Westernized mask developed in post-war Europe might be. Copeau explored aspects of mask work to help train his actors,[45] developing the Noble Masks, to open the actor to simpler, less self-conscious movement and gestures, whilst his interest in Noh Theatre and its masks was to forge a connection with ancient and ritualistic forms of theatre. As Dr Coldiron reminded me, exploring the use of diverse cultures to innovate movement and mime is a complex topic. However, the aim to distil theatre and its expression by focusing on body, space and narrative is an attempt to identify common threads that unify theatrical practices. For instance, there is scholarship which looks at the parallels between Ancient Greek Tragedy and Japanese Noh Theatre (Smethurst, 2015).[46] The mask work I have described focuses on the act of performance and transformation, but Dr Coldiron has also identified some evidence of altered states of consciousness in the masked performer, which are more likely to occur with the incorporation of music and dance.[47] And as she points out, being taken over by a character can happen in 'straight' theatre too. The mask teachers from the Lecoq/Michel Saint-Denis traditions are sometimes negative about the power, or trance-like properties of the mask. However, once you consider its place as part of modern and postmodern mime, working silently can intensify narrative, both for the audience and the performer.[48] It can lead us to experiencing a story, as well as intellectually understanding it.

---

[45]For more detail on Copeau, see Chapter 9.
[46]https://www.the-noh.com/sub/jp/index.php?mode=db&action=e_index&class_id=1
[47]See Dr Coldiron's book, *Trance and Transformation of the Actor in Japanese Noh and Balinese Masked Dance-Drama*.
[48]See *Modern and Post-Modern Mime* by Tom Leabhart.

I started this chapter by saying the reason I work with the Neutral Mask is to seek a deep, emotional and imaginative expression that is silent and physical. My own experience of mask work, with students, is that they find its liberation more profound and mysterious than I anticipate or even wish. My interest in teaching mask work is to open a stronger physical and imaginative life in the actor; I am not interested in them developing Lecoq-like theatre (unless they want that). The rules and games I developed were to keep a sense of proportion, and a path of learning to support that. But mask work is connected to its origins, and to work with a mask will always tap into something bigger than ourselves.

Neutral Mask was developed by Lecoq, and he refers to it as a development of the Noble Mask, that Copeau discovered. But its application is creative, designed to reflect the here and now. The premise of the mask can't be ignored – that the artefact of the 'Neutral Mask' is unique and developed solely for one purpose: to respond to what is in front of them as if for the first time. The act of renewal every time happens each time you wear it.

All mask work focuses on gesture and action and asks us to be generous towards the audience. It takes the actor into an exploratory, mimetic and open state of theatre and focuses their attention on the expression of their body and the play of their imagination through their choice of action and their use of space.

The seeds for this are in Copeau's earlier work but as Dr Coldiron shared with me:

> Lecoq's pedagogy, though it owes a clear debt to Copeau's earlier work, is finally more successful in its production of self-sustaining theatre ensembles; ... Lecoq was more fascinated by his students' own journeys than either Copeau or Saint-Denis, and therefore able to let them go their own way.[49]

The innovation of Lecoq's Neutral Mask wasn't to make theatre based on mime, but to let students go their own way, with depth and passion. I'd like to think that study of the Neutral Mask helps them to see the world around us, and connect to their imaginations, to create theatre which audiences 'feel emotionally'.

---

[49]*Coldiron*, *Trance and Transformation* and taken from email conversations with Dr. Coldiron.

12 Neutral Mask and Chorus

Into Chorus work

The Neutral Mask is magical. I remember putting it on in Shona's class and going on a profound journey and experiencing, for the first time, what it means to speak through my whole body.

Eric Sirakian, Actor and RADA Graduate

This chapter looks at how to teach Neutral Mask and considers its connection to Chorus work. It looks at the dynamic between the protagonist and the Greek Chorus, reframing Greek tragedy as ensemble theatre. I developed these approaches when teaching in drama schools, some of which came from working with the Chorus in professional productions.

Both Neutral Mask and Chorus work have been described in *The Moving Body*, and there are examples in the video, *The Two Journeys of Jacques Lecoq* (Carosso, 1999).[1] The techniques I describe have been adapted for actors more interested in text-based, or psychological acting.

The personal and the poetic

Students and actors go on a surprising journey in Neutral Mask. There is a mask, there is their body and there are some exercises, and somehow the actor makes a piece of theatre. This requires a leap of faith, to step into a completely new way of thinking.

The story of what the Neutral Mask encounters flows through them empathetically, with actions both amplified and simplified. The actor digs into deep undiscovered parts of themselves, transferring the passion they would use speaking poetic text into movement which has a similar emotional depth. The scale of the response reflects the scenarios, which are often epic, or based on the movement of the natural world. This 'physical text' is contained by the formality of how to wear the mask effectively, and the classes are taught through a series of structured improvisations to keep this work steady and clear.

The other obvious way to explain the Neutral Mask is that teaching it also informs the actor on how to work with a mask in a performance. Mask work in performance needs the actor to bring the design – the form – of the mask to life. A mask brings their own life on stage, expressed in its own use of time, rhythm, tempo. If there is another character on stage at the same time, the tempo and action of the mask will usually dominate the stage.

---

[1] Drama Online https://www.dramaonlinelibrary.com/video?docid=LO-Masterclass&tocid=LO-Masterclass_6312189988112

A mask will introduce a tonal shift from naturalism to heightened drama, whether tragic, comic or surreal.

The body's response: The physical text

> You are looking out of a window.
>
> You see a tree and it starts to rain. Soon the rain is pouring down.
>
> In a film, we could film your face, cut to the rain, zoom out to the woods, then back to your face to see your reaction. You might shut the window
>
> In a play, you would play an action, maybe you would close the window, say a few words to describe what you see. There might be sound effects.
>
> Now convey this in silence, wearing a Neutral Mask. Through the body. But how? What the mask sees, can only be conveyed in movement. The rain and the tree, even the woods far away are as important to the story, as the mask. This is Neutral Mask work.

*

I gave a workshop in Ireland on the Neutral Mask and on the last day the group made a piece about a shipwreck, using a fisherman's song they knew. They worked 'as if' they were masked, using the movement of the sea (see below) through dynamics and rhythm, to create a ghost story. To evoke the shipwreck, the fishermen sang the song quietly in harmony, moving like 'mist' from the back of the stage, as the fisherman looked out to sea. This vocabulary had been explored in the workshop and allowed them to think poetically. By conjuring what they see physically with their bodies, Neutral Mask also helps actors create poetic images, usually reserved for text, in silence.

Neutral Mask work can create a vocabulary for theatre and for acting. The actor's expressive freedom explored in Neutral Mask will flow into the theatre, giving directors, writers and actors new ways to think about how to stage and make meaning. The register of Neutral Mask work is poetic and epic. The actor's connection to it is personal.

*

The delivery of Neutral Mask in a drama school

The exercises I describe below are for the Neutral Mask, designed for a drama school training. But they are also for professional actors. The warm-up exercises prepare the body, by working with the breath, and some collective exercises help actors/students amplify their movements and use the space more freely. Neutral Mask and Chorus work often extend to working with text and with the voice.

When working on Greek tragedy or Shakespeare I often use 'analogy'[2] to explore the text. Neutral Mask, Chorus and the elements are exciting to teach alongside rehearsal exercises or theatre texts. At RADA, this was how I structured the delivery of these classes.

---

[2]Moving *like* something.

Neutral Mask, Chorus and elements alongside text projects

- **Neutral Mask** for epic theatre or Greek tragedy.
- **Chorus work** for Greek tragedy and plays with big casts that need transformations from one scene to another. (At RADA, chorus was equally useful for David Hare's *Stuff Happens* as for Horvath's *Tales from the Vienna Woods*.)
- **Elements** for complex text, particularly Shakespeare, where the imagery refers to the elements. Many scenes are set in storms, tempests, forests.
- The **elements** can also be useful for plays with mythical elements, where it is useful to find ways for actors to work poetically, rather than literally.[3]

Neutral Mask for actors: benefits

Neutral Mask can be a pathway to make new theatre or your own theatre. In drama schools, I used it as a movement director on Third Year public productions, as the actors shared an understanding and vocabulary when working as an ensemble, to clarify action and intention through the body and out into the acting space. This clarity can be reduced into smaller, more precise physical responses, for naturalism.

The relevance for the modern actor is, the Neutral Mask can 'unmask' and repair a fear of physical expression, perhaps by moving us away from enculturated norms to something more essential and authentic. Its work on balance and calm can help the actor find this and make them feel differently about their movement.

*

The Exercises

How to introduce the Neutral Mask?

In the first class I show the mask and pass it round the group, asking them to handle it with care. The Neutral Mask is presented to the movement class, as an artefact, handcrafted and made of leather. This is a new experience for me and the students – to share how a physical object asks our body to change: this is an experience all actors have when the designer shows them their costume or the props they will be using. Like so many exercises I record in this book, training that helps an actor's stage technique can be artistic as well as practical. The student handles and 'feels' the mask, and 'looks' at it, and considers how they might wear it and move in it.

I explain that I work with the Sartori masks, because they were uniquely designed for Neutral Mask work, and so are the best masks to carry the body's openness and the actor's curiosity. The form of the mask has a life the actor needs to tap into. The expression of the mask is the clue that gives the actor information for their interpretation, like dialogue or a text.[4]

---

[3] This is about how to bring the body into play without working literally. How do you play being poisoned by a magic garment – perhaps by moving as if you were fire? For the witches in *Macbeth* how do you convey them appearing then disappearing – maybe as if they were air and the use of dynamics.

[4] I don't overlook how expensive Sartori's masks are: I believe the workshop now sells less expensive versions.

Sartori's Neutral Mask is a full mask, covering the whole face. We discuss how this might feel for students or actors. Some might say they are unable to cover their faces. We discuss options to approach this.[5] I talk about the idea of the empty space, and the body in the space (a set without décor) to create meaning, and how much contemporary theatre derives from these principles. I talk about masks, and what they ask of actors (radical transformation).

Then I explain the simple principles of Neutral Mask work.

You take the expression of the mask into your own face. This will change your physicality and inform your responses to the exercises.

Many find the mask quite formidable to look at, as its expression isn't recognizable. The eyes are wide, the eyebrows raised, the mouth slightly open and the nostrils also open. Many remark it looks like an alien. All these comments are positive, as it means the students share this experience of novelty together. No one looks like the Neutral Mask! It is the spirit, its qualities and its responses that you must interpret – not a character.

Sartori's masks are all different, some larger, some made of a darker leather, but all with the same expression, which is slightly asymmetrical – the two halves of the face not quite matching. No face is completely balanced, and sculptures or masks which depict a harmonious face are presenting either a hero or the idea of 'perfection'. This is not what the Neutral Mask is intended to convey. Instead, each person that wears the mask will bring out a slightly different expression, which comes from their physicality, not from the 'body as hero'.

Introducing the mask in this way helps students view it as a physical 'text', to be unearthed and discovered. The more I gave this introductory talk; the less students appeared to fear or resist the ideas it asked them to explore.

First exercise: how taking the expression of the mask into your body changes you

- The actors sit quietly on the floor in a circle and allow their spines to lengthen, and their bodies to relax.
- I show them the mask and ask them to take on its expression without putting it on. Eyes wide, eyebrows raised, mouth and nostrils slightly open.
- Then they look at the space in silence. This takes quite a long time.

This moment is very precious. The quality of silence and connection between all of us, sitting in a circle as we take on the mask's expression and then *look* at a space we might know well, discovering it 'as if' for the first time, is powerful. Sitting in silence, we have found a different point of view, just by changing our physical expression, which has changed our inner tempo, our breath and our emotions. Actors need to give themselves this preparation time when putting on the mask to start an exercise. Students describe their sensations, and (without wanting to pre-empt what you might feel should you do this exercise) they are usually the same: I felt curious, time felt slower, I noticed things I hadn't noticed before, calmer, excited, more open.

---

[5]There are ways to make this work for actors not wanting to work with the masks. See below for how-to exercises 'as if' masked.

The First Exercise wearing the mask

First, I explain how to do this, and then ask two or three students to get up each time, to try this out in front of us. I usually do this before a warm-up, or any physical work. This is deliberate on my part. I want the actors to approach the mask as if they were acting. I want them to use their movement work instinctively.

I never put the mask on myself, because they need to discover how to do this for themselves.

- Stand-up and turn with your back to us.
- Hold the mask at arm's length to look at you and for you to contemplate the mask.
- Breathe and relax as you take its expression into your face, making sure that as you open your own face you aren't holding tension and are balanced on your two feet.
- Then turn the mask so that the inside of it is facing you and gently guide it onto your face by placing the elastic on the back of your head and gently sliding the mask down from forehead to chin.
- Make sure the hair isn't trapped and that the eyes are in line with the eyes of the mask.
- If the mask is too big, you can put some sponge in place either in the mask or behind the elastic.
- Now turn into the space and start to move. Let your impulses guide you. Discover the room and explore what the mask asks you to do. Make sure your eyes are lined up with the eyes of the mask. Remember to breathe!
- Take the mask off.

The sensations the actors have wearing the mask for the first time vary, but often this can feel very freeing, and playful, with some saying they felt less self-conscious than in a movement class. The actors watching are also encountering the power masked expression wields in a playing space.

Physicality

The Neutral Mask is an acting exercise, not a movement exercise – so the actor's imagination and responses are as important as their movement.

But for the prolonged exercises that follow I always start the classes with a warm-up with exercises from Pure Movement. Focus (where they are looking) and breath (as in not holding the breath, when they move), are important. Here are some of the exercises I might select for a warm-up for a Neutral Mask class.

- Breathe and roll down the spine, and roll up again.
- Ripple through the spine from hanging down – this starts with a little pulse from the knees and gently ripples through your back, with hands gently raking the ground in front of you, as if it was sand.
- Gentle undulation from hanging down – knees, hips, chest, nose, then gently drop down.
- From standing, reach the arms up into High, suspend and fall forwards and return, in Tree Topple to open the arms out into Wide with a whispered 'hey' to get the breath and the space connected.

- Then take one swing from wide, across and back to expand the back and encourage your body to open even more. Make sure you stay centred, not pitching forwards.
- Stand with feet in wide. Open arms wide and welcome the space, breathe out and imagine you are looking at an expanse of space, maybe a horizon.

How to engage the whole body

There are useful training exercises to allow actors to practice 'looking' through the eyes of the mask by moving their heads when they see something. This shifts the weight and changes the angle of the torso.

Principles of engaging the eyes through the head/mask

- The whole body looks.
- The whole body pays attention.
- The eyes are part of the body, not isolated.
- When the eyes move, the head moves.

This is how 'carrying' the mask conveys an actor's physical imagination.

The next warm-up exercises involve the torso, with the limbs flowing out from the centre.

Neutral Mask warm-up exercises engaging the space and the body and the head

1 The eyes and head survey a vast landscape together

- With arms wide (not too high) and legs wide to balance the width, breathe out.
- Turn the head slowly from right to left, with your eyes leading, breathing out as if surveying a horizon.
- Finish with your head facing front. Turn the head from left to right, finishing front.

2 Letting go and finding volume to start to walk as if you were a stag in the forest, or a god

- Stand with feet in wide, arms out. Release the arms and drop down to hang off the spine, with the full weight of your body, with very bent knees, so that the head is free, and the weight of the body is dropped between your legs.
- Slowly build up through the spine, allowing the weight to stay dropped through your legs but at the same time, lengthening and opening out the spine.
- Feel the volume of your body and torso, as you bring your legs closer together, to walk in the space, with a slow, free pace, looking out in front of you. Feel how you have increased in size, as if you are a titan, or a stag in a forest. Balance the arms with the legs as you walk to find an easy rhythm with the arms working with the legs.
- Experiment with increasing and decreasing the speed but without losing a sense of volume or taking up space, justifying the tempo changes.

3 Space, torso, lunges

- This develops out of the walking, or moving swiftly (not running) exercise as described above.
- Stand on the spot.
- With strong sweeping and fluid movements, discover the space by reaching up to the ceiling, or dropping down into a squat, reaching with a wide forward gesture to the floor with both arms. Make sure that each movement comes from the torso and into the arms, rather than just gesticulating. It is a whole body movement.
- Stand and reach forward, taking this to into a lunge, to increase the sense of reach, then reach in both directions, then in diagonals.
- Keep the body and the torso open and try and lengthen out of the hips when in a squat.

4 Travelling through the space with lunges: what do you see?

- Travel through the space.
- Drumbeat: stop and discover the room with the strong sweeping gestures described above, but in response to the question, what do you see?
- Use all the different levels and dimensions.

5 Working with bamboo sticks

- Develop this exercise by working with short bamboo sticks, which you hold in either one or both hands.
- Reach out with the sticks, to define the end of your space.
- Every gesture you make in the Neutral Mask reaches beyond your fingertips
- This is extension, not tension or stretching.
- When you reach forward with the sticks you will find this takes you into a lunge. The sticks are at the same level as your arms and parallel with the ground.
- Down into low with knee bends with a long spine.
- Imagine the sticks come from the centre of your body, radiating outwards.
- Explore ways of moving to keep the body open by using the sticks as part of your body. Maybe you are an animal or an insect. Maybe reeds in the wind.
- Work in pairs and create a space and an action.
- Take the sticks away and see if you can maintain the sense of extension and reach.

The Neutral Mask inhabits a much bigger space: we find this through extension and activating the torso to move in different planes. Let the breath be part of the movement. Increase the tempo of these journeys and play with the rhythms of these extensions.

6 Travelling sequence: what do you see, using your breath to tell the story and activate the movement?

This is a useful exercise to connect the torso and the head to the legs and the feet. It is not 'masked' but played as if 'masked'. Your gaze is looking out as though you are on a journey, looking at seas, mountains, maybe even dragons or monsters. You are bending your knees and changing your focus through a series of lunges to side and, changing the angle of your torso to follow your gaze.

1. Stand with your feet a little wider than your shoulders. The feet should be turned out sufficiently so that the knees track over the feet. Breathe out and sink into a bend, looking forwards – think 'Wow!'
2. Breathe in sharply and turn your head to the right, as if you have seen something surprising – think 'What?'
3. Travel to the right, breathing out smoothly to cover the journey of travelling. Your right knee will be bent, your left will be straight. You will end with your head turned to the side, but your torso still facing front. 'Wow!'
4. Breathe in sharply to turn the torso to the side, so that the whole body: head, torso, hip, knee is looking to the side in a lunge through the right foot. The face is in profile to the front (so if wearing a mask, the mask is still in play). Think: 'I need to see more' (let the back foot pivot, so as not to put strain on the knee).
5. Breathe out as you hold the position: the exhalation will keep the body active as if you have seen something amazing that holds the attention. Think: 'Wow!'
6. Breathe in and turn the head centre; the body is now in torsion, with the torso still to the side, head facing front. 'What?'
7. Breathe out, with the body still facing side, but travel back to the centre by bending both knees. This is an interesting movement as you are travelling back to where you started, but part of the body is still turned away from the front. This can look curious, comical, quizzical – 'Wow!'
8. Breathe in and turn the torso to the front, to join the head and the knees – 'I need to see more'.
9. Breathe out as you hold this position, again as if you are looking at something in front of you. 'Wow!'
10. Breathe in and look to the left and repeat the whole sequence to the left, until you come back to centre – repeat all connections with breath, intention, tempo and rhythm.

Observations

Work in pairs, one person observing the other.

Ask them what they see? Is there a story? What is amusing or touching? Keep the eyes in play and focus them with ease. What you look at is coming to you, rather than you piercing it with your gaze.

The specificity of the body's movement clarifies what the spectator receives.

Developments

- Ask the actors to create a story for themselves. What do they see when they turn their heads, does this change the breath, or the speed?
- Reverse the breath and see how this changes the story. Breath out as you turn your head, breathe in to travel, breathe out to turn your body. This creates narratives.

Teaching points
It is the punctuation and accents in the movement, and where the mask is looking, that tells the story by how the actor uses their breath.

Other warm-up exercises for Neutral Mask: imagination, storytelling and identification

These games help actors find a playful physicality, developing their understanding of movement qualities. They introduce the use of dynamics and observations from the natural world or from everyday actions to create physical character or story. These classes are also physical improvisation classes.

1 I see it, move it, I become it, and then I find out who I am

This is a physical way to explore 'mimesis' – as previously described – that is interactive and improvisatory. It uses 'analogy', moving like something, to create a character or a situation.

- Hold an imaginary feather in the palm of your hand, perhaps a goose feather, light and downy. Blow the feather into the air, and 'watch it' floating until it drops to the ground. As you watch, take its movements into your body and become the feather. Make this into a character. Amplify parts of the movement of the feather that capture your imagination and move round as the new character you have become. Introduce yourself.
- Imagine you have a huge vat of clay in front of you, the clay is viscous and stretchy, good for moulding into pots and sculptures, but dense enough that when thrown on the floor, or potter's wheel, it would land with a splat, immovable with a strong dynamic, and no rebound. As you pull the clay out of the vat, take on its physical properties by taking the weight, elasticity and dynamic of stretching clay into your own lunges and leverage. You are the clay. When you throw the clay on the ground, it is a push or a thrust – the gesture and action have the same quality as the clay you are handling. Who are you? Make the movements more human and find who you might be. Now you are thrown onto the ground as if you were clay. Minimize the movements but keep their quality. What is happening?
- Take a bowl of water. Gently wash your face, allowing the water to trickle down your face. Tracing the water's journey with your fingertips, take on the movement qualities of water. Let it escape its boundaries, flowing from face to shoulders to torso to knees, until you become the water. You flow, you swirl, you stagnate. Who are you? What kind of person? Make the movements smaller and smaller but keep the essence of the movement inside you. Try to pick something up or do a domestic task, as if you were water.
- Light a candle and watch it glow in the dark: feel the glow inside you; or take the soft movement of the flame into your body. Who are you? Light a firework, and take the spitting, quick, fiery movement into you. Who are you?

Characters can appear from these movement explorations. Refine them further inwards, until they are recognizably human. Remember the premise of the exercise – I see it and I become it – which starts with a simple activity: blowing a feather, lighting a candle, throwing clay on a potter's wheel. The discovery of a character is here developed from action.

2 Technical guide: when moving as these 'elements' each 'element' will have an opposite force – play the opposites

> They push, they pull.
> They rise, they sink.
> They open, they close.
> What is the weight factor? Can it have its opposite?
> The tempo and the rhythm? And the opposite.
> They move, they stop.

3 Improvisation with your character

- The actors use these ideas as triggers to find character and situation. Rather than staying with the perfectly 'embodied' activities, some leaps in the dark will be made that make sense to the actor. The only test is, do we believe it?
- These exercises also give scope for an actor's originality and expression. Let the expression go as far as is playful.
- Let the characters introduce themselves, tidy the room, sing a song, teach someone else how to do something.
- Allow the actors time to inhabit these discoveries – encourage stillness as part of their actions.

4 Partner work

- One student blows an imaginary feather, the other is blown *as* the feather. This is great fun, as you have to say 'yes' to what your partner suggests and adapt dynamics and impulses to someone else's story.
- Then explore these 'dynamics' as if this was a relationship, someone is making the feather character take off (love?) and fall to the ground (despair?): or the candle character glow (maybe with pride): or the clay character emphatic and perhaps full of angst (arguing with a partner?).

The connection to the Neutral Mask

I don't always teach a Neutral Mask class as a pure Neutral Mask class. I like to apply abstract ideas to playable actions and choices. Working like this can help the actor connect to the mask afterwards. Actors will decide how deep or playful they want to go. I show them how to get there and what it might be used for, and they do the rest. There will often be a joyous sense of adventure in these exercises.

The space is alive: and how dynamics make us move

This next exercise introduces the actors to the space as their acting partner and creates some experiences from which to build Chorus work. They are playful, with the accuracy coming from exploration, rather than analysis.

1 The great outdoors

- You are on a journey in the great outdoors. Where are you, and how is this affecting your journey? The only rule: you must fully physicalize your journey.
- For instance, you are hiking across a moor, what is the terrain? Is there a cold wind?
- You are walking through a stream. How fast is the water flowing? Do you need to balance on rocks or stepping stones?
- You are climbing a mountain, how do you have to pull yourself up, how much do you need to push into your legs?
- Add sports: You are canoeing, windsurfing, skiing, mountaineering, parachuting.
- Encourage the actors to choose journeys that would take them out of their comfort zones. Or the journey is epic, and they are on a mission and must physicalize the journey 100 per cent to get the holy grail or slay the dragon.
- As they physicalize the journey, they will be embodying the elements. If they are crossing a stream, the water will need to be in their body. If battling against the wind, its force will change their physicality, as they press against it in a strong lunge.
- They are living in the outdoors. They aren't describing the outdoors.
- Do these journeys as a team, as if on a reality TV show.

Teaching points

They will notice what they encounter on the journey will change the way they move – their breath, their tempo, their use of space and their rhythms. They will use the dimensions and pathways through space. They will be pulling themselves up or pushing against the wind. Encourage them to work with pulling or pushing. Encourage them to use the full range of their body, with lunges forwards and backwards. The physical space of mountains, rivers, trees, offer physical resistances to the human body: encourage them to imagine what the physical resistances of this journey are. They can speak, shout, sing. Very often students will create their own mythical stories without prompting.

2 The morning routine

This is first a solo exercise, then a group exercise.

- On your own in the space, re-enact how you woke up this morning, made breakfast, showered, cleaned your teeth, prepared your bag and left the house. Make the actions clear and specific and make the sounds of the activities – the taps, the toothpaste, the toaster – and let the sounds feed into the dynamics of the movement.
- The objects need time to be played – which your body responds to: the toaster pops up, the tap is turned on, and so on.
- Next you will share this in a group of three or four people.
- Elect one person to re-enact their morning. They must leave space between each activity, so that the group can physically embody this activity. They become the duvet, the taps, the water, the toothpaste, the toaster etc. It is a development of 'I see it' and 'become it' but there is an element of tag-relay to it.
- The rule is that no one touches each other, and the actor has to say 'yes' to detailed offers the ensemble might make – for instance, the toothpaste needs a lot of squeezing, or the toast might catch fire.

- How do the actors transmit this information to each other? The actors will need to work with complicity.

The solo event has become a scene where the space is alive, and the actors are working as one.

These warm-up exercises or Neutral Mask influenced exercises can be adapted. The emphasis is on exploration, with everyone working in the space at the same time. Sometimes students can work in front of each other, with the teacher offering suggestions; or they can break into pairs or little choruses or to create sequences to show each other.

Exercises wearing the Neutral Mask

Technical notes about how to wear the mask

- The mask must be visible to the audience.
- Preferably be performed solo.
- Preferably without preparation, as an improvised response to a provocation (which is why warm-up preparations are important).[6]
- The mask is in a large space, and 'coins' the images they see in front of them, as if they had never seen them before.

The audience

- The audience might feel they are in an epic space, a theatre like Epidaurus in Greece perhaps.
- Try to have the audience sitting as far away as possible from the mask, so the actor has space to move.
- Make sure students watch supportively – explain to the students that they need to watch with empathy, as if they are doing the exercises themselves.
- This might be the first time an actor has worked 'truthfully' in this register, or seen this way of working.

Remind the students of what is innovative for them in these exercises

- The mask helps actors explore with openness, curiosity and simplicity.
- There is no conflict, and the dramatic action comes from the physical expression of the mask's journey.
- The mask is not a character 'reacting' to their environment, with a back story and an objective.
- The actor is communicating what they see through the mask.

How to give feedback

Very often the audience and actors are affected quite deeply by the mask. I let people speak and talk about what they have seen. I let the actors share their sensations in the mask, even

---

[6] Sometimes it is fun to let the actors run through the exercise for themselves in the space with no one watching (and in a big group), so as to open up their imagination.

the negative ones, and only comment on what I saw. Every exercise in the mask will offer remarkable actions and responses in the actors.[7]

The exercises, written below, are deceptively simple. Every event, if fully alive, is a powerful piece of dramatic action. Even poetic. The power of a simple action executed with connection to an empty space is wonderful.

Neutral Mask exercises

1 Waking up for the first time

> Methought I was – there is no man can tell what. Methought I was, and methought I had, –[8]

There are so many instances in plays which start with a character alone on stage, waking up. Bottom (in *A Midsummer Night's Dream*) for instance: his surprise and gestures are written into the text as he half remembers being an Ass. Here is the exercise where the mask wakes up for the first time:

> Ask the student to put the mask on as described above.
> Then to lie down on their side (so we can see the mask in profile).
> The mask is asleep on their side – the body has to be genuinely relaxed for this, the breath flowing, the limbs inert.
> You wake up for the first time.
> You have been asleep for a long time.
> What does it mean to wake up for the first time?
> The openness, the exploration, the wonder?
> What do you do? Where are you?
> What do you find?

Encourage the actor to investigate the physical activity of waking up. Stretching, opening out and then the curiosity and playfulness when they see the space. If you try this at home, you might notice how hard it is to genuinely relax, then genuinely wake up: the impulse is often to plan when to wake, to be ahead of the action. The mask is asking you to be inside each action as you do it.

Remind the actor of:

> *I see it and then I respond. How do you punctuate seeing something. Give yourself time to take in the space and then bring it to life through your actions..*

2 Waking up scenario

> The mask is asleep on their side.
> You wake up for the first time.
> You are on a sandy beach.

---

[7]See Simon McBurney's introduction to *A Moving Body* (Lecoq, 2002 [1997]), on the importance of being able to 'see' well.
[8]Bottom in *A Midsummer Night's Dream*, Act 1V, Scene 1 (Shakespeare, 1984).

You discover the sand, how it moves when you play with it, what it does.
You see the sea.
You see the horizon.

Questions for you and the students:

- Remind the students of 'I see and I become it'.
- Remind them to work with curiosity and openness.
- The space you are in has dynamic – the sand when you lift it up and let it fall, the sea when it moves, the horizon as you notice its breadth and its distance and its space. Nothing is inert. Everything has life.

3 Stone

The mask starts with its back to the audience:

The mask turns into the space.
How do you enter with a mask?

The mask turns, then the body follows:

- Think of turning into the space as arriving somewhere.
- Once the mask is visible, the action has started. The first action could be stillness.
- You turn by letting the head lead you, the mask sees first, and the body follows.
- Once you see the first image, remember the idea of 'I see and I become'. There is suspension, followed by action, or a gesture to express the sea and the horizon.

You see the sea; you breathe the sea; you start to move like it. This can take a long time.
You move towards it and then *suddenly* you see a stone on the ground.
You pick it up and throw it as far as you can into the sea.
You stand and watch it land and the waves breaking on the shore.
Standing and watching it land, is as much an activity as throwing the stone.
You take another stone and find different ways to throw it.

There are many changes in this piece; encourage the actors to take this as far as they want.

4 Sea

The mask turns and sees the sea.
Where are you?
You are in a deep ocean – you see and become the ocean.
What kind of ocean is it? Is it the Pacific, the Channel, the Mediterranean?
The mask *is* the sea as it moves as the swell and the waves – and the mask also 'sees' the sea.
Gradually the sea becomes rougher, and the waves become higher.
This goes into the mask's body.
A storm breaks and the mask and the sea are travelling closer to the shore, the waves hit rocks, they crash onto the beach and get pulled back powerfully fast.
The mask is thrown up and down with the waves, maybe onto rocks, maybe under the waves, until eventually the sea throws the mask onto the beach.

The mask lies for a moment looking at the world from low down, then is compelled to stand.
As they stand, they can see the sun high in the sky.

5 The Bird

The mask turns and sees a bird in the sky, high above them.
They watch the bird – what kind of bird? A lark? An eagle? – this needs to be clear.
The bird flies in the sky and the mask takes the essence of the bird's flight into its own body. (Every actor and every bird will be different.)
The bird lands at some distance from the mask. The mask watches it and then approaches it and lifts it up.
It looks at the bird at close quarters and feels its heart beating as the mask holds it close.
It sets the bird free and watches it fly away.
Until the only thing the mask can see is the sky.

This takes time.

6 The Tree

The mask turns and sees a dense forest.
They must push aside branches and climb under and over logs.
It is dark in the forest. Will this affect how they move?
There is light as,
They come to a clearing and they see a tree.
The tree is specific. What kind of tree? How old? How tall?
They become the tree, gradually growing from the roots, through the branches and into the leaves.
There is the sky above and the earth below, and the mask sees over the heads of animals and people.
Some animals live in its branches and its trunk.
The tree expands with water from the earth and sunlight from the sun.
Time passes: the leaves fall.

*

The next two exercises are more like 'études' and might need some preparation time in class for the actors to absorb the activities before they improvise them. It is best for them to be done solo. Everyone needs enough time do these exercises, they will need space to travel forward on their journey.

7 The Neutral Mask journey

The mask travels through the forest.
They come to a clearing, they see a tree.
Lightning strikes: the tree catches fire and becomes ash or cinders.
The mask runs away and sees a lake or a wide river.
The mask jumps into a lake or wide river, in which they swim, and which takes them to the foot of a mountain

They emerge from the water to climb the mountain until they reach a plateau or a high
   plain, where they see the bird.
They watch the bird fly, catch it, and set it free.

Teaching points

This needs a lot of action and change of rhythm and tempo. It needs stillness, and changes of pace. The movement qualities for each event embody the elements. The students could do this journey in phases. The exercise could be used as a way into students devising staging for scenes from plays, or their own scenarios. The technique in the Neutral Mask is really stretched here. The more open and alive and in the moment the actor is, the easier it will be for them to access these physical changes. Dexterity and musicality come into this sequence. The themes in this journey are challenging both imaginatively and emotionally. The journey is epic, and the events the mask encounters powerful and transformative.

The Goodbye

When Lecoq introduced this exercise he would talk about the immigrants leaving Sicily to travel to New York, arriving at Ellis Island. Maybe he saw this when he was in Italy? It was a vivid description of families jostling at the harbour, with their suitcases, and children, sending their son or daughter to escape poverty and seek their fortune, and waving their last goodbye as the ship sailed. It was an image that captured me, because, sadly, it is timeless. Every day families are separated and forced to leave their countries.

The mask comes to a jetty or a harbour, to see someone very important to them leave
   on a ship, for ever.
The mask will never see this person again.
When they arrive, they think they have missed them. They push through the crowd,
   looking for them. Then they run down the jetty as they see the ship about to leave.
   They wave until they see their friend or lover or parent/child waving back.
Each share waving together, the mask and the person on the ship.
But the ship moves further and further away.
The ship departs and the mask keeps waving until the ship slips over the horizon, their
   wave carrying this sense of distance.
BEAT.
What do you do once the ship is no longer in view?
How does your hand come down, your body let go, your knees buckle.
What happens to your breath?

This last exercise moves into an emotional and psychological form of storytelling. But it is still the action which carries the narrative. Pushing the crowd out of the way, the rhythm and tempo will channel the anguish and anxiety of having missed seeing your loved one. Watching the boat disappear over the horizon, and mirroring that as your breath sinks, or your knees give, will mirror perhaps the sense of loss and separation. Something happens to us, and it is expressed physically.

*

Let the actor interpret all the exercises in their own way: how long they stay with one image, how quickly they pass through another. The mask helps the actor find their own impulses, so each exercise will be unique.

In one class, an actor took off their mask at the end of the Goodbye exercise and wept. He said he saw his father who had just died, who he had never fully grieved for. These exercises tell our shared stories deeply. I have had many powerful responses which, to remind us of Lecoq's quote, are often to do with people connecting to the struggle in their own lives when they meet the full open and considered expression of the mask. Every exercise carries the potential for a story which carries a more complex meaning.

*

After the exercises, I ask the students to share with the group what they saw. There are often revealing observations about the actors: 'I saw a side of you I hadn't seen in your work before', 'you were stronger', 'you were so funny!'

Students will often really let go in these exercises, particularly the tree catching fire or the storm at sea. The actor is physically embodying specific ideas, which are often quite dynamic and violent, but it is important that the mask doesn't get dislodged, or the actor gets too out-of-breath. You can guide the exploration by side-coaching to remind them to breathe or find suspension.

Cool-down after wearing the mask

At the end of each exercise, I ask the actors to stand and breathe and imagine they are looking at something that relaxes them.

Then I ask them to take the mask off.

The expression on the face is telling.

If they stand fully present and open – that will often suggest that they really 'carried' the mask.

Boundaries and debriefing with the group

I reiterate that students can take the mask off whenever they want. I work with a 'cool-down' approach at the end of a class, not just for the actors wearing the mask, but also for those watching to share, if need be, all responses. This helps de-mystifying the work. However, the spirit in most mask classes is usually exploratory and surprising[9] and, as I mention in the last chapter, students often become interested in the ancient power of mask work in general.

These exercises can all be adapted and developed: the mask on a train journey, the mask in a fairy story, the mask in the city.

The Chorus: Ancient and Modern

I learned the rules of Chorus work from Jacques Lecoq, particularly his innovation of 'the Plateau' or balancing the space exercise. For Greek tragedy, Lecoq proposed that the Chorus used the stage space in response to the hero. For ensemble playing, the Chorus can take over the space to tell their own stories, dynamically through movement – in Greek

---

[9]See below for how I have dealt with anxiety wearing a mask.

Figure 10 *Stuff Happens* by David Edgar at RADA, student production, directed by Ed Kemp, movement Shona Morris. Photo credit RADA/Linda Carter.

tragedy this takes place in the choral odes, but it can be used for narration, or setting a scene (a market, or a football match for example). I teach the Plateau, or balancing the space, to set this up, but here I focus on the dramatic potential of the Chorus – so will feed in ideas of the Plateau if it helps explain how the ideas can be played.[10] I have used many of these approaches when working with movement to stage group scenes.

Though Greek plays are frequently taught in drama schools, is it necessary to include the Chorus? Modern productions of Greek tragedy, rarely work with a chorus, preferring to concentrate the focus on the journey of the protagonists.

In 1997 I was asked to direct a Greek tragedy at Rose Bruford, and I wanted to find a way that would feel relevant to the students, by including the role of the Chorus. The Chorus is made up of ordinary citizens and are a counterpoint to the gods and protagonists. I was fascinated by the mixture of naturalism and ritual they brought to the drama, creating an exciting lifeline into a contemporary world. Consider the change of tone the arrival of the Chorus in Ted Hughes' adaptation of *Alcestis* by Euripides brings, as they enter after Death's exit, following his/her outburst that s/he will take possession of Alcestis, the Queen of Thessaly.

Death (roars)
This woman is mine.
And she is mine forever
Death exits. Enter Chorus

---

[10]Please see *The Moving Body* (Lecoq, 2002 [1997]) for a more detailed description and how to teach it.

Chorus 1
Will Admetos want to see us, at a time like this?
I never heard this house so silent.
Chorus
Is that good or bad?
Is that the careful silence of the sickroom
Where life still hangs on by a thread?
Or the silence of death? The final silence
Of the damp cold stone?[11]

The questions they ask are simple but evocative. The Chorus is speaking poetry, as they consider the silence of illness or death around them. This is a collective response, but the questions are planted in an everyday reality. But without an epic use of the space, the questions could seem bathetic. The Chorus has to take its place dramatically, once Death has left.

I started to teach Greek Chorus to bring these ancient plays to life, by focusing in depth on how the Chorus and the protagonists share the same dramatic space, in which to communicate their different points of view.

The Chorus is outside of the action. They can be political in their questioning of the state and the actions of the protagonist, and existential in trying to comprehend man's place in a pitiless world. The Chorus asks questions that we might ask, which makes them often appear more 'modern' in these Greek plays than the protagonists.

Below I refer to research I did when working with Annie Castledine on Sophocles' *Oedipus* (Sophocles, 1978), at Cambridge, and conversations I had with Simon Goldhill, Professor in Greek Literature and Culture, and Director of Studies in Classics, at Kings College Cambridge. Much of this explanation is sparse, as I am focusing on physical action and storytelling, and some basic facts about Greek drama.[12]

*

In a Greek tragedy, the role of the Chorus is different to that of the protagonist, so each party expresses themselves in different registers.

The protagonist is an 'actor' and usually a 'noble' tragic hero familiar to us from myth or legends: other 'actors' will also take on the role of messengers, gods, antagonists. The Chorus represents the citizens and is outside of the story. The Chorus was played by real citizens of Athens, trained over a year, by a Choragus, or choreographer. The celebrants or participants were trained to move, sing and dance in unison. 'Real people' occupy the same space as the mythical and thespian figures they observe, but both call on the gods. The 'noble' protagonist relates to the Chorus, hierarchically – letting them speak, but rarely heeding their advice. The protagonist's main concern is their own fate, rather than that of the citizens their actions might affect. The Chorus has a perspective that keeps changing, reflecting the reversals in the plot, which changes their physicality and alters the content of the choral odes. They anticipate or predict what might happen, but they cannot change the

---

[11] *Alcestis* by Euripides in a version by Ted Hughes (Hughes, 1999).
[12] For more detailed understanding read *The Faber Pocket Guide to Greek and Roman Drama* by John Burgess (Burgess, 2005).

outcome. They speak to the gods in the choral odes, reaching up to them, or kneeling in supplication: or address the protagonists across the space, seeking balance or resolution, and ask all to remember the importance of the laws of the gods, to protect the interest of the citizens. They are like the audience – bearing witness – but their text when speaking to the gods can be poetic, lyrical and musical, so they are also celebrants.

When the Chorus speak the odes, they flood the performance space, to address the gods, or express their hopes and fears, as one. They take over the performance space, but only when the protagonists or actors aren't there. When they speak to or observe the protagonists, the main actors, or even the subsidiary ones, they retreat or balance the space.[13] Their physicality shifts according to what they say and who they speak to. Their dramatic volume on stage also shifts. They are an 'entity', representative of a community, speaking for us, when they confront or advise. They could be captives, women, elders, keepers of holy shrines – but their interests are shared, and they voice 'our' concerns, by speaking for us.

Dramatically they also give the performance its texture, changing its rhythm, because many of the odes were accompanied by music, movement and song. Fifteen people moving and speaking poetic text as one is physiologically thrilling for an audience. It provides sonic and physical dynamics and elevates the action.

*

The plays were staged once a year, in an amphitheatre, in the open, in front of thousands of citizens, during the Festival of Dionysus.

This re-imagining of sunlight, and an empty stage, reminds us of the spatial freedom of these dramas, with landscape and nature as their backdrop. Movement and nature. The acoustics in the Greek amphitheatres were very good (and still are), so you would hear the wind in the trees, birdsong, insects, water, as the plays were played out of doors, in the blaze of the sun. A sonic, visual experience.

The actors' voices were amplified in the masks, accompanied by movement and gestures equally amplified, and they were elevated onto high boots, *cothurni*. Each actor was 'larger than life' and each mask had clear characteristics to express their role in the drama – old, young, heroic. With no more than two actors to play all the parts, the art of transformation was central to their acting techniques, which would alter movement and voice for the different characters. By contrast, the Chorus was usually human and not masked, their dramatic function an intermediary between the action on stage and the audience. Their movements and the actions to fit this landscape would be simple and dynamic. The pathways in the amphitheatre – in a semicircle – would also be flexible, circling, dynamic. The plays were written for these spaces. Even the music was portable – flutes, drums. Nothing is static here, all shifting alive, flooding the amphitheatre. I have always been fascinated how the dramaturgy of Greek tragedy was determined by the theatre spaces they were performed in. The way the actors moved brought the drama with its epic themes of family, war, the battle of the sexes, and destiny, to life. This can be overlooked if we focus on the plays as purely poetic literature – they are poetic and mythic, as dramatic action.

---

[13] In the Ancient Greek tragedies they would go into the orchestra, surrounding the acting area; in Lecoq's re-working on the Chorus, they would balance the space, but cluster together.

What can Greek Chorus teach drama schools?

When I joined RADA in 2015, I was asked to help re-imagine their second-year Greek project. The director of training and I wanted students to expand their technique, imagination and physicality to embody the demands of Greek tragedy. I referred to my experience of working with Greek Chorus at the Stratford Festival Theatre, and discoveries I had made working with Annie Castledine on *Oedipus Rex* in the Cambridge Greek play in 2005. The Cambridge Greek play is performed every three years in Ancient Greek by students and alumni of Cambridge University and the actors are trained to speak the text by Greek scholars. Castledine and I worked from a transliterated English text against the Greek, while directing the actors in the complex rhythms of Greek poetry. The combination of ancient and modern led us to a reimagining of how to update the themes of the play, while keeping in touch with its origins.

Castledine reimagined the whole play from a contemporary perspective, reversing the genders, and placing the play in a political context. All the male roles and Tiresias (who is possibly intersex?) were played by women. The men played Jocasta and the Priest.

We rehearsed the Chorus separately, while casting them as bereaved citizens rather than elders. We gave them a function, to hold Oedipus to account for the death of their loved ones in the plague. The plague was both a mortal illness and also the symptom of a diseased state. The play is also known as *Oedipus Tyrannus*. The fear of speaking out against the tyranny of the state we referenced as the silent demonstrations for the 'disappeared' in South America at the time: staging them holding photos of the 'disappeared', leaving the shoes of their loved ones on the stage, and lighting candles at makeshift shrines. Professor Simon Goldhill corroborated that the Chorus's function in Greek plays was civic and often 'political', with the Chorus in Oedipus 'the most political'.

Castledine was aware of Lecoq's version of chorus work, and she wanted me to infuse our work on the Chorus with this vocabulary. I trained the Chorus to work collectively, balancing the space with the principle that the dramatic weight of the Chorus is equal to that of the protagonist. As the protagonist moves, the Chorus answers as an entity, balancing the space across from them, producing stage dynamics that come from the action and the text, rather than from choreography.

I suggested these approaches might be useful for teaching Greek tragedy at RADA, with the role of the Chorus an important part of how to understand these plays. This would be a synthesis of ancient and modern approaches with an epic style of playing, but giving the Chorus a contemporary identity, and a reason to break the fourth wall and speak to the audience – their point of view, political and civic, as well as religious. The director of training agreed we should try this. We did it for seven years. The Chorus gave the play a contemporary context and each actor would play a main role and be part of the Chorus.

Working in Greek had given me insight into how the rhythms and sounds of the ancient language triggered movement and action. For the Chorus, a foot of verse was a line of verse, which would be moved to, almost as if it were music. The Greek celebrants of the original Festival of Dionysus would 'step out' the beats of poetry. The accents, or steps would alter on account of the different verse forms: iamb, trochees, spondees, anapaests, dactyls. By mirroring these accents with movement, while speaking the text, the rhythm of the steps might change to match, suggesting stepping through mountain paths or jumping over rocks. You could stamp on a strong beat, or run on a light beat. Belinda Quirey (1976), in her book[14] on popular dancing, cites the chain-dance (holding hands and walking or running in a line) as the first Western dance, going back to the Minoan civilization in Crete (1400–1200 BC), and described by Homer in *The Iliad*. I refer to it here for the significance of the footwork and because there is evidence to suggest that the original celebrants of Dionysus were young men and women, who danced and sang the ancient myths and legends of Greece by moving in semicircles antiphonally. This is in the structure of the choral odes, written as strophe and antistrophe. As well as two directions moving antiphonally in response to each other, Quirey refers to two rhythms in Western dancing, determined by our heartbeat and the breath, manifested in chain-dances (or farandoles).

> Our feet coming down on the metrical beat, make the same type of rhythm as our pulse. And above this base our upper bodies respond to the phrases of the melody with the free-flowing arc of our breathing. (Quirey, 1976)

Working with the strong beat of the verse would determine the step (the rhythm), and working with the meaning and sound of the words would determine the breath and vocal expression (the melody).

I worked with the voice teachers at RADA, to connect a similar approach, but less 'classical'. The meaning of 'the choral odes' was also in the sound of the words, and the meter in the rhythm of the verse, which in turn affected the physicality of the actors. This approach liberated the choral speaking and helped make it an emotional and physical response that expressed action, 'set' in an outdoor space. Rather than standing still when the chorus was speaking, they would move, expressively and with a dramatic purpose.

However, understanding the choral odes is very hard, and finding the shape of how to express the meaning in ways that are dynamic and intensely alive, even harder.

Using dynamics and analogy in Chorus work

Lecoq's Chorus Exercises, especially the plateau, used dynamics[15] and the how to move through the theatre space to animate and reinvent the Chorus. The dynamics of movement and expression in the Chorus, often mirrored those of the elements, nature and matter or even molecular forces, to reflect the text. We had studied many of these movement techniques, and how to amplify and simplify them, in the neutral mask work. My work on Chorus has developed from this, using analogy, moving 'like something', or moving in surprising patterns. Many of us are familiar with how Lecoq's exercises have been distilled into ideas like 'flocking', or 'the shoal of fishes'. It is true that being able to do either of these choral exercises well takes a lot of practice, but it can make the dynamics predictable, and not in response to the text.

I like to take these analogies further. The Chorus is a group of people (or sometimes supernatural beings) and is responding to what is happening in the story, so these responses need to mirror the dramatic action and journey. The front of the Chorus is the centre of

---

[14]Belinda Quirey (1976), *May I Have the Pleasure*, London: BBC.
[15]Dynamics have already been discussed in this chapter and previous chapters

gravity, who all can see, and who sets up the movement. But if the Chorus changes its orientation, there is a new leader. A protagonist can travel into the heart of the Chorus, to try to break them apart, and they can fall outwards, then eddy like water to the opposite side of the stage, crossing in front of each other to re-form, as a mirror image facing the protagonist.

A Chorus can simply breathe together to express anguish, anticipation; travel forwards to a suspension, to express a prelude to speak; emphatically address the audience, to express their views about the protagonist.

I discovered how the dynamics of vocal delivery could palpably change the movement of the Chorus and used 'analogy' to make this more surprising – the dynamic of glass shattering, or ice melting, or blood congealing – to find the 'rhythm' or musical dynamic of an idea. Consider this image: where the Chorus describes a man's fall from power or security and asks Zeus to wreak vengeance. In the verse below, from *Oedipus Rex*, imagine the chorus as starting in stillness on the first line, then slowly expanding upwards and outwards on the second and third lines, to shatter like glass breaking on the last line as they call for the end of tyranny. The image of a glass being lifted and smashed.

> Nothing can stop his fall
> His feet thrashing the air standing on nothing
> And nowhere to stand he plunges down
> O god shatter the tyrant. (Sophocles, 1978)

The Chorus share the dynamics together, moving in unison, but as the glass shatters, each person in the Chorus will have their own journey: one will fly across the space, one fall directly downwards, several will fall outwards. The Chorus has shattered apart. Their cry of 'O God shatter the tyrant' becomes personal for each of them. Then re-connects.

The development of dynamics and analogy to create stage action preceding speech

You can use the dynamics of the sea to show a group suddenly flooding the space. The Chorus starts at the back of the stage, clustered in a group breathing together, then the 'wave' swells as the group accelerates down to the midpoint in the stage, suspends, then decelerates as the front of the Chorus spreads forward and outwards and the back of the Chorus spreads backwards and outwards, to settle into stillness. The space is full of a crowd of people. The wave has crashed onto the shore.

You can use the image of a wave retreating to make characters mysteriously disappear, like mist, or the witches in *Macbeth*. They start spread out on stage, balancing the space. Then they retreat, with an acceleration to the centre (the front moving back, the back moving forwards) where they suspend: and then they decelerate backwards together, to hover, then accelerate backwards to the furthest corner, like a vortex.

The Chorus can be explored more expressionistically, in relation to a protagonist, by working across from each other. The protagonist is opposite the Chorus and looks to the right: The Chorus in response looks to their right; there is a tension across the space, not mirrored, but oddly echoed. Using these principles of opposites to create emotional and physical dislocation, the Chorus can raise itself up as the hero/ine sinks, and if the hero/ine sinks the Chorus rises.

I have used this tension dynamically. The Chorus is a group, one behind the other, and if it looks sideways, the faces will strain to see, one behind the other. If the Chorus then travels swiftly like a flock of birds from upstage right, swirling round through the centre to upstage left, the leader will be pivoting almost on the spot once they have reached their position, with the group swirling behind in an ever-increasing curve, and the person on the end often arriving last as an afterthought, but pulled by the dynamic, almost out of control.

In Greek tragedy the Chorus always has an identity. When I was working at RADA, the students would often decide this identity to give the play its context. They each then found their character and a back story to inhabit their place within it. This would mean that the movement would be choral, but their responses individual.

These approaches can be collapsed into stagecraft, for actors in big group scenes. At the Stratford Festival Theatre in 2003, I was invited to work on Shakespeare's *Henry VIII*, to work on the crowd scenes, and the pageants. One crowd scene was the trial of Katharine of Aragon, and the director Richard Monette created a rhythmic staging for her entrance that mirrored her anxiety. As the Queen entered, one actor dropped a document on the floor, another fanned themselves, two exchanged positions, one whispered to someone, one person ran across with an urgent message for a petitioner. The stage was full of a flurry of anticipation, a sense of fear, expressing the Queen's anxiety. The actors' tempi were quick, their actions varied; the Queen's progress was slow, ponderous, full of dread. This to me was a masterclass in how to craft the emotional life of the Queen, by giving the actors separate actions, in counterpoint to her entrance. It was like a piece of music, and the mood was brilliantly established, as she took her place on stage.

These examples come from working with the Chorus as a collective entity, to find their dramatic life through movement. The work I describe is Chorus work, and is developed through a series of training exercises. The actors take their responses off each other, rather than working to beats and choreography: the moves are determined, but the impulses come from them. This approach to Chorus work is reliant on actors being able to move with impulse and expression, and being able to work as a collective – which is the subject of this book: why movement training for actors is essential for theatre.

However, for actors and directors to trust that this will work, and be secure in a performance, time needs to be given in rehearsal, or in classes at a drama school.

13 Actors and play and end notes

My aim has been to de-mystify Actors' Movement and make it accessible both as a practice and as a ground-breaking subject in its own right through considering the context of its principles, and exercises. Every teacher breaks down exercises in ways that make sense to them, and I also teach in a variety of ways, depending on the day, the students, what class they have just come from. The exercises are a palette from which classes, ideas, physical development can be gleaned. This is not a codification but a provocation for the myriads of possibilities in our physicality. Stability. Elasticity. Volatility. Dynamic. Responsiveness. Feeling, above all feeling. Inertia. Observation. Stillness. Breath. Letting go and recovering.

There is a richness in training.

Movement taught me to relate to the world, through sensation and feeling, and consider how to translate that into action, and into theatre, through the body. Inevitably that places movement in a context – social, cultural and political. Everywhere we see the power of the body to communicate and to change the space around them. Artists use this power in their performances – as do politicians. A performer raises a contested flag and chants a slogan that ignites hope for some, fear for others, but the action has created responses that surge through a crowd like a tsunami, entrenching strongly held views on all sides. Power through forward energy. One dimensional, confrontational.

A herd of animals – puppets – travel with quiet intent through a city, their existential fragility in the cardboard tatters that make up their bodies. Puppeteers keep them alive, breathing with them, initiating their movements with empathetic shadow moves of their own. The animals stand and observe the city with wonder. We stand with them. Contemplation. Three dimensional, thoughtful.

An artist galvanizes a crowd with a spark, a move, a physical display, its oxygen feeding an audience to release into dance, freedom, joy – release, three-dimensional, explosive.

The space we live in is performative. Instantly images are made, and actions activated and then commented on.

Our streets are full of energy, anger and tumult. Actors and artists change the space they inhabit, and many actors now choose to use this power politically. Let them choose wisely, they have more power than they realize. Let them understand the 'meaning they are making'.

The space.

In the introduction I asked – 'how can a student take charge of their training?' Perhaps through understanding the purpose of the work, and physically committing to the training, and the classes, which will lead them to make their own work. Bridging the gap that helps a student commit to their training is pedagogy. I recognize that there are many elements I haven't covered, especially those of identity politics and its intersectionality with gender. But I have proposed an alternative: that the actor learning resilience and craft can apply that to whoever they are, and at any point in their lives. I have also proposed that movement training is a radical experience for the actor, one of growth and development, that will continue for the rest of their lives. But the pedagogy needs to change to meet the students where they are now.

Teaching a movement class is a strong and powerful act from teacher to student. It demands a lot of the teacher – to donate their energy and expertise to the group in the room, and breathe life into their bodies, through the dynamism of words, movement, wit, humour, energy and above all a relentless pursuit of technique and craft. Teaching movement is hard. Monika Pagneux once told me 'il faut avoir de la force' to teach movement.

Every time I teach a class, I prepare physically and mentally to shift my focus from myself to the other. But the students need to be able to receive what is taught.

So, this book is not about codification but about another question. How to teach movement in drama schools for the theatre that students will encounter, or change? Drama schools have changed and are changing, and it remains to be seen whether they will continue in their current form. But despite the tsunami that swept many of us away, willingly or unwillingly, drama schools as institutions prevail. As I write, I hope there is a future for the detail of the actor's movement I record here. I suspect the same questions will always prevail: how to get a student to engage with their training? And what is the best training for a particular time, place and student?

The price of a pedagogy is that it isn't a theory, or a curriculum – it relies on committed practitioners to work with students every day over a long period of time, with an embodied practice that is tested through practice-based research. Drama schools need to invest in their teachers and continue the spirit of enquiry – as we discovered new pedagogies and exercises in the 90's and 2000's – only this time, make sure it is funded and recorded. They need to help teachers find practical ways to work inclusively with the students they encounter who present with the mental health issues, and anxiety and fear of moving that go beyond the classes. Movement teachers and counsellors in drama schools can research together how to enable the students to fully participate: practice-based research that is as calibrated and considered as the movement exercises that are taught; expanding movement training from a synthesis of dance and movement, to connect to the issues many students face today.

For movement teaching to continue in the way that I encountered it and first taught it, it must be recognized as a professional pedagogy, and an embodied understanding of students' development. It holds a vital place in training. And it has contributed to the making of theatre and determined what an actor's metier in modern theatre is.

Although writing this book has been much harder than I imagined, it stands as a record of a body of work I have been immersed in, and which has been part of drama school teaching for several decades. This is not an eponymous system, but a window into a practice that is intrinsic and extrinsic to theatre and not often written about, nor consistently researched. The book charts my practice and how I changed it and searched for how it could evolve. This now urgently needs practice-based research to take us into the current time.

I owe a debt of gratitude to Trish Arnold. She trained me to think physically about how a body expresses thought and feeling and goes deep inside the actor. From my work with her, I learned how to break exercises down, and build them up again. I have never seen myself as a technician, but she gave me a technique that was only for an actor and helped me see myself as a technician for acting.

*

I started the book with a rehearsal. I end with two movement classes.

*

1 Expressive Movement: The four contrasting elements

The four 'elements' – air, fire, earth and water – connect the actor to immediate strong emotional dynamics. You 'inhabit' the element, and this changes your mood, or your identity. Below are condensed versions of how to approach teaching these exercises analogously – moving *like* something. The previous exercises in this book have suggested ways to apply them in other classes: the work on movement qualities has also introduced us to the elements. Movement qualities informed by the elements are – in my experience – a creative and spontaneous way to find changes of weight, rhythm and tempo that Laban's effort actions also introduce.

Air

This can be taught by objects that move in the wind, and we have already looked at these.

But what is the force and character of the wind, its changeability, its mercurial nature, how it shifts in weight, tempo and presence?

Take the idea of flying a kite: hold on to its string and feel the force of the wind pulling the kite and lifting you up. Your feet are planted, as you resist the wind, but the play of the wind reverberates through the string, in a dance of balance and loss of balance. Gradually become the kite set free from the ground and move through the space pushed and pulled and lifted and dropped by the wind. Prepare for this by reminding the students of lunges and sinking and rising to the floor safely.

Fire

Start with the breath of fire as it sparks before it ignites. Explore the spitting, spurting and sudden sounds and movement that comes from this (a firework is a useful analogy). Let the sparks and flickers affect your body, particularly your spine, as the fire grows to become a conflagration.

Earth

Lie on the ground. You are like a bog that moves. This mud or bog is moving with air pockets that bubble up and disperse; you are viscous, cloying, formless, dense. Find the sound of the mud, its weight and its movement. Gradually emerge from the mud, but stay as mud, sliding, drooping. Using your levels, knees, all fours, rolling, roiling. Sculpt yourself into a figure or creature from mud. The Jewish Golem was said to be made of mud; the Goddess Gaia came from mud; images of soldiers from the First World War, like the painting *Mud* by Gilbert Rogers. Mud is earth, powerful and perhaps full of feeling.

Water

As preparation, do an undulation through the spine (knees – hips – chest – nose – release and find a continuous way to move). Stand with your feet balancing your body, knees soft, and start to move from your knees and pelvis, travelling up into your ribs and torso; water also bursts its banks and has no boundaries (like air) when it isn't contained, but its volume is all through your body. Allow yourself to rise and fall like water, allow your head and upper body to move sideways, undulating, one part on one side, one on another – you are everywhere, enveloping, flooding, expanding. Water is powerful, sensual and changes or subsumes other elements. Feel and explore the expansiveness of this. Move the dense flow of water over a cliff to crash as a waterfall into a fast-flowing stream, which now tumbles over stones, find the sound of all this. What text goes with this?

Pure Movement class: A 2-hour session as part of input on The Tempest

Movement classes in drama schools can also be taught as a preparation for rehearsal and to research its vocabulary. This is taken from my notes of a class I taught for the Shakespeare project at a drama school. The exercises had been planned in some detail, but some of the notes below were written up after the class, to reflect on what had worked, and what hadn't worked as well.

> *Movement Class November 20*
>
> Our movement class today is loosely connected to a rehearsal exercise of *The Tempest*. The students are working on a series of scenes, and the director is keen to explore the world of the play. I come at this 'sideways', so as not to impose any outcomes. I will run some movement improvisations to prepare them physically and imaginatively for rehearsal. This class combines Pure Movement and Expressive Movement.

The exercises

Warm-up exercises
- Roll down the spine breathing out and roll up.
- Trot in the space to loosen out.
- Stand with eyes closed – this is a new game where people are gradually woken up to join the group (like the end of *The Tempest*).

You can only open your eyes if someone taps you on the shoulder, then you join the group.

One person walks carefully round the room, taps someone on the shoulder who joins them.

The game continues with one person joining at a time, swelling the group.

The others stay with their eyes shut, and the actors start to play – they stand round someone for a long time, then maybe move on and move back to tap them, or blow in their faces; they are allowed to hum and distract them, but they must keep their eyes shut.

The idea is to keep a sense of surprise.

At the end, eleven students stand round the one remaining with eyes closed, who seems unaware they are the last.

I signal to let the room be still for as long as possible, until someone in the group can't resist the temptation and taps them on the shoulder.

Eyes open, surprise, hilarity, lots of words tumbling out.

- To change the energy, the students play Run–Stop–Go, balancing the space. I ask them to 'stop' at different levels, see someone reach towards them, then change direction in one movement.
- Same game, but now they are running on Prospero's island, and I add the idea that either Ariel or Prospero has made them stop – the levels change, and actors add elements from Neutral Mask warm-up (without me asking).
- Either the Ariels or Prosperos work together to make them stop: when they stop they are bewitched and reach out and change direction in one move …

- This takes 2–3 minutes, maybe 5 at most, because all of this has been covered in other classes.

Pure/Spine

- Bounces down for 8, hang off spine, breathe out.
  Squat by dropping pelvis with head still hanging, then lengthen legs lightly (imagine a balloon is attached to your sit bones).
  (NB: Adaptations offered for a student with an on-going problem with sciatica).

- Stretches, High, Wide, and Forward.
  Fast and playful with breath.

- Pelvic Rock and circling of pelvis into Bird and Bear*.[1]
  Bird is spine hollow, with arms wide and elbows and knees soft-upright.
  Bear is spine rounded but reaching forward (still standing), with arms curved.
  Movement is led by tail bone, arching and rounding, movement rippling through the spine, supported by knees and breath, arms move into their positions through a swing.

- This leads into an undulation from hanging down – knees, hips, chest, nose, flowing down onto hands and knees.

- On hands and knees:
  Round and hollow
  Animal drinking and tortoise undulation
  Flow into cobra
  Then back through plank* (if arms are strong enough)
  Into downward dog, walking hands back to hang off spine
  Release there for a while
  Roll up and breathe
  Shake out
  This is one flowing activity.

Swings

- These are delivered light and free, and only take about 15 minutes. No dramaturgy and no fussy corrections.

- *Tree topple with extra circle**
  Lift arms up high
  Swing down and up in one movement
  At the top do an extra arm circle suspend and repeat
  Swing: 1 and 2, circle suspension
  Swing 1 and 2, circle suspension

---

[1] An asterisk indicates an exercise not covered in the book but described in these notes.

Feel the length of the spine and the looseness in the neck and head
Work with softness and breath.

- *Pendulum swing with arms in parallel*
  Start with feet parallel and one arm suspended forward and one suspended back
  Swing arms with a soft knee bounce
  1, 2, 3 and change direction on the fourth swing as the arms come up to the top
  (NB: arms will be circling in counter motion to each other)
  Allow the torso to move with the motion
  Briefly use the exercise to play with the idea of being on a ship in a storm and trying to reach for the rail or the rigging.

- *Release and breathe*
  To get the breath back, open arms wide then drop down with soft knees and hang in between your legs
  Unfurl and stand up.

- *Leg swing*
  Keeping the breath soft, gently elongate through the spine, lifting one leg in front and balance with the opposite arm
  Swing the leg for 8 counts with arms swinging in parallel to balance
  Place leg down
  Change direction imagining you are walking on Prospero's island
  Do the same on the other side.

- *Arrow swing from the two diagonals*
  Split the group into two, one half goes in one corner, the other in another corner
  You go in groups of two, opposite each other, with the two diagonals crossing
  Swing by starting with right arm behind and left foot in front
  Swing – forward and back
  Full circle forward (with a gallop)
  Full circle backwards (with a gallop)
  Four full circles galloping with a hey at the end.

Improvisation

Lie on the floor to listen to the third movement of Kodály's Háry János Suite.

The third movement starts with a refrain on the zither, and bells. There are instruments that could speak to the different characters. Some of the rhythms are distorted. The sound world reflects Caliban 'this isle is full of noises'.

Split into groups, with characters who have scenes together, and use the music to find the physical life of one of those scenes – play with the action and your responses. Bring the scene to life, using the stillness and rhythms of the music, either to push or pull you, or to be another voice in the scene. Pay attention to your character and your motivation. Try to find how the music and the text move you and change you. Scenes the students chose to explore were the appearance of the Harpy ('You are three men of sin'); The shipwreck at the beginning; Ariel leading Ferdinand through the Island.

*

Conclusion: The future – How to keep searching

I have interwoven conversations and threads of reading and research throughout the exercises in this book, which alongside the bones of my pedagogy, illuminate my reflections on how to teach movement.

My focus is on 'Physicality and Acting: Movement Training as a Catalyst for Change'.

When I was teaching and learning my craft, the shadow of the Second World War was a galvanizing force that drove many of my generation forward. We questioned the status quo and wanted to distance ourselves from the past. Maybe the issue is that movement training has never been permanently admitted to the status quo and now it needs to be, to fully develop and get proper support from institutions to research it as a contemporary pedagogy.

Movement training is radical – it can expand a text outward into the space: or it can make a text with the body as a starting point. And most importantly, it can help an actor to find physical life and expression, both as the character they play and as themselves.

Many of us are teaching a craft we know is essential to an actor's development. Many of us are teaching a craft that had previously changed how theatre was made.

Does the provenance of this technique come from the patriarchy as defined by the Judo-Christian tradition in the Bible?

> The woman, says the Law, is in all things inferior to the man.
> Let her accordingly be submissive, not for her humiliation, but
> that she may be directed; for the authority has been given by God
> to the man.[2] (Flavius, 1926)

The paradox is that the provenance of many of our movement techniques started with men and were passed on by women, with those practices still attributed to men. But the movement practice I teach was, and still is, a pedagogy translated into a methodology crafted, piloted and trialled by women. Women who taught movement were disproportionately the pioneers in movement teaching in drama schools.

This book celebrates that.

My own practice – which I developed – owes much of its 'thinking' (because movement is thought) to male innovators, from Laban to Sigurd Leeder, Lecoq, Grotowski. But the 'authority' doesn't have to stay with 'the man'. Many of us have changed these influences radically. Litz Pisk, with originality and creativity, developed a style of teaching and way of working that was dramatic and physical and entirely unique, not paying tribute to any 'masters' or 'history'. Trish Arnold pioneered her own pedagogy, involving the use of the breath in the swings, adapting the work of Sigurd Leeder and Lecoq. As I suggest earlier, the Free Dance practitioners were often outliers and originators as well as educators. For my

---

[2]This is quoted from 'Dybbuks and Jewish Women', in *Social History, Mystery and Folklore* by Rachel Elior. It is taken from *Against Apion*, 2:24 by Joseph Flavius, who was explaining the Talmud to the Romans to whom he had defected. As Elior points out, this was also taken up by Paul and is part of the New Testament as well (Flavius, 1926).

own part, I have rejected Laban, and I question the shadow of his legacy. And I question the value of theory over practice and advocate for more research. Many more teachers continue to adapt and develop this practice.

So, the book celebrates the pedagogues. The workers at the chalk face.

Hierarchy – despite the social and political changes of relatively recently – still moulds how our institutions work, particularly in drama schools. Spatially it is boring. Up and down. Command and control. Who gets to speak, to make the rules and keep outliers outside. I have advocated for research to change the structures and to illuminate what movement for actors is, how we can continue to teach it and engage with our students in our training institutions – the intersection between technique and artistic autonomy and new teachers.

The body.

Freedom, breath, space, dynamic and transformation.

Bodies

An actor is only ever a body in a space with a story to tell alone or with others.

The history of the subject of movement training for actors can only be realized by its practitioners and its pioneers – mainly women, outliers, sometimes refugees and often non-conformists. And new teachers. We don't need hierarchy for this.

If any of these exercises and observations can serve that 'catalyst for change', take, take, take. And make, make, make.

We have been silent far too long. We must come out of the shadows and take up space in our training institutions.

Over to you.

References

Arnold, T. (1997, 24 February). Trish Arnold's Notes.
Arnold, T. (n.d.). Trish Arnold. *Reverberations*.
Auden, W. H. (1987). *Selected Poems*. London: Faber & Faber.
Austin, J. (2022, 3 December). *The Dark Hidden Origins of the Alexander Technique*. https://connectingupthedots.com/2022/12/03/dark-hidden-origins-of-the-alexander-technique/
Badham, V. (April 2015). Review of Endgame: 'Innovation choked by Samuel Beckett's strict staging edicts'. *The Guardian*.
Ballinger, L. (2023). *Trish Arnold: The Legacy of a Movement Training for Actors*. London: Bloomsbury.
Barrault, J.-L. (1972). *The Memoirs of Jean-Louis Barrault*. London: Thames & Hudson.
Beckett, S. (1965). *Waiting for Godot*. London: Faber & Faber.
Berkoff, S. (1999). My Metamorphosis. *The Independent*. https://www.independent.co.uk/arts-entertainment/my-metamorphosis-1110231.html-
Bradby, D. (2009). Roger Planchon Obituary. *The Guardian*.
Brecht, B. (1978). *The Mother*. London: Methuen.
Burgess, J. (2005). *The Faber Pocket Guide to Greek and Roman Drama*. London: Faber & Faber.
Carosso, J. N.-G. (Director). (1999). *The Two Journeys of Jacques Lecoq* [Motion Picture]. Paris.
Churchill, C. (2008). *Plays 4*. London: Nick Hern Books.
Clapp, S. (2016, 27 November). Review of the 'Shakespeare Trilogy'. *The Guardian*.
Coldiron, M. (2004). *Trance and Transformation of the Actor in Japanese Noh Drama*. Lewiston: Edwin Mellen Press.
Collective, T. B. (1968). *Our Bodies Ourselves*. New York: Simon & Schuster.
Congreve, W. (1999). *The Way of the World* (New Mermaids), 2nd edn. London: Methuen Drama, A & C Black Publishers Ltd.
Cros, J. T. (1962). *Divided Loyalties*. London: Hamish Hamilton.
Eichler, J. (2024). *Time's Echo*. London: Faber & Faber.
Evans, M. (2009). *Movement Training for the Modern Actor*. New York: Routledge.
Evans, M. (2017). *Jacques Copeau* (Routledge Performance Practitioners). London: Routledge.
Evans, M., and Kemp, R. (2016). *The Routledge Companion to Jacques Lecoq*. London: Routledge.
Ewan, V., and Morris, S. (2023). Mission Statement. *Conservatoire Conversations in Movement*.
Filippakopoulou, I. (2024, 2 January). Facebook Post. London.
Flavius, J. (1926). *Against Apion*. London: Heinemann.
Gaunt, H. (2021). *Strengthening Music in Society: The Way Forward for UK Conservatoires*. Conference, 16 December, Silk Street Music Hall, Guildhall School, London.
Ginther, A. M. (2023). *Stages of Reckoning*. New York: Routledge.
Guardian. (1975). Interview with Litz Pisk. *Arts Guardian*.
Hagen, U., with Frankel, H. (1973). *Respect for Acting*. New York: Macmillan.

Hanley, E. A. (2017). *The Role of Dance in the 1036 Olympic Games: 'Why Competition Became Festival and Art Became Political'*. International Society of Olympic Historians (ISOH). http://ISOC/uploads

Harris, J. G. (2021, 23 June). *Jewish Women's Archive*.

Holman, R. (2016). *German Skerries*. London: Hern Books.

Hughes, T. (1999). *Alcestis*. London: Faber & Faber.

Jays, D. (2023). Obituary for Michael Gambon. *The Guardian*.

Kampe, T. (2025). 'Tracing Fertile Ground.' In *Modern Dance – Revisited* 2025, 346. Seiten.

Karina, M. K., and Kant, M. (2004). *Hitler's Dancers: German Modern Dance and the Third Reich*. New York: Berghahn Books.

Latham, D. (2023, July 27). How Is Movement Important in Theatres (S. Morris, Interviewer).

Leabhart, T. (1998). *Modern and Post-Modern Mime* (Modern Dramatists). Basingstoke: Palgrave Macmillan.

Lecoq, J. (2002). *The Moving Body*, rev. edn. Routledge. Originally published in French (1997).

Lee, L. (1959). *Cider with Rosie*. London: Penguin.

Lehmann, H.-T. (2006). *Postdramatic Theatre*. New York: Routledge.

Mackinnon, I. (2023, July). *Empathy and Difference*. Conservatoire Conversations in Movement at Central School of Speech and Drama, London. Taken from S. Morris's notes.

Miller, S. (2024, March). What Makes a Dance Teacher. Taken from S. Morris's notes.

Mirodan, V. (2016). 'Lecoq's Influence on Drama Schools.' In Mark Evans and Rick Kemp (Eds), *The Routledge Companion to Jacques Lecoq*, 208. London: Routledge.

Mirodan, V. (2018). *The Actor and the Character, Explorations in the Psychology of Transformative Acting*. London: Routledge.

Montague, L. (2023, June). Training at Old Vic Theatre School (S. Morris, Interviewer).

Morris, S. (2017). Shona Morris Diaries.

Moss, S. (2013, 13 June). Article A-Z of Wagner: J is for Jews. *The Guardian*.

Murray, S., and Evans, E. (2023). *Mime into Physical Theatre: A UK Cultural History 1970–2000*. London: Routledge.

National Drama. (2023). *National Drama's Response to the Arts in Schools Review*. Nationaldrama.org.uk

Newlove, J. (1993). *Laban for Actors and Dancers: Putting Laban's Movement Theory into Practice*. London: Nick Hern.

Nicholas, L. (2007). *Dancing in Utopia: Dartington Hall and Its Dancers*. Alton: Dance Books.

O'Loughlin, O. (2024, 27 February). 'Drama schools can radically reimagine theatre's future'. Interview with Josette Bushell-Mingo. *The Stage*.

Pearce, D. M. (2024). Embodied Ecological Awareness and the Pedagogy of Jacques Lecoq. *Theatre Dance and Performance Training*, 15(3), 375–94.

Peck, L. (2021). *Act as a Feminist: Towards a Critical Acting Pedagogy*. New York: Routledge.

Phillips, M. (2024). Altruism Not Activism Can Help Loneliness. *The Times*.

Pisk, L. (1975). *The Actor and His Body*. London: Virgin Books.

Pisk, L. (2018). *The Actor and His Body*, 4th edn. London: Bloomsbury Methuen Drama.

Pisk, L. (n.d.). Archive of Litz Pisk. Held at Central School of Speech and Drama.

Quirey, B. (1976). *May I Have the Pleasure*. London: BBC.

RADA. (2020). *RADA Students Anti-Racism Action Plan*. London: Royal Academy of Dramatic Art.

Rilke, R. M. (2004). *New Poems*. Manchester: Carcanet Press.

Rudlin, John. (1986). *Jacques Copeau*. Cambridge: Cambridge University Press.

Schama, S. (Director). (2025). *The Road to Auschwitz* [Motion Picture]. BBC.

Shakespeare, W. (1980). *Hamlet*. London: Penguin.
Shakespeare, W. (1984). *A Midsummer Night's Dream*. Cheltenham: Stanley Thornes.
Smethurst, M. (2015). *Greek Tragedy and Noh: Reading with and Beyond Aristotle* (Greek Studies: Interdisciplinary Approaches). Lanham, MD: Lexington Books.
Sophocles. (1978). *Oedipus the King*, ed. by W. Arrowsmith. New York: Oxford University Press.
The Guardian. (2023, August). Chrissie Hynde.
Veirel (Director). (2024). *Riefenstahl* [Motion Picture].
Wardle, I. (1978). *The Theatres of George Devine*. London: Eyre Methuen.
Winearls, J. (1958). *Modern Dance: The Jooss-Leeder Method*. London: Adam & Charles Black.